Journey of the

BITTERROOT GRIZZLY BEAR

Journey of the
BITTERROOT GRIZZLY BEAR

THE INSIDE STORY OF A GRIZZLY REINTRODUCTION EFFORT AND THE JOURNEY OF A REMARKABLE YOUNG GRIZZLY

IAN MCALLISTER

Steve Nadeau

Patricia Entwistle, Editor.

Book design and typography by Meggan Laxalt Mackey, Studio M Publications & Design, Boise, Idaho.

Cover photo by Ian Mcallister.

Library of Congress Cataloging-in-Publication Data
Nadeau, Steve, 1956 —.
    Journey of the Bitterroot Grizzly Bear:
    The Inside Story of a Grizzly Reintroduction Effort
    and the Journey of a Remarkable Young Grizzly

Summary:
"In the *Journey of the Bitterroot Grizzly Bear*, author Steve Nadeau creates a compelling insider's look at a unique grassroots recovery effort that encouraged leaders in conservation, industry, and government to collaborate on a proposal unlike any other in Endangered Species history. In the West, politics often override scientific judgments, but the demise of this optimistic proposal was not necessarily a defeat for grizzlies. Alongside the author's historical account of the recovery effort, Nadeau weaves a fascinating tale of the journey of BB, a remarkable young grizzly and recovery pioneer who survived the gauntlet in his travels from the Canadian border to central Idaho. He became the first grizzly in 60 years to find his home in the 5500 square miles of wilderness landscape in central Idaho, and his path marked the way for other bears to follow. Biologists, students, and others will enjoy this close-up look at the beauty and mystery of grizzly bears, as well as the science, conflict, and politics surrounding them as they attempt to establish a new home in the "wildest heart" of the American West."

Includes index of names, organizations, and abbreviations; bibliographic information; timeline; maps, illustrations, photos; and glossary of terms.

Published by **BB PRESS**
The Bitterroot Grizzly, LLC   Boise, Idaho

ISBN 978-1-0878-7249-0

FIRST PRINTING 2020
IN THE UNITED STATES OF AMERICA

DEDICATION

For my mother, Jackie.

I thank her for her encouragement, love, and support, and for showing me what courage is. She instilled in me the love and joy of animals and sunsets.

CONTENTS

*The grizzly bear is a symbolic and living embodiment
of wild nature uncontrolled by man. Entering into grizzly
country presents a unique opportunity—
to be part of an ecosystem in which man is not
necessarily the dominant species.*

—Stephen Herrero, 1970

FOREWORD

ROCKY BARKER

GRIZZLY BEARS WERE ON THEIR WAY OUT of the lower 48 states when Steve Nadeau graduated from high school in Maine.

That year, 1975, grizzlies were listed as threatened under the federal Endangered Species Act (ESA), and a new era began in the northern Rockies of Montana, Idaho, and Wyoming. Before then, the giant brown bears were considered remnants of the Old West, ghettoed in Yellowstone and Glacier national parks and some of the roadless lands around them.

Nadeau was a lot like many young men and women of my generation. He loved wildlife and sought a career devoted to conservation and a life in the outdoors. Even though he lived in the wilds of Maine, he was drawn to the wildness that remained then, and still remains, in the American West. His odyssey took him to Yellowstone National Park, ground zero of the grizzly bear crisis that landed the bruins on the threatened species list.

The National Park Service had shifted its management to seek a "reasonable illusion" of primitive America in its parks. Feeding bears along its roads and allowing them access to garbage dumps collided with this new naturalness approach, and in the early 1970s,

Yellowstone abruptly closed the dumps and instituted a sanitation campaign in its developments and campgrounds to keep bears away from human foods. Nadeau took a job in 1976 as a night security guard in Fishing Bridge Campground.

Nowhere in Yellowstone or arguably in the lower 48 states were bears and humans thrown together in more conflict. Bears starving after the closing of the dumps regularly raided the campground built in the middle of some of the richest grizzly bear habitat in the park.

Like meth addicts, the bears did almost anything to get at the human food they had learned to eat. They smashed coolers, broke into cars, ripped up tents, and terrorized the people who got in their way. Nadeau was seeing up close the human-bear conflicts that are at the center of grizzly recovery efforts.

Studying and managing these conflicts became Nadeau's calling, and over the next 40 years he participated in a recovery effort that attempted to raise grizzlies from the brink of extinction to a possible but still uncertain road to recovery today. Nadeau led grizzly research projects in Glacier National Park, ran large carnivore management for the Idaho Department of Fish and Game, helped develop a mandated plan to reintroduce grizzly bears into central Idaho, and led Idaho's gray wolf management program.

Grizzly numbers have risen to more than 2,000 from only hundreds that were counted in the 1970s. Grizzly bears have expanded their range by 34 percent over the last decade, putting grizzlies on the edge of cities like Missoula, Montana, and communities like Jackson, Wyoming, and Coeur d'Alene and Driggs, Idaho.

I have had a front row seat for the grizzly comeback since I came to Idaho in 1985, after answering an ad from a newspaper offering a job covering "Yellowstone grizzlies and Three Mile Island nuclear cleanup." In that position as environmental reporter for the

Idaho Falls *Post Register* and later, in a similar position at the *Idaho Statesman* in Boise, I got to see grizzly management up close.

I watched a grizzly sow and her cubs chasing elk at Antelope Creek near Mt. Washburn and a trio of young bears standing in front of hundreds of tourists near Mammoth Hot Springs in Yellowstone. I watched several grizzlies eating berries on a steep slope next to Many Glacier Hotel in Glacier National Park. Later, I went to Kamchatka, Russia, to write about the big brown bears that patrolled the rivers and lakes, living off the salmon just as they had in Idaho a century before. I got to know John and Frank Craighead and told their stories, along with stories of the men and women seeking to preserve biodiversity across the Pacific Northwest, from bears and wolves to salmon, steelhead, and northern spotted owls.

I covered Nadeau as he and others developed one of the first collaborative efforts between conservation groups and the Idaho timber industry to reintroduce grizzlies to the Bitterroot Mountains. Today, Idaho Timber Co., the largest purchaser of federal timber in the United States, has one of its executives on the board of the Idaho Conservation League, and collaboration on forest policy is routine.

Thirty years ago, biologists couldn't find a single grizzly sow with cubs in Island Park, the Idaho town west of Yellowstone. Now it's crawling with bears. Still, the federal government hasn't been able to remove them from the federal threatened species list, even though it is clear they have recovered.

Idahoans near Yellowstone went from complaining about the return of grizzly bears in the 1990s to sharing their wild communities with them. People in Island Park in particular have learned to live with grizzly bears, much like folks in Montana always have.

A new generation of Idahoans relish the state's wildness and want to make room for its wild creatures—but also want a place for humans. Still, in the 22 million acres of wilderness and roadless lands in central Idaho, they have not made room for these creatures that still generate both fear and awe.

Nadeau is arguably the bruin's best advocate in central Idaho, and in *Journey of the Bitterroot Grizzly Bear* he tells the story of one recovery pioneer that found his way into this wildest heart of the American West.

Rocky Barker is the author of two books about endangered species and Yellowstone, *Saving All the Parts* and *Scorched Earth*. He retired from the *Idaho Statesman* in 2018.

ACKNOWLEDGMENTS

I OWE MANY THANKS to the hard work of all the people who were involved with the Bitterroot Recovery effort, and all those who still are. I owe a thanks to my editor, Pat Entwistle, who came out of retirement to edit this manuscript. She had her hands full and did a wonderful job. I also would like to thank Meggan Laxalt Mackey of Studio M Publications & Design for her encouragement, assistance in helping me understand the steps in book publication, and for the final book design.

I would also like to thank my reviewers, Dr. Hilary Cooley, Jamie Jonkel, Wayne Kasworm, Dr. Sterling Miller, Herb Pollard, and Rocky Barker whose collective comments improved the manuscript and provided me with encouragement. Dave Cadwallader helped me pack into and locate the site where the Bitterroot bear (BB) was discovered. I would like to thank my wife Kara for her early reviews and suggestions, continued support, and understanding.

I would especially like to thank my late father, Leo, and grandfather, Leo, Sr. for teaching me to be a woodsman, and to respect and appreciate nature.

ABBREVIATIONS

BB	Bitterroot Bear
BCH	Backcountry Horsemen of Idaho
BE	Bitterroot Ecosystem
BESC	Bitterroot Ecosystem Subcommittee of the IGBC
BLM	Bureau of Land Management
CBA	Conservation Biology Alternative
CIG	Citizens' Involvement Group
CMC	Citizens' Management Committee
DOW	Defenders of Wildlife
ESA	Endangered Species Act
EIS	Environmental Impact Statement
	DEIS: Draft Environmental Impact Statement
	FEIS: Final Environmental Impact Statement
FR	*Federal Register*
GIS	Geographic Information System
IDFG	Idaho Department of Fish and Game
IGBC	Interagency Grizzly Bear Committee
LOC	Legislative Oversight Committee
MFWP	Montana Department of Fish, Wildlife and Parks
MVP	Minimum Viable Population
NCDE	Northern Continental Divide Ecosystem
NEPA	National Environmental Policy Act
NOI	Notice of Intent
NWF	National Wildlife Federation
ROD	Record of Decision
ROOTS	Resource Organization on Timber Supply
RSF	Resource Selection Function
USFS	U.S. Forest Service
USFWS	U.S. Fish and Wildlife Service

PROLOGUE

IN THE REALM OF GRIZZLY BEARS:
A UNIQUE RECOVERY EFFORT FROM AN INSIDER'S PERSPECTIVE

WHEN YOU ARE IN THEIR REALM, grizzly bears don't let you not think about them. They have a way of occupying your thoughts when every turn in the trail might be where you encounter the next grizzly. They have a way of hiding in the closet of your mind and opening that door in the quiet hours before you fall asleep. The sounds you hear at night just might be a grizzly rather than a deer licking the salt from your sweaty backpack.

Fear, when controlled, is nothing but a whetstone to our senses—making them sharper and more capable. When uncontrolled, fear can dominate our imagination and actions, and limit our abilities to cope, to understand, to make good decisions. Because of their reputation as killers, grizzly bears can make you feel either fearful, or for some, more alive. You forget about the pain of hiking when your senses are engaged; you leave your world and enter their world of predator and prey. With honed senses and experience, fear is eventually replaced by alertness, thus allowing you to feel more at ease and more fully able to enjoy the realm of the grizzly bear.

These are the thoughts and words of a biologist who spent many years working with or near grizzly bears in Yellowstone, Glacier National Park, British Columbia, and Alaska—and eventually using what he learned in an attempt to recover grizzly bears in central Idaho. That recovery effort siphoned the knowledge, experience, and research from dozens of scientists and hundreds of citizens to try to bring grizzly bears back to a place from which they had been missing for more than 60 years. This story chronicles that unique recovery effort. It also brings to life the story of a real grizzly bear that found his way into the Bitterroot Mountains after a remarkable journey of self-discovery. It is about the incredible physical and behavioral traits of grizzly bears and the tiring politics of environmentalism versus industry. It is about the hopeful and innovative efforts to seek common ground and work together to try and solve the puzzle of recovery. It is the story of how environmental pragmatism and purity became enemies. It is also my story—a biologist who spent 40 years working toward grizzly bear recovery, 30 of which were with Idaho Department of Fish and Game (IDFG).

I have always loved and been fascinated by wildlife and, in particular, bears. My journey began when I graduated from high school in 1975, the year grizzly bears were listed under the Endangered Species Act. Although northern Maine, where I grew up, was a wild place, I longed for something different, wilder, and with a bigger sky. After undergraduate school at the University of Maine, I moved west to Montana to find a new home, a home where grizzly bears roamed. After earning an M.S. and gaining experience with or near grizzly bears in Yellowstone, Glacier National Park, British Columbia, and Alaska, I was hired by IDFG. It was meant to be. There, I was lucky enough to be stationed in the middle of the most remote part of Idaho: the edge of the Selway-Bitterroot Wilderness. This was where the U.S. Fish and Wildlife Service was considering an effort to recover grizzly bears.

For the next 20 years, I helped develop the plans and documents that would lay the foundation for recovery in the Bitterroots.

During the entire period of 1988 through 2008, I collected all the Bitterroot grizzly bear recovery records in hard copy and electronic files. I helped coordinate and conduct meetings, kept minutes, and participated as a primary contributor to all the major grizzly bear recovery and management efforts. I was the only IDFG employee who worked on the recovery effort in the Bitterroots for that entire period, so all the files floated to me and are in my possession.

Beginning in 1994, following completion of the Bitterroot Chapter of the U.S. Fish and Wildlife Service's Grizzly Recovery Plan, I began thinking about how important this effort and the story of recovery could be. I wanted to eventually write a book about the events and the people involved during that tumultuous period. I also began to realize how my life was intertwined in mystical ways with grizzly bears. So in retirement, I finally was able to focus on the book.

This book is really a combination of two books. One is a nonfiction account of the recovery of grizzly bears in the Bitterroot Ecosystem (BE) from my insider perspective. The other is a short novel inspired by a true story of a young grizzly bear that was born in the Selkirk Mountains of northern Idaho and journeyed to the Bitterroot Ecosystem—the first to do so in 60 years.

The Bitterroot Bear (BB) that inspired this story was a real bear. I took the liberty of creating BB's life as it may have been from birth until the fateful day in September 2007 when he was discovered. We know most of the facts surrounding the day he was discovered, but what took place prior to that day, we could only speculate. The story follows a likely path he took from the Selkirk Mountains, where his DNA proved he came from, to the Bitterroot Mountains some 200 miles away. His journey changed how we thought about and managed the recovery process in the Bitterroot Ecosystem.

Bears are remarkably intelligent, and their behavior proves it. In many ways, their behavior is similar to that of humans and our pets, and of course, in many ways it's very different. We know they have the capacity to reason and think in a rudimentary fashion, to play, and to feel joy and pain. Their responses to stimuli can often be remarkably similar to humans. But they are also much different from humans in so many wonderful ways, while struggling through their life and death events. The morals, ethics, and laws of human society cannot be confused with the natural laws of the wild kingdom. This is a grizzly bear's life in Idaho from a biologist's perspective. It is not a Disney story. I hope you enjoy it!

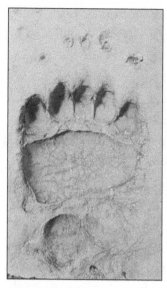

Plaster cast of the 4-year-old Bitterroot Bear's front paw. Claw marks extend 2" beyond toe pads; main pad measured 5" wide. In contrast, black bear claws are almost always 1.25" long.

The recovery story, however, is factual, and is based on hundreds of files I have in my possession that span 20-plus years of grizzly bear recovery efforts in the Bitterroots. I felt it was important to tell the inside story and what it was like being in the center of the grizzly bear (and wolf) recovery controversies. I used my hundreds of files and emails to create an accurate portrayal and timeline of both the primary recovery effort from 1988 to 2001 and the post-recovery effort from 2001 to 2008.

A vast number of good people worked hard on the recovery, and even though I was unable to include everyone in this book, I have listed in an appendix the names of those whose efforts and affiliations were recorded. Their efforts were important, and I enjoyed working with everyone involved. Also, I tried to take into account that opinions differ, and resulting policies can tend to reflect personal or political biases. This story has villains and heroes, and depending on your perspective, they could be the same person.

And finally, some readers might see the story of grizzly bear recovery as a powerful and irresponsible government forcing a dangerous animal on them, their community, and their families. Others might see it as a way to make wilderness truly wild and complete. Some might see it from a purely scientific or legal perspective of species recovery, and some, as an attempt to correct historical mistakes. I am not sure where I fall on the spectrum, because I understand or believe in aspects of all of them.

All I know is that the great bear is, in my view, one of the most incredible species on the planet; and that in itself is at least deserving of a place in our hearts and minds. And if we can find a place for them there, then we should be able to find a place for them in the largest contiguous wilderness in the lower 48 states.

This book is for all those who have labored for grizzly bears, simply because they deserve to be here with us.

Author Steve Nadeau in his "bear's den" surrounded by files used to write this book.

CHAPTER 1

THE DEN

A FULL MOON CAST LONG SHADOWS across the snow, and the subzero nighttime temperatures crystallized the moisture in the air. Despite a cloudless sky, a light snow fell. Howling of wolves could be heard in the distance, as the pack moved through the creek bottom, looking for a meal. A snowshoe hare quietly moved in the shadows of an old whitebark pine snag, unaware that seven feet beneath it, a 300-pound grizzly was giving birth.

The summer of 2002 had been ideal for bears in northern Idaho, and huckleberries had been plentiful. In October, the female grizzly had also found the carcass of an elk that had been wounded and lost by a hunter. She gorged on the remains for three days until a big male grizzly took what was left of the carcass from her. Her *hyperphagia*, or pre-denning period of overeating, had passed as foods became scarcer. She had been feeling very lethargic for a few weeks, and her appetite began to wane as the cold temperatures and shorter days brought changes to the mountains. Leaves of the aspen and huckleberry bushes had long changed color and fallen off, as had most of the berries. Elk hunting season had ended and elk were migrating to lower elevations. Flocks of geese could be heard overhead voicing their excitement for their long journey south.

The female entered her den in very good shape, having put on well over 100 pounds since last spring. It was late October when the first real snows began falling at 7,000 feet. She had located her winter den site over the previous few weeks, after searching for the perfect spot. There, she dug a hole under an old whitebark pine snag on the eastern side of a ridge, high in the Selkirk Mountains of northern Idaho just south of the Canadian border. The westerly winds had already begun blowing snow over the entrance when she started to pull bear grass into the den. The dirt left from her excavations at the entrance became muddy as she worked and then slowly disappeared as the snow accumulated.

As the wind-blown snow changed the landscape from fall to winter, she moved into her den. Inside was warm and dry, with bear grass and chewed wood chips insulating the floor. Her den entrance was only a couple of feet wide and about four feet long, and the bowl was about five feet in diameter and a little elevated from the entrance. It was big enough for her to completely turn around and stand in. The entrance quickly became covered with snow and her tracks were now obliterated. For the next six months, this would be home.

Inside the den, changes to her system began taking place along with the seasons. As she slowly fell into a deep sleep, her respirations slowed to only a few per minute, her body temperature dropped a couple of degrees, and her heart rate slowed down. Her circulatory system changed as her blood pressure increased slightly and a decoupling of the atrium and ventricle slowly occurred. Her heart now worked on two chambers rather than four. Her system moved from storing fat to burning fat. Humans would lose about 1 percent of their muscle mass daily if they didn't eat or move. But the chemical and organ changes in her system will allow her body, over the next six months, to live on fat while losing only 25 percent of her muscle and no calcium from her bones. Her body will miraculously recycle her urea and blood waste created by her metabolism. She won't defecate or urinate, as her kidneys and liver clean the blood without the need to drink water. Her last meal of grass will slowly move down her digestive system and create a little fecal plug. But unlike a true hibernator such as a ground squirrel, she can be awoken quickly if need be. Her system has evolved to allow her to do that to protect herself or her offspring.

The female was in full lethargy as her body rested and underwent another important change: She was pregnant.

She had found a mate several months earlier, in June—a big male that had tended her for over a week, at first keeping his distance but finally coming in close. The big old male was persistent in fending off smaller bears until finally she accepted him. His huge jaws bit her neck and back, and his long claws raked her underside as he mounted her, inducing ovulation. This occurred multiple times over the next couple of days.

An egg dropped from the ovary during mating, allowing the male's sperm to fertilize it. The eggs would not fully implant in the uterus until she entered the den months later. This type of "induced ovulation" allows the female to mate with several males, thus potentially producing offspring from multiple fathers. In the bear world, this is good for two reasons. First, genes from the most dominant and healthy males get passed on, and second, the offspring are less likely to be killed by that male if he is familiar with the female and has bred with her.

Among many impressive physical traits, the big male had some "wandering" genes in him. He had moved south into the U.S. Selkirk Mountains from the Canadian side a few years prior when establishing his home range. He was now the dominant male in that part of the Selkirk Mountains and roamed nearly 500 square miles annually searching for food and mates. Bears don't have a territory that they defend against other bears. Instead, they defend a personal space around them. A bear's home range typically overlaps with those of many other bears, but large males tend to dominate and other bears tend to avoid them. That allows dominant males more access to females and prime feeding sites.

The female's body was in good shape, entering the den with enough body fat not only to feed herself but also to provide the nutritional needs of offspring. Her body mysteriously knew this. The sperm from the big male was healthy and viable and, together with the female's eggs, formed two blastocysts. Fertilized eggs in bears do not implant immediately in the uterus like most mammals when bred. If she were not in good condition, the blastocysts formed during summer breeding would not implant at all and would be sloughed out of the uterus or be reabsorbed into her system once in the den. She was, however, in excellent health and condition, the blastocysts did implant, and soon she was pregnant with two growing fetuses. Her body could not possibly guess how the summer and fall foods would fare and what condition her body would be in when entering the den. So the body's "decision" to become pregnant waited until the final facts were in, thus preventing starvation for both mother and offspring.

One of the fetuses developed into a male, and one into a female. Within a few weeks, the fetuses were almost a pound each, which was big enough to want to be out of the womb. They were born that cold January evening and entered the world with no expectations other than to find a nipple. The female licked off the afterbirth, and with her muzzle, pushed the squalling, hairless, and blind newborns toward her teats. After a few false tries and more squalling, BB and his sister found the nourishment they needed. The contented mother pulled her massive arms around her hairless, rodent-sized offspring and allowed them to nurse while she dozed. Thus was the start of a young bear's life, unremarkable for a bear but remarkable for us. BB was going to be a very special bear.

CHAPTER 2

BEARS AND ME

I WAS BORN IN CENTRAL MAINE and grew up on the Canadian border in a small town along the St. John River. It flooded almost annually, as the great ice packs of the frozen north let go of their firm hold of winter and proceeded to cause havoc on their way downriver, bullying anything man-made along the way.

"Ice out" was an event in northern Maine. We would wager on when the car placed on Long Lake ice in January would eventually fall through rotten spring ice, which caused a timer to record the exact date and time. It predicted the arrival of spring much more accurately than that silly groundhog way down south in Pennsylvania. Spring in that part of Maine was actually known as black fly season. You only ventured out in a short-sleeved shirt if you had a death wish.

We lived farther north than most of the Canadian population, a fact that could be seen in the craggy, weathered faces of the locals. The locals were French Catholics of Canadian descent and spoke a broken *Franglais*, a French/English dialect. The Acadian history of the valley dated back to the lengthy wars between the French and the English. Displaced Acadians moved from Nova Scotia to northern Maine and all the way to Louisiana and became known as Cajuns.

My father worked as a customs and immigration inspector on the border, and although English was his first language, he was also fluent in French and Franglais, as was my mother, who was actually born in Quebec. The average family was quite large to help with the farming. I never got an accurate count of my neighbors' family; I think it was around 15. Our family was small by comparison, only four kids: three strapping boys who all grew to over six foot three by high school and an older sister to worry about us and keep us in line. But the Northwoods were as big and welcoming as the large Acadian families, and they were home to me.

As early as I remember, I was in the woods. When I wasn't playing basketball, I was hunting, fishing, hiking, canoeing, building cabins, and disappearing from morning until dark with a hunting knife, ax, gun or rod, and a peanut butter sandwich. I graduated from high school in 1975, the same year grizzly bears were listed as threatened under the Endangered Species Act. I was always fascinated with bears, but they didn't become my totem until I was in college.

I was working toward an undergraduate degree in wildlife management at the University of Maine and came home over Thanksgiving that first fall. Deer were very scarce in northern Maine, but it never stopped me from hunting them. One day, I was out deer hunting and had just walked up a hardwood ridge. I stopped and quietly watched the surroundings, hoping a deer would make itself visible. I heard the sound of shuffling leaves coming from the same ridgeline I had just walked, and I immediately thought, "There's my buck!" Instead, to my surprise, a nice big black bear was walking with his nose to the ground in the exact tracks I had just made. My immediate thought was, "That bugger is tracking me!"

I was perfectly willing to shoot a black bear but never had. I pulled up my lever-action .30-.30 rifle, aimed it at the bear, and waited for the right shot as he plodded even closer. About that time, the bear stopped and turned his head to look at me, maybe 20 yards away. I stared into his eyes, down the barrel of my rifle, and I swear to this day his expression turned from a nonchalant, "This is an interesting scent," to "Oh crap!" as he recognized the fix he'd just stepped into.

I was stunned at the human-like expression and just stared at him with my mouth open. He slowly turned his head and seemed to tiptoe in slow motion—probably hoping I hadn't seen him—until a large beach tree stood between him and me. Then he made a 90-degree turn and exploded over the ridge out of sight.

My rifle was still at my shoulder pointed at the beach tree when I regained my senses, but I could not get that vision out of my mind. The almost human-like expressions on that bear's face haunted me and made me want to find out more about them. That was the start of my bear totem and formed the direction of my career in wildlife management.

I returned to the University with a new goal in mind: I wanted to learn about bears. Roy Hugie was getting a PhD at the University of Maine, conducting the first black bear study in the state. I set my focus on the project, got in touch with him, and asked for a job as a volunteer. He pretty much blew me off at the time, so I volunteered on other graduate student projects—a coyote study and a pine marten project. I vowed to pester him again, but in the meantime, I learned as much as I could about bears.

The summer after grizzly bears were listed and after my first year in college, I got a job as a night security guard at Fishing Bridge in Yellowstone National Park. On the way to Yellowstone, a couple of my high school teacher friends who worked in Yellowstone recommended that my traveling companion, Jeff Thibodeau, and I take a detour through Glacier National Park in northwestern Montana. They said it would be worth the extra time.

Glacier National Park

Our detour was filled with many firsts for me, like seeing the snow-capped Rocky Mountains for the first time (thinking they were storm clouds in the distance), glaciers clinging to the sides of mountains, elk, mountain goats, mule deer, and my first grizzly bear tracks in the snow. We followed those long-clawed tracks to Iceberg Lake, a misty high-alpine lake shrouded in fog, and saw where the bear had crossed the snow-covered alpine tundra and made its way up a slope and over the next pass. I envisioned the bear that had made the tracks and shuddered at the thought of having stood in this spot as the bear walked past me. Would it have walked away, or run from me, or maybe even mauled me?

I had heard about grizzly bear maulings and, as a kid growing up, read about them in *Outdoor Life, Sports Afield,* and *Field and Stream.* That was part of the western lore that was so appealing to boys from the East who wanted to become men in the West. The thought of a bear attack was probably in almost every person's thoughts when hiking in Glacier Park for the first time. It was in my mind for sure, but I was more enthralled at the possibility of just seeing one and learning how they eked out a living in that rugged high country. They totally occupied my thoughts while I was hiking or sleeping in my tent that summer, my first summer in the West.

Grizzly bears didn't let you not think of them. They were always present in your mind when you were in Glacier or Yellowstone; they were not as visible as the mountains but were every bit as spectacular and omnipresent. Grizzly bears were mythical, powerful, unapologetic, and beautiful. They were the epitome of wild country and demanded your attention.

Even if you didn't see grizzly bears, you felt their presence and they made every day special because they were there. You were alive, looking, listening, smelling, and feeling like a prey animal must feel every day. You heard and saw more because of it. You began to understand how things worked when you really paid attention. You didn't just walk with your head down, focusing on the pain in your feet and shoulders and ignoring the intricacies of your surroundings. When a turn in the trail could be where you encountered the next bear, every turn was special. The snuffling you heard outside the tent could have been a grizzly bear, not just a mule deer licking your sweaty backpack. The discomfort that bears created slowly waned as you became more experienced with them and their backyards, but it never really totally went away. If it did, you were at least careless, if not a little crazy.

Back down at low elevation, I remember Jeff getting a bit freaked out when we saw a black bear walking across the road in front of us near Apgar village; so we flagged down a ranger car, and Jeff excitedly explained the "close encounter." The ranger calmly asked us, "Wow, that close, huh? What color were his eyes?" He laughed with his partner at our expense, as he drove off. I smiled at Jeff as he realized that he had overreacted and we probably had little to worry about. I wanted to become so familiar with bears in Glacier that I too could laugh at tourists who were afraid of a little black bear.

I was so taken by Glacier National Park that I told Jeff it had changed my life, that I now had a "grand plan." I had a goal, and perhaps a premonition, that I would come back to Glacier and lead a grizzly bear study.

Yellowstone National Park

I was excited to be in the West and have a job in arguably the most incredible wildlife mecca in North America—Yellowstone. It just so happened it was one year after grizzly bears had been listed under the Endangered Species Act in 1975. I remember watching the *National Geographic* show of the Yellowstone grizzly bear research being conducted by twin brothers Drs. John and Frank Craighead.

That particular episode had the brothers immobilizing a big grizzly and placing one of their homemade radio collars on him. The bear woke up before they were ready, and they had to run to their old red station wagon to escape! I watched in awe as the big grizzly charged and hit the car with his head and body, rocking it and the brothers inside.

That episode was one of my earliest impressions of grizzly bears and wildlife research (excluding *Mutual of Omaha's Wild Kingdom*, which I watched religiously every week as a kid). It was exciting and manly and, for a woodsy kid from Maine, very attractive. Without realizing it at the time, it was enormously influential in my career path. If you could have a job doing stuff like that, then I wanted in.

The Craighead brothers, who had pioneered grizzly bear research in the park, had just been unceremoniously ousted over their beliefs that the park should not shut down the garbage dumps cold turkey. That was a time when park management and philosophy was changing from a place that allowed feeding bears from car windows and roadside dumps to a place where bears were wild and not familiar with or conditioned to human foods. Managers understood that feeding bears was wrong and that park wildlife should be wild; it was not a zoo or petting farm. The Craigheads, however, were sure that most bears in Yellowstone used the dumps and that as a result of closures they would become food-stressed and would cause many problems with people.

Well, they were right on that count. One of the densest grizzly populations in the world had just been cut off cold turkey from the highest nutrient source of food in the ecosystem; they were upset, and they were hungry. And I was a 19-year-old night security guard that summer of 1976, there to witness all of it!

As a Yellowstone Park Company security guard, I was given a flashlight, a clock around my neck to punch at each of the stations, and a laundry truck to use if I didn't want to walk the circuit. My job was to make the rounds, making sure no person or animal was causing trouble, breaking in, or having issues.

Across the street was the Fishing Bridge campground run by the National Park Service. This was a place where people camped in tents and left their food in coolers, on picnic tables, or in their tents and cars. They cooked fresh fish in bacon grease, left food scraps in fire rings, and provided every other enticement you could possibly create for a hungry bear. My office was in the main concessions building, and it was usually the only light that was on in that area at night. It was also only 50 yards across the road from the Fishing Bridge Campground.

In August, grizzly bears, as usual, decided it was time to hit the dumps, but the dumps were gone. So, as the Craigheads predicted, they hit the campgrounds instead. Grizzly bears ripped into coolers, cars, and tents; they injured campers and otherwise caused a great deal of damage, havoc, and panic. Rangers patrolled in their cars, set large culvert traps, told people how to store food, and rescued those stupid enough to try and scare a grizzly away.

I had the luck to meet and befriend a couple of the night-shift rangers and rode with them on their patrols. I remember once watching a female grizzly with two cubs pick up a tent and shake it like a box of cornflakes to get everything out of it. I watched bears flatten coolers because they couldn't get the lid up and try to get into cars before the rangers could scare them off.

One night, an elderly man tried to shoo a bear away by waving his red flannel shirt at a cub that was too near his camper. The cub gave a little bawl, and the female turned on him. He almost got back inside the camper door when she grabbed him. She was standing on his chest with her mouth over his head when rangers arrived and scared her off—just in time to avoid his untimely demise. Many nights, fearful campers ran into my office to avoid marauding grizzlies. I remember one young couple who hysterically screamed that one of the bears "was as big as a Volkswagen, and not at all friendly!" It was an exciting month of August for a kid from Maine. I was hooked!

I returned to Yellowstone in 1979 after a couple more years of wildlife biology classes at the University of Maine and summers as a whitewater canoe guide. This time, I was a Park Service employee working on the helitack team. We were responsible for the initial attack and suppression of wildfires in the park. Additionally, we handled helicopter work around the park, including moving grizzly bears and traps into the backcountry.

District Ranger Dale Nuss, affectionately called "Nasty Nuss" by the guys working for him, had for some reason befriended me. He showed me the prototype aluminum culvert trap that could be sling-loaded to remote locations for trapping and releasing bears. He had developed a remote cable system so the door could be lifted without having to stand on the culvert. This was a real advancement for the rangers responsible for releasing upset grizzly bears. I also met a few of the Interagency Grizzly Bear Study Team members, including Jamie Jonkel, son of well-known grizzly bear researcher Dr. Chuck Jonkel. Jamie was a crusty-looking character even back then, with a battered cowboy hat and the look of someone much more weathered than his 19 years. And he knew bears.

Yellowstone and its bears became important to me, and I spent much of my free time in 1976 and 1979 watching and learning about them. I hiked and backpacked many miles by myself and with others, learning about Yellowstone's backcountry and wild-life. One time, I caught a bunch of cutthroat trout, placed them in a pillowcase, and hung it where I could safely watch from a hundred yards away. I waited many hours with another friend to catch a glimpse of the big bear in Pelican Creek, whose tracks I had seen many times while fly fishing there. That was illegal and I knew it was pretty stupid, but at the time I thought it was harmless because it was miles away from the nearest campground or road.

A large bear found the fish, but not while I was watching. The pillowcase had been ripped along the bottom by a razor-sharp claw, and all its contents had been released and scarfed up by the hungry fellow. His large tracks in an anthill under the tree recorded his activity. Those hours were not wasted; anytime you could hang out in Yellowstone's backcountry learning about bears were very good hours.

During my last few years at U Maine, I was finally able to work with Roy Hugie and his team on the black bear study. At first, he took me on as a volunteer, then as a work-study student. I trapped bears, followed them into their dens, chased them with hounds and

Steve Nadeau with black bear cub, near Baxter State Park, Maine, 1979 (southern black bear study area). First Maine black bear study conducted by University of Maine and Maine Inland Fish and Wildlife Department.

radio-collared them, and otherwise got the bear experience I so desired and my totem demanded. I also worked with a lifelong friend, Brad Allen, a fellow undergrad at U Maine and later a graduate student at the University of Montana. He had studied bears in Maine and was a career biologist with Maine Inland Fish and Wildlife. Bears were truly interesting to me, and my desire to learn more about them pressed me westward and made me surround myself with those more knowledgeable about bears than I was.

Moving West to Work with Grizzlies

I graduated from U Maine in May 1980 and moved to Montana. It was hard to leave Maine, my family, and my friends, but the draw of the West and grizzly bears was just too big. I had a job in Glacier National Park studying mountain goats. I met the park research and management staff and spent many days hiking the mountains and trails of the park. I particularly eyeballed the bear management team as a future job possibility and befriended the rangers on the bear team. The next summer I was offered a job on the bear team, which meant I could finally work with grizzly bears!

The first U.S. Fish and Wildlife Service (USFWS) Grizzly Bear Recovery Plan was started in 1979 and finished in 1982. It was based primarily on research conducted from 1975 through 1980 near Glacier and Yellowstone, the years I attended college. From 1981 through 1982, I worked on Glacier's bear team and was selected as the West Lakes Region team leader in 1983.

I had some great experiences learning about grizzly bears, watching them for hours on end in Bear Valley, keeping bears and people apart at Granite Park Chalet, and otherwise hiking the trails, talking to the public about bears, and enjoying life as a young bear ranger in Glacier, one of the most beautiful places on earth. We trapped and moved bears, investigated bear maulings, and unfortunately, even had to kill a bear or two that got into trouble. We helicoptered around the park and rescued lost and injured visitors, handled bear issues, rode horses into the high country, patrolled McDonald lake by boat, and otherwise did things young men usually only dream about. I was literally living the dream!

During that time, I became enthralled with the idea that we had a very dense grizzly bear population in the park, especially around Granite Park Chalet from July through September. I was curious about nighttime bear movements in the area around the campground below the chalet, which was the location of a 1967 mauling and the subject of a book called *Night of the Grizzlies* by Jack Olsen. Part of my job as a bear ranger was to make sure backpackers who stayed in the campground kept a clean campsite to avoid attracting nocturnal visitors.

Author on horse patrol as a bear management ranger at Trout Lake, Glacier National Park, Montana, 1981.

Every night before dark I would go down to the campground and basically tuck the campers in. I would tell them not to worry about bears around their tents, even though we had just been watching grizzly bears in Bear Valley, a short distance away. I would then return to the patrol cabin below the chalet, shut and latch the steel door, and check the shotgun hanging over it before I went to bed.

I felt a little hypocritical sleeping in the safety of a cabin and telling campers not to worry. We really didn't know what bears were doing at night, whether they walked the trails close by, avoided the campground, or sniffed their way through it looking for food. That really bothered me, as well as the rest of the team. So, I started a small study with the blessing of the park and conferred with the new bear biologist for the park, Kate Kendall.

I began by raking trail sections in the evenings, around and in the campground, so I could see bear tracks made overnight. I spent many hours scanning the chalet, campground area, and Bear Valley with binoculars. In September, I used a night-vision scope to watch the flats below the chalet at night. I spent hours sitting in my favorite spot on a little cliff on the rim of the valley, watching bears feeding and interacting. I often saw as many as a dozen bears at a time during peak huckleberry season in late August and early September.

After weeks of collecting data, my research showed that when people were present in the campground, the bears avoided it! They would walk by the campground on the trails at night, only a few yards from the tents, but they didn't stop to investigate. They only investigated the campground when people were absent. That was quite a relief to me and to the other rangers tasked with watching the area. It was comforting to know that the bears had developed a pattern of avoiding the campground and people and that our clean-camp mantra appeared to be working.

I had several close encounters with bears during that period, but I always tried to avoid female grizzlies with cubs as that was the one thing I feared the most. One sunny September morning, I was sitting against a blow-down snag glassing for grizzlies when I heard the snuffling of a female with cubs as they walked a few feet behind me. They moved around and below me, feeding on huckleberries, apparently unaware I was just a few feet from them. As the family fed, they moved below my perch, facing me. I froze, with my binoculars glued to my face, staring at the mother's eyes, afraid to even breathe. When she stopped moving, she was at the base of the ten-foot cliff I was sitting on. She was so close her head took up my entire view. Her prehensile lips delicately selected the berries from the bush, better than my fingers could have, and an occasional flash of a large yellow canine tooth erupted from her lips, reminding me of her flesh-eating capabilities.

Suddenly, she paused, stopped chewing, and with a huckle-berry leaf sticking out of her mouth, looked up at me. She stared at me for the longest few seconds of my life. She was 20 feet from me, and her eyes fixed on me like I was a big huckleberry. I feared they'd find my Park Service badge in a grizzly turd the next morning. My heart was pounding so loudly I was certain she could hear it! Then, for some unexplainable reason, she put her head back down and contin-ued feeding. As she and her cubs slowly moved away from me, I was able to exhale and quietly start breathing again. It took a while for the adrenaline to stop coursing through my veins and my shaking to stop. As soon as she moved out of sight, I scrambled back to the trail, happy to be alive and exhilarated that I had survived another encounter!

But I was also very curious about her behavior. Did she see me and not worry because she was habituated to people and saw me as a non-threat? Did she look at me in my green and gray uniform and think I was a stump? These heart-pounding experiences happened regularly enough during my days in Glacier that I became enthralled with bear behavior and language. How I survived without a scratch baffled me but made me want to learn more about them, especially their behavior and what led to confrontations and injuries. Was I lucky, or was there something I did that kept me safe? Why did bears run from some people and not others? Why did some bears attack people and others let you hang with them just a few yards away? Was it the bear or was it the humans? It was very confusing to me as well as to park managers, and I wanted to try and figure it out.

Doug Peacock was a notorious bear photographer, filmmaker, and acknowledged bear expert, who later authored the book *Grizzly Years*, based on the years he spent as a fire lookout. Doug had spent a few summers on Huckleberry Mountain Lookout, but in August I think he spent more time watching grizzly bears than looking for smokes. He was the only other guy I knew in Glacier who was as interested in bear behavior as I was. He filmed bear-on-bear encounters and tried to decipher their language. That was something I was interested in and had studied for hours near Bear Valley.

On Doug's days off he would often seek out beers (instead of bears) in the local watering holes. Whenever our paths crossed at Frieda's Pub in West Glacier, we often discussed bear behavior. We had several discussions about how to understand their intricate behavior patterns and how to interpret them.

One evening, Doug made a comment to me that really made me stop and think. He said, "You damned biologists, you spend too much time trying to prove something and not enough time learning!" I think he had a point. If you get too wrapped up in statistical significance, you may miss something that is very important, just not statistically significant. And if all you do is collect data points, you may forget to look around and see what's happening. That was a naturalist's perspective, not a researcher's, and I had to respect it.

Doug kept a bottle of whiskey and a .44 magnum in his briefcase that was always by his side when he was in town. He always said you should never have a gun in bear country because it made you act stupid. One night I asked him about the .44 and the seeming hypocrisy of his statements. He smirked at me in his burned-out Vietnam-vet way and said, "The gun isn't for bears, it's for people!"

Doug was a Vietnam medic who hung out with other reclusive 'Nam vets of the era. Those often mentally wounded vets disappeared into the mountains of northwestern Montana to escape the rat race and try to heal. They idolized Doug, who by this time was a notorious symbol of the "Earth First" eco-terrorist movement and a known grizzly bear advocate. A character known as George Heyduke, from the book the *Monkey Wrench Gang,* written by Doug's friend Edward Abbey, was supposedly based on him. Whether or not he actually did any of the things credited to him in the book, he seemed to enjoy the notoriety of the association. At heart, however, he was a loner.

Doug's friends were more than a little weird. They would call me the "bear mauler" rather than a bear ranger, and a few times I had to leave the bar to avoid getting into a scuffle with them. One of the guys was a big bruiser who insisted on hiking in Glacier with a "bumbershoot," otherwise known as an umbrella. A story was once written about him in the local newspaper, *The Hungry Horse News*, relating that he had scared a bear away by quickly opening the umbrella and hiding behind it. Apparently that encounter made him a bit of a bear expert, or so he thought. He was heard regaling the story multiple times to whoever was slow enough, or drunk enough, to listen. Characters, all of them!

Grad School

I became a little depressed in 1983, watching my friends get older and still working seasonally at Glacier Park in the summer and Big Mountain Ski Resort in the winter. They were starting to show the wear and tear of that lifestyle when they were still in their 30s and 40s, and most had no Plan B to rely on when their knees finally gave out. They were smart, happy, healthy, and young, but those days don't last forever. In them, I began to picture my future—and it scared me.

So, at the age of 26, I began submitting grizzly bear research proposals to Glacier Park. The science staff did not want to allow me to do research without a university backing, and they were very leery of outside researchers anyway. Because I had worked in the park for years, I felt I had an "in" and could convince them to let me do some research, perhaps continuing what I had started as a ranger. I began to investigate how to get into graduate school.

For a few years, between seasonal jobs, I had volunteered on graduate-student projects at the University of Montana and got to know the wildlife students and professors. I attended bear conferences and meetings and got in with the bear people and professors. Many became my close friends. I spent so much time in Missoula with my friends, the "bear" graduate students, that some thought I was already a graduate student. One day, Bernie Peyton, a grad student who was defending his thesis on Andean Spectacled Bears in Peru, asked me when I was defending. I hadn't even been accepted to grad school yet! That was the peak time for students conducting grizzly research at the University of Montana. Dr. Chuck Jonkel, The Border Grizzly Project, and the Montana Cooperative Wildlife Research Unit trained and mentored such noted bear biologists as Don Young, Harry Carilles, Mark Haroldson, Jamie Jonkel, Carrie Hunt, Marty Smith, John Hechtel, Tim Thier, Rick Mace, Chris Servheen, and many more.

When I finally did apply to school in 1984, it was with some financial backing from the Park Service, who had finally accepted one of my many proposals, contingent upon acceptance by the University. Dr. Bart O'Gara, a noted scientist and great human being, was also head of the Montana Cooperative Wildlife Research Unit at the time and became my major professor. Bart saved my bacon when Cliff Martinka, the chief scientist at Glacier National Park, told us one month before I was to begin my field studies that he was pulling my funding because of new park research priorities. I was shocked and disappointed to say the least! Bart, however, saved the day; he said he wasn't going to be the bad guy and told me I was accepted to school if I could find my own funding. Additionally, I had to continue working to get a study proposal accepted by the park.

So I went to work and obtained most of my own funding through grants, odd jobs, and Teacher Assistantships and finally got a study off the ground the following year, which ultimately resulted in my thesis, entitled, "Habitats and Trail Situations Associated with Grizzly Bear-Human Conflicts in Glacier National Park."

The park supported my work by providing me with as many C-rations as my field tech, Norval (Rick) Armstrong, and I could eat, and they gave me free parking, camping, and access to park observation data. Not quite the $10,000 per year they had originally discussed, but at least I was doing research on grizzlies in Glacier! After many fits and false starts, in 1985, I was finally the head of a research project, in line with my ten-year grand plan. A life lesson I learned through all this was that persistence can eventually pay off.

Through my project, I developed a system that could predict grizzly bear conflict sites with up to 86 percent accuracy. It required my visiting historical conflict sites and mapping bear foods, sight distance along trails, proximity to water, and time of year. When seasonally available bear foods, short sight distance along the trail, and close proximity to water all occurred at the same time and place, hikers were more likely to encounter a bear close-up. Foods attracted the bear, the sound of water masked the hiker's noise, and the short sight distance prevented the hiker or bear from seeing very far ahead.

I also looked at five years of grizzly bear conflict and observation records in the park. With that information, I was able to determine that grizzly bears that were habituated to people along high-use trails were less likely to injure someone than those bears encountered on low-use trails or off trail. This was a counter-intuitive result that helped the parks understand the nature of habituation: a bear that was habituated to people likely wouldn't react to an encounter with surprise and defensive behavior, which can precipitate most injuries. Until then, managers believed that a habituated bear was the more dangerous bear.

During the summer of 1985, while I was conducting my field research, I took Dr. Steve Herrero on a hike to Granite Park Chalet. Dr. Herrero was a University of Alberta wildlife professor, grizzly expert, and author of the book *Bear Attacks: Their Causes and Avoidance.* We saw several grizzly bears that day, including a few at very close range. He was quite impressed and exclaimed, "What an incredible laboratory you have here!" I had to agree. We spent hours discussing grizzly bear behavior and trying to make sense of it all. Dr. Herrero later told me he used the results of my research to help design hiking trails for Parks Canada that were aimed at avoiding bear conflicts in Canadian National Parks.

Glacier Park, as far as I know, did not use my research as I had envisioned. I hoped, however, that it had helped park managers further their knowledge and understanding of grizzly bears and human conflicts. Glacier National Park has an incredible resource in grizzly bears, and conducting research there was an honor enjoyed by few others. I trust park managers are still doing everything they can to reduce conflicts, with or without my research.

After spending five years working in and near Glacier, I needed a change. I had lots of ideas to improve bear management in the park, but I think the park and I had reached a logical time to part ways. I had gained important life experiences in an incredible location, and it gave me a better perspective of the National Park Service and the real world of wildlife research and park management.

Although I absolutely loved Glacier National Park and had earlier seen myself as a wildlife manager there, I never returned as an employee or researcher. Instead, I looked elsewhere for work but spent many vacations hiking and watching "my" grizzly bears near Granite Park Chalet and Bear Valley and marveled at them and the incredible place they called home.

During the summer of 1986, after my M.S. field work in Glacier, I was hired by Dr. Chris Servheen (who also co-chaired my graduate committee) and the U.S. Fish and Wildlife Service (USFWS) to trap grizzly bears in British Columbia in the North Fork of the Flathead River, assisting famed grizzly bear researcher Dr. Bruce McLellan. We trapped many bears that summer, placed collars on some giant bears, radio-tracked bears on the ground and by fixed-wing aircraft, and otherwise learned

Author conducting research for M.S. thesis, Bear Valley, Glacier National Park, Montana, 1985.

about grizzly bears and biology by listening to Bruce expound upon his ten years of research just north of Glacier National Park. I turned 30 years old on a day in late October when we caught three grizzly bears. A grizzly for every decade I'd been alive on the planet! It was a long and exciting day, capped off by a nice birthday dinner and cake made by Bruce's lovely wife, Celine—not a bad day.

My First Permanent Job

In the fall of 1987, following graduation, I was offered a job working for the Idaho Department of Fish and Game (IDFG). Serendipity, providence, or luck put me in the right place at the right time, and Idaho gave me a chance. After a few months of training, I became a Conservation Officer stationed at Powell in the heart of the Bitterroot Mountains and the Bitterroot Grizzly Bear Recovery Area. I had always wanted to be a game warden and thought the idea of being a real Rocky Mountain warden with horses and all the trappings sounded romantic and exciting.

Powell was one of the most remote patrol areas in the state, and it was perfect! I knew that I didn't want to be an officer forever, but the training and experience would greatly benefit me in my career and life. Powell had a year-round population of about 60 people at the time, mostly U.S. Forest Service (USFS) employees, a few Highway Department staff, the Lochsa Lodge owners and employees, and a State Highway Patrol officer. It had a one-room schoolhouse with eight students and a dedicated and enthusiastic teacher. It was another dream job that finally included health insurance, a steady paycheck, and a Department-owned cabin to call home. I was 31 years old, and everything I owned fit in my truck. My Labrador retriever, Niki, and I were starting an adventure that, for me, would last 30 years.

During the winter of 1982 and summer of 1984, I'd spent time in the north-central Idaho backcountry with Timm Kaminski, Don Young, and Jerome Hansen on a wolf project. We hiked, skied, snowshoed, and flew helicopters, as we howled our way through the wilderness and tried to document wolf presence for USFWS and IDFG. Much of that time was in what would later become my new patrol area—an area that was about the size of Delaware.

By 1988, as the new Conservation Officer, I was already familiar with much of Idaho's backcountry and couldn't wait to explore it further. My patrol area was 95% roadless, so I got some horses. I spent many days, weeks, and months over the next few years exploring the Bitterroot, Clearwater, and Nez Perce National Forests in what was called the Selway-Bitterroot Grizzly Bear Recovery Zone.

The one thing that bothered me about the Selway-Bitterroot Wilderness and surrounding forests was that, despite having incredible elk and deer populations and plenty of black bears, cougars, and other wildlife, it felt dead to me without grizzly bears. I would hike with my head down, not paying attention to my surroundings. I didn't have that little feeling of possibly running into a grizzly, the feeling of not being on top of the food chain, that little bit of tempered fear that makes one feel especially alive. I was missing that feeling that mountain men, Native Americans, and Lewis and Clark had and the feeling you get in Glacier, Yellowstone, British Columbia, and Alaska.

These beautiful mountains, lakes, and streams were vacant of the most dominant animal in North America. Miners, livestock producers, hunters, and government trappers had done a pretty good job of removing predators from the Bitterroots, and by the early 1900's, the once plentiful wolves and grizzly bears had breathed their last breath there. I could almost hear the mountains mourning their passing like a parent losing a child. The Bitterroots were incomplete. The forests were missing the grizzly, and so was I.

As part of my job and because of my experience and interest, I spent time looking for grizzly bears and their sign. There were rumors that grizzly bears might possibly still exist in the Bitterroots, and the USFWS wanted to find out if that was true. I was responsible for trying to verify their presence whenever someone reported a grizzly bear sighting. I looked at many black bear pictures, tracks, and scats that were supposed to be grizzly and listened to many "grizzly bear" stories.

There were, however, a few pretty credible reports. One time I spoke with a guide who had worked in the North Fork of the Clearwater River up Kelly Creek. He said that he had seen a grizzly bear that stood up and looked at him while it fed on a dead horse. According to him, he saw the long white claws and distinct hump. Another time we got a good report from an outfitter who saw a grizzly feeding in the huckleberries in the upper Kelly Creek country. Dan Davis, the Clearwater Forest biologist, hired a helicopter and flew the berry fields that September. I took my horses and hauled a prototype trail camera up near Rhodes Peak and Cache Saddle, still following that report.

The first trail cameras were developed by Tim Manley, a bear researcher and manager from Montana. In those days the cameras had a large riding-lawnmower-type gel battery, a camera with 36 pictures on a roll of film, and a motion sensor, all stuffed into a surplus military ammo can with holes cut out. Each weighed probably ten pounds. If the battery got low, the camera malfunctioned and shot through all the film. If a moth or branch flew around in front of the sensor it would shoot through the roll. Despite all that, we occasionally got a few good animal photos.

I set the camera on a likely game trail near Cache Saddle. A short time after setting the camera, it snowed. With hunting season in full swing, I couldn't get back up to retrieve it, so I contacted Mike Stockton, the local outfitter, and he rode up to get the camera in late October in "belly-deep snow."

Upper Kelly Creek habitat, southeasterly from Kidd Lake, northern section of Bitterroot Recovery Area. Inset: Huckleberry bushes along trail in Middle Fork of Kelly Creek.

Although there were no photos of grizzly bears, the exercise was worth it to me to learn a bit about that country. In my view it was some of the best grizzly bear habitat in the Bitterroots and in Idaho, much like Glacier Park. It was, however, thick with black bears, and their food habits were quite similar to grizzly bears. After that trip, I always thought that if a bear came from Montana it would likely walk through Cache Saddle and find the huckleberry fields of Williams Creek or upper Kelly Creek.

I worked with the USFWS and IDFG biologist Greg Servheen in 1991 to hire a couple of technicians to place trail cameras throughout the North Fork of the Clearwater River. I helped them place a few but mostly just provided location ideas to the crew. They spent several months but couldn't find any evidence of a grizzly.

From 1984 to 1992, I spent thousands of hours on horseback and on foot in the Selway-Bitterroot Recovery Area, and the best spot for grizzly bears in my view was in the upper Kelly Creek country. There were lots of locations and large swaths of the recovery area that looked ideal, but that upper Kelly Creek area seemed remote, full of available food, and had previously been the location of some credible grizzly sightings. It just looked like they should be there.

In 1991, after much deliberation and soul searching, I left my job and career as a Conservation Officer and took a promotion as a biologist with IDFG in McCall. There, I was able to explore what would eventually become much of the southern part of the recovery area in the Frank Church-River of No Return Wilderness. In 1992, I moved to Lewiston as a regional biologist and got back into the Bitterroot Recovery effort as the regional IDFG biologist. I served as the Department's expert on grizzly bears for the team and provided staff assistance to the Bitterroot Ecosystem Subcommittee (BESC) as well as to my Regional Supervisors who often chaired the BESC for years to come.

The 1982 Grizzly Bear Recovery Plan referred to the Bitter-roots as an "Evaluation Area in need of more research." That seemed like a calling to me. The USFWS wanted to develop a separate "Bitterroot Chapter" (Chapter) for the Recovery Plan by late 1993, to outline how grizzly bears could be recovered. I was part of the team to develop the Chapter, and that was when the Bitterroot grizzly bear recovery effort started to get interesting.

Author with a black bear cub at the Idaho Department of Fish and Game office in Lewiston, Idaho, 1993.

CHAPTER 3

BB: THE EARLY YEARS

BB AND HIS SISTER GREW RAPIDLY, doubling in size in just a couple weeks. By the middle of February, their eyes were open, making it easier to find the nipples and mother's milk that was full of the nutrients and fat they needed to grow. BB's little body was now covered in soft gray baby fur. He began walking around the den earlier than his sister, and he regularly crawled over his mother's head and body, making it difficult for her to sleep for very long.

By March, both of the cubs were becoming restless. When not wrestling with each other, they explored every nook of the well-constructed den. It was dark most of the time, but the days were becoming longer. Some light filtered through the snow into the den as the sun made a higher arc in the sky. Soon, the snow started melting and water began dripping into the entryway. BB explored this too, but because he found it cold and uncomfortable, he hurried back to the warmth of his mother, shivering as he nestled in.

The snow had melted enough by mid-April that the female decided it was time to head outside. The cubs had grown to about ten pounds each by now, though BB was a bit larger than his sister.

Their activity was similar to that of a puppy. They had incredible high-energy moments of biting and tussling with each other, followed by feeding, and then falling sound asleep.

The female was becoming eager to let the rambunctious little fur balls run around outside. She had lost a great deal of weight nursing the cubs and living off her fat for six months. She was now noticeably thinner, with her hip bones sticking out. She eventually began to dig and push her way through the remaining snow and through the entrance until the sun suddenly burst into the den. The cubs were confused at first as the female squeezed her way out of the entrance and stood outside.

Until now, the cubs' world had been the cozy little den, and although very curious, they were also a bit afraid. But their mother's soft mewing slowly coaxed the cubs to the entrance. BB was the boldest and moved up the entrance toward the sunshine first. He stood at the entrance as his blue eyes got used to the brightness of sun on the snow, but it didn't take long for him to begin exploring. He soon began sniffing and biting at the branches of the subalpine fir trees nearby. The snow was cold on his feet so he picked them up with an exaggerated high-stepping motion that suddenly made him lose his balance, causing him to career downhill for a few feet until he slid into the fir saplings below. The slide was exhilarating to him so he did it again and again, scrambling up the hill and sliding and tumbling down; all the while, his concerned mother looked on.

By now, BB's sister had emerged and huddled next to her mother, nervously watching her brother. She slowly walked toward BB, sniffing at the snow and the muddy little paw prints he had left during his escapades. BB saw his sister and ran up to her, knocking her downhill. She didn't much like that and began bawling to her mother. The female watched briefly, then turned and began to slowly move upward toward the ridgeline. The cubs soon followed, but not before BB gave his sister one more good body bump, sending her tumbling and bawling another complaint to her mother.

Once they reached the top of the ridge, the world seemed to change. The sun was brighter and warmer now as they faced south-west. The female closely watched her cubs as they scrambled in her tracks, falling into the depressions she created when she occasionally punched through the crystallizing spring snow. They were young and still weak and struggled to climb out of her tracks and the depressions in the snow.

The female could smell green grass growing in tree wells, and where snow had been blown off the slopes and melted, well below where they stood. She knew it was time to eat, and although food would be available farther down, the cubs were not quite ready for the dangerous move. She too was still very weak from the long winter, having lost both fat and muscle. This was enough activity for their first day outside, and the female cautiously worked her way back toward the den to give the cubs more time to strengthen and learn to walk on the snow. When she eventually decided to leave the den for good, the walking would be treacherous for the little fur balls, and she instinct-ively knew they all needed to get stronger first.

Every day for a week, the female and her two cubs would emerge from the den and play outside. Occasionally she would walk them across the slope and up the ridgeline to bask in the sun. Then they would explore a little and return to the den and nurse. The cubs were becoming less interested in going back into the den and com-plained loudly whenever she did. They would run in circles, chasing each other in the den and making it impossible for the female to rest as they passed her head time and again. Finally, she decided it was time for the move. She slowly made her way over the top of the ridge, heading to one of the green patches far below, while the cubs did their best to keep up.

The going was slow and a bit treacherous for a small cub making its first journey into the world. But it was all so exciting! The cubs were able to keep from sliding too far down the snowfield by stepping in their mother's footprints. Although the snow was crystalized into a corn consistency, the mother's heavy body made sufficient indentations for the cubs to have a place to step, and they had already learned how to crawl out of the depressions or walk around them during the previous few days' excursions. BB carelessly stepped out of the tracks once and, to his mother's horror, slid quickly downhill. But like a mountain climber would use an ice ax to come to a stop, he instinctively rolled over on his belly and dug his little claws into the snow—a trick he had learned when wrestling with his sister near the den. Once stopped, he was able to scramble back up toward his mother and sister.

The little family finally reached the safety of the grass, and the female began to eat her first food in six months. She wasn't very hungry yet because her stomach had shrunk so much, but her body knew it needed nutrients. She had lost nearly 100 pounds, and nursing the growing cubs was demanding more calories than she could continue to produce for much longer without eating some food. The cubs watched her grazing at first, then began playing again. They didn't yet know what solid food was, and it would take a little while for them to experiment. Though the grass was only a few inches tall, it was enough for the female to fill her empty but shrunken stomach. It wouldn't be long before night fell, and she had to find a suitable nest to spend the night. Temperatures still dropped below freezing at night, and if it snowed or rained, the cubs could easily become hypothermic.

A patch of trees served as a nighttime windbreak and would provide some warmth when the temperatures dropped and the thermal winds began sliding down the mountain. As the female moved toward a patch of fir trees, she stopped and sniffed the ground and began digging. A squirrel midden lay beneath the surface, and she could smell the contents. The squirrel had cached some fat-rich pine nuts, and they provided a quick snack for her. She moved deep into the trees and began digging a shallow nest by flattening the ground and then piling some dry duff and grass on the spot. She was already tired, and the lethargy from six months in the den had not totally left her. Her muscles were weak, having lost a quarter of their size and strength over the winter, and her body was still trying to adjust.

The cubs were tired and very hungry. The mother lay back in the nest and presented her nipples for the cubs. They fed ravenously for several minutes until they were full. The female turned her heavily furred back toward the mountain where the cold thermal winds began to whisper downhill and laid her tired body down. She had a full belly from her first meal of the new season, and the contented cubs snuggled up beneath her hair and remaining fat folds and immediately fell asleep.

The next morning the female awoke to a light frost on her back. The cubs had buried themselves deep under her fur and found a nipple to suckle. Once the cubs were fed, she stood up and moved out to the early morning sunlight to gather some warmth from the rays. The frost was melting off the grass patch as the sun grew warmer, and she began feeding as the cubs played. Soon, she started moving downhill again, toward the sound of a creek where she knew higher-quality food would be. She traversed through an avalanche chute that still had ten feet of snow and a collection of broken trees and splinters. She stopped and lifted her nose to the air. She smelled something familiar —rotting flesh.

She soon spotted the hind leg of a moose sticking out of the snow. The coyotes had already feasted on what they could reach and had tried to dig deeper in the snow to retrieve the rest. However, the avalanche had created an icy tomb for the cow moose, and it would take all the bear's strength to remove the heavy frozen body. She began digging and pulling at the carcass. Slowly she made progress and ate as she worked, while the cubs watched and tried to help.

BB found the smell fascinating. When a chunk of meat went flying past him, he instinctively ran to catch it. He picked it up in his mouth and it tasted strangely good to him, but his little baby teeth could not rip it apart in pieces small enough to swallow. Instead he played with it by tossing it around and carrying it to his sister to play tug-of-war.

Meanwhile, the mother feasted. This was just what her body needed, but her stomach was not yet ready to accept it after digesting nothing for six months. Shortly after gorging on about 10 pounds of meat, she vomited. She sniffed the pile of regurgitated meat until her upset stomach relaxed, then ate it. She did not give up on the carcass either. She continued to tug and eat until she had consumed enough meat to satisfy her for the time being. This time it all stayed with her.

Then she moved away from the carcass to nap in some trees. She put herself in a spot where she could see the carcass but was upwind in case unwanted visitors were attracted to the smell. In that fashion, she could see anything that approached the carcass from downwind, so she could either protect the carcass or flee, depending on the situation. She knew coyotes were in the area but they didn't bother her as much as the wolves or other bears. Her young cubs were totally dependent on her for everything, and they hadn't yet been faced with danger. That was about to change.

All three bears were fast asleep when a noise woke the mother. She was immediately alert, and her nose and ears pointed to the direction of the sound. A bear's eyesight is about as good as a human's but their sense of smell is 10,000 times better. Their hearing is also better than a human's, but the nose is the business end of the bear.

All her senses were fully focused on trying to figure out what had made the sound.

Slowly, the hair on her back bristled and she quietly gave a grunt of alert to the cubs. Their instincts took over and they hustled up the tree they had been sleeping under. A black bear slowly walked out of the low end of the avalanche chute toward the moose carcass. When it got to within ten yards of the carcass, the female lunged toward the unsuspecting bear. The bear practically turned inside itself at the view of the 250-pound female making a full charge at him! The black bear flew in the direction it had come from, just as the female closed the distance. He was only a few feet from the edge of the forest when she made a lunge at him that came up just short. She roared a warning as the lucky black bear barely escaped serious injury.

The female knew the location was not very safe, but she also knew the food was very important to her and would provide more sustenance in just a few days than weeks of grazing on grass and forbs. So she decided to continue to feed and try to defend the carcass for a while longer. Coyotes were more focused on the meat than they were on the cubs, but she had to keep a watchful eye on them at all times. She didn't trust the cubs to stay in the tree while she fed, so she kept them close by her. The coyotes were a dangerous nuisance but had learned to keep their distance until she was done feeding. There was plenty to eat, and the female was making more available for them all the time. All they had to do was be patient.

This went on for a few days—gorging, sleeping, gorging, and sleeping. At first, the female's body was having difficulty with the heavy meat diet, but her diarrhea turned into dark meat scats within three days. She was already putting on fat, and the rapid weight loss common in spring was, for the time, reversed. The cubs fed well too, as the female's body produced more milk on the high protein diet.

By day three, the carcass was pretty well exposed and blood stains on the snow attracted aerial scavengers such as ravens. The sounds of the ravens attracted additional scavengers, and soon a wolverine was attacking the carcass while the bear rested. The sounds and smells, however, attracted another animal— this one much more ominous to the female and her cubs.

A large male grizzly was working his way up the creek bottom when he caught a whiff of rotting meat in the distance. He slowly made his way up the draw toward the smell and heard the telltale calls of ravens. The old male made a direct line for the carcass, secure in his dominance and ability to fend off any other animal in the area. He could smell the female bear's scent mixed with the meat smell, and she smelled familiar. He walked mightily out onto the avalanche chute so all could see him and loudly rumbled a few times for good measure.

The female also recognized the male as the one she had mated with the previous summer, but she was not going to take any chances with him. Rather than chirping for the cubs to climb a tree, she immediately started to move away. She pushed the cubs ahead of her as she retreated into the forest, quietly leaving to avoid any conflict. It worked. She got away with the cubs, and after a few hundred yards, she slowed down a bit. The cubs were running as fast as they could to keep up but had difficulty crossing the rough terrain.

The mother kept moving as fast as the cubs could follow until she felt far enough away for safety. The cubs were exhausted, and once the fright dissolved, they began to whimper. The female now felt comfortable enough to allow them to briefly nurse. Afterward, she moved up a small draw toward a midslope basin she knew would be safe from the male and would provide good forage for the family. For the next couple of weeks, this would be their new home.

Many forbs (flowering plants) had just started to develop in the basin, but the grasses were already tall. Lush angelica, cow parsnip, and horsetail grew around the small creek. These and other foods would provide sustenance while the cubs grew. Soon they would be on hard food, supplemented with mother's milk. This took time to learn as the cubs watched the mother foraging. Their little teeth were just getting big enough to chew on leaves and grasses, so they tasted a few. Eventually, they found some dandelions, which BB really enjoyed. The cow parsnip was growing quickly and, before many days, was as tall as the female, providing good protein and nutrition to the family.

By late May, BB weighed around 15 pounds, about the size of the Chinook salmon that were making their way up the Idaho rivers farther south. His sister weighed only about 12 pounds, and BB took advantage of that. He quickly tired of beating on his little sister, though, so he began exploring as much as his mother would let him. He climbed trees of all shapes and sizes. He walked out on logs over the creek and enjoyed plunging into a small pool, splashing around and doing it again and again. He would run up to his mother, jump on her back, and then run off before she cuffed him. He was getting strong and independent from all the play. Although his sister was smaller, she knew how to flip BB when he attacked her. She would let his weight roll the two of them until she landed on top and then sank her little teeth into his nose. That would cause BB to snort and back off for a while, giving her some space.

After a few weeks, the small basin that had provided good forage for the little family was starting to get used up, and what was left was quickly becoming less palatable. The female knew it was time to change locations. She liked the higher alpine basins, away from the male bears, and knew which one was best. But the journey wouldn't be easy. It would require a dangerous river crossing, and the rivers were flowing near their peak. She had to make a decision soon but was delaying it as long as she could. She wasn't sure the cubs were ready yet.

She slowly moved down the draw toward the river, foraging along the way. She knew of a good crossing in the river where it was wider and a little slower and not quite as deep. At low water it was an easy walk across, but right now it was flowing deeper than she liked. It made her nervous. She decided not to try it that day and instead continued to feed along the banks. Nightfall was coming soon, and she chose to stay in a grove of trees near the river until morning. The cubs were enjoying the backwater pools, and there was enough food here for the night, so they bedded down.

It was the first of June. The female woke up as the morning sun began poking through the cedar branches. She soon moved back out to the grassy riverbank, where they foraged for a short time. The water level was noticeably lower this morning, as the nighttime temperatures had dropped and the snowmelt had slowed down. The cubs were slightly bigger and stronger, but she still wasn't sure they were ready for the treacherous crossing.

She was contemplating the perils of making the crossing when she heard a branch snap behind her. She spun around and between them and the trees a huge male grizzly was staring at her. Her back was to the river and she was trapped! The cubs sensed the danger and nervously crawled under her belly as the female backed toward the river, her jaws popping a warning sound. This was a high-stakes bluffing game, and the male knew it. She would fight to the death to protect her cubs, but the male was almost twice her size and not afraid of any bear. This male was on the very edge of his home range, and the female did not recognize him. This was danger.

The male began walking stiff-legged toward her in a sideways fashion, showing his bulk and size, and looking first at the cubs and then at her. He had big open cuts on his face and neck from a recent battle; it was mating season, and he had been battling for the rights to breed. He surmised this female was not receptive, but the cubs looked like easy food.

The female knew she had no chance against this male, and the only escape route was the river. She spun around, and with BB on the upriver side and his sister on the downriver side, she made the plunge, expecting the cubs to follow. The male made his charge to the shoreline as the cubs jumped in. The female spun around to meet him and give the cubs a chance to escape.

The cubs were terrified and started to swim out into the river, but they were confused and turned to look at their mother. The female attacked the male in the face where he was already cut and ripped a larger tear, exposing his cheekbone. The male quickly countered and roared as he rose on his hind legs in the water and delivered an awful blow to the female. She rolled sideways just as the enormous paw swiped her side and the claws raked her ribs. Out of the corner of her eye, she saw the cubs just out of reach of the male but still confused as they swam in the backwater pool.

The mother turned so he had to position himself with his back to the cubs. Just to her left there was an upturned tree root tangled with driftwood. The tree was lying down, and between the root and the trunk she spotted a small space just big enough for her to dive into and escape. The male was now angry, and adrenaline was coursing through his veins and heavily muscled body; he regrouped and readied for a deadly charge. She waited just long enough for him to move and then dove toward the root wad. He exploded after her and bit into her haunch just as she dove under the tree. She yanked forward, and her momentum forcefully pulled his head into the tree trunk, making him lose his grip. She immediately scrambled out the other side and ran by the cubs while plunging into the river. The cubs quickly followed.

The current quickened as she moved away from shore. The cubs could not keep up and began moving downstream with the current. Their little heads were barely above the water. The female looked back at the big grizzly, who by then was sitting by the root wad, still stunned from hitting his head. She circled back below the cubs so they could climb onto her back. BB immediately crawled up onto her shoulders, but his sister was already weakening from the current and was coughing from inhaling water. Their mother kept trying to get the small cub to crawl up onto her, but the cub was too weakened from the cold water and current. The mother's body created a bit of an eddy for the cub to swim in, but this only worked briefly until the current became too swift, and the female began floundering.

Like a tick, BB hung on for dear life while his sister's life-and-death struggle unfolded. They were almost all the way across when the little cub slowly separated from her mother, moving downstream, with her head alternately above and below water, until finally, her little head disappeared. The female charged to shore with BB on her back. She ran up onto the bank and shook furiously, forcing BB to fall off. Then she took off down the shoreline, calling for her cub, jumping in at times and once pulling on a floating stick, thinking it was her. She continued her panicked search while ignoring BB. He followed her as best he could but soon lost sight of her as she frantically searched for her lost cub.

BB fell further behind until he was all alone and very frightened. The only thing he knew to do was to call for her. Finally, he found the nearest tree and instinctively climbed it until he was high up in the cedar tree and felt safe. There, he clung to a limb, whimpering and waiting for his mother to return. His baby fur was matted with mud and water, and he was very cold. The shade of the cedar tree and light breeze made him even colder, and he shivered involuntarily to stay warm. BB was hungry, scared, and cold, and hypothermia was a real danger. He had never been without his mother and sister before and had never been this hungry and cold. His mother had always returned after a short while, especially when he or his sister called.

All of a sudden, BB heard something below the tree and immediately called out, thinking it was his mother. But instead, it was the big male that had crossed the river in pursuit, once he had regained his wits. The male sniffed below the tree and circled it a few times. Then he stood up on his hind legs and leaned against the trunk, sniffing where BB had climbed. The male shook his enormous head side to side, trying to shake off the headache he had received from the tussle with BB's mother; the flap of bloody skin on his cheek flopped as he shook.

BB remained quiet, shaking in fear and cold at the sight of the bear. His feet and baby claws could barely hold onto the tree in his weakened state. Suddenly he lost his grip and slipped off the branch, falling toward the waiting male. As he fell, he bounced off one branch and flipped toward the trunk. With his energy stoked by fear, he was able to grab the next branch with one tiny paw, halting his descent. With his little front legs extended, he was able to reach with his hind feet over the branch and right himself; he then moved over the trunk and started climbing. He climbed higher than he had before, until he could no longer see the giant bear at the base of the tree. Finally, the big male moved away from the tree and away from the direction BB's mother had gone.

Eventually, it started to get dark. BB had been in the tree for hours, and shards of sunlight coming through the branches helped his fur slowly dry and his shivering to become less violent. Pretty soon he decided to try and move farther up the tree. He got lucky again; there was an abandoned pileated woodpecker's nest hole just above the branch he was sitting on. His body was still trembling, and it was getting colder outside as he climbed up to the hole and was able to climb in. It was warm and dry inside, and finally his shivering ceased. He poked his head out of the hole, still listening for his mother if she should call. He fell asleep hungry, whimpering, and dreaming about his mother's milk and the terrible bear that had tried to kill her. And he dreamed of his sister.

Later, BB was woken by a noise at the base of the tree and poked his head out. It was now dark, but he could just barely make out a gray form walking around the base of the tree. Again, he thought it was his mother, so he gave a quick bawl. It was not his mother; instead, at the base of the tree, a wolf was looking up at the cub. Even though he didn't know what it was, BB recognized danger and quickly pulled back into the hole and stayed quiet. He heard the wolf sniffing for a while, and then it was quiet again.

BB finally settled down, and although he was lonely, he felt safe and warm and fell into a fitful sleep. When it was almost daylight, a howl in the distance woke him up again. BB was even hungrier now but also very scared. He waited until daylight, and as the sun poked through the branches, he became bolder. His hunger was getting the best of him, so he decided to climb down and look for something to eat. He didn't, however, want to get far from the safety of his tree. He slowly descended to the base of the tree where he could see some vege-tation about ten feet away. He moved over to it, cautiously sniffing for any signs of danger. Once he began eating and the hunger pangs slow-ly subsided, he soon forgot about how scared he was—until suddenly a noise startled him. The wolf had returned.

BB instinctively hunkered down in the grass as he focused on the wolf at the base of the tree. The wolf sniffed at the tree trunk, then the ground, and quickly began tracking BB's scent toward his hiding spot. The cub's short life had been full of danger already, but this was about as bad as it could get.

A cub alone with a wolf would last only seconds, and fear screeched through BB's body. He couldn't defend himself as the wolf drew closer and, without thinking, BB bawled as he made a break for it, running away from the wolf while looking for a place to hide or a tree to climb. His little legs moved as fast as they could but were no match for the wolf, who easily caught up to him in a few long strides. The wolf reached him just as BB dove into a patch of devil's club.

BB let out a terrible cry from both fear and pain as the thorns dug into his little body and the wolf's fangs snapped shut, just short of his butt. But in his haste to grab the cub, the wolf's nose got the full force of the thorns. He yelped in pain and pulled back momentarily. BB scrambled farther into the thorns, bawling as he went.

The noise from the skirmish was loud but not as loud as the roar that BB heard coming from behind him. Just as he turned to look, he saw a huge brown form moving at a speed and ferocity he had never seen. The roaring blur charged into the wolf with such speed and force that the wolf didn't have time to move.

BB's mother had searched for her female cub for many hours, pacing up and down the stream, moving farther away from BB as she searched. Her instincts were to protect the cub that was in danger, and she knew the little female was in deep trouble. For the time being, BB was safe. She could not give in to the idea that the female cub was dead—not yet.

She crashed along the shore, moving farther downstream while swimming out into the river back and forth in panic. Eventually, exhaustion and her aching wounds were getting to her. Her pain and instincts had narrowed her focus and for hours had closed off her thoughts about BB. She rested on the bank, long after the sun had set, until reality sank in. Her female cub was gone. She had done everything she could, but it wasn't enough.

As clarity began to slowly seep into her tangled brain, she remembered BB. She turned to find him and called for him, but he wasn't there. Her thoughts raced back to when she last saw him—hours ago and miles away. Once again, she panicked.

The female began moving back upstream the way she had come. She couldn't remember all the crossings, and the distances were only a blur in her memory, but she remembered where she had fought with the big male and where she last saw BB. She headed back in that direction with her nose to the ground. She was bleeding from the cuts and bites she had endured during that fight and had developed a limp as the muscles in her torn rump stiffened. Along with the long and difficult search for the female cub, the injuries and loss of blood had weakened and slowed her. Her fatigue was overwhelming, but she plodded on. She could smell her own tracks and blood off and on, but no BB.

The location was unfamiliar to her, but the direction she needed to go was clear. Her head was pounding and her weakened legs moved slowly, but still she continued her search. Her drive to find BB was all she needed. Her instincts took over as her senses were on high alert.

The going was slow and she needed to stop occasionally to rest and lick and clean her wounds. Flies had landed on the open sores and laid eggs, and pus was starting to form. The pain was taking its toll.

Finally, as the first gray streaks of daylight began to filter down along the river bottom, she recognized where she was. She was not far from where she had last seen BB. She began zigzagging up and down the bank and through the brush along the river, slowly making her way back upstream, searching and sniffing for his scent. Every now and again she would give a grunt or other call and stop and listen for a response. She continued her slow work upstream, until she heard it.

At first a muffled cry alerted her to a place a short distance up the bank—then she heard the sounds of something else. She recognized her cub bawling and what sounded like the yelp of a wolf. In a heartbeat, 10,000 years of grizzly bear evolution funneled into a location above her kidney called the adrenal gland. All the pain and fatigue were suddenly gone and were replaced by incredible anger, fear, power, and instinct. Her blood pressure spiked, causing it to suddenly accelerate through arteries and capillaries and into her thick muscles. The adrenaline caused tunnel vision; her target became clear.

The loss of one cub was too much to understand, and the pain of that loss weighed heavily on her. The second cub was in danger, and his simple cry had transformed her body into a deadly killing machine, hurtling forward like a boulder plummeting down a mountain.

BB's mother crashed through the brush without knowing what she was attacking; it was simply a dark form in the shadows, but it was hurting her cub. Her speed and force were so great the wolf barely had time to look up before she was on him. She crushed his back with the first blow and bit into his neck and skull, tearing flesh and bone with every bite. There was nothing left but fur, blood, and crushed bones, but still she continued ripping and tearing and roaring. The wolf was dead within seconds, but her fury lasted much longer.

Finally—eventually—a soft sound slowly filtered through her rage: it was the whimpering sound of her cub. Her deep gasps continued as she finally stopped the attack and caught her breath through her blood-drenched mouth; she slowly started to gain control of herself. She looked over to where the sounds were coming from, and slowly, out of the maze of devil's club, a small cub's face appeared.

BB had seen the "force" rush by him, and he had cowered motionless as he witnessed more fury than he had ever seen before. His mother instantly crushed and dismembered the wolf, and it frightened him. This was not how he remembered his mother, but he knew it smelled like her. He was unsure what to do, so he stared at the horror through the stems of the devil's club until things slowly settled down, and then he began to whimper.

Finally, his mother looked at him through her bleary bloodshot eyes and came forward quickly. At first BB was afraid and backed up, thinking she was going to attack him too, but as he cowered, she stopped and started licking his little head. It was a powerful reunion that BB would always remember; peace had finally returned to him and his mother. They were together again.

CHAPTER 4

HISTORY OF GRIZZLY BEARS IN THE BITTERROOTS

IT IS IMPORTANT, I think, to review the early years of grizzly bears in the Bitterroots. There were some locals and others who claimed there were never grizzly bears in the Bitterroots. One such figure was former Congresswoman Helen Chenoweth. Helen famously said she didn't believe Idaho Chinook and sockeye salmon were endangered if she could buy salmon in a can at Albertsons. She also said grizzly bears were schizophrenic.

Helen was a colorful anti-grizzly bear personality during the Environmental Impact Statement (EIS) writing period of the early 1990's. But there were many more people thinking that if there never were grizzly bears in the Bitterroots, there could be and should be no recovery. In their opinion, it would be a newly introduced population. For the EIS, we needed to document a history of grizzly bears in Idaho from the archives.

Grizzly bears were once very common in the western United States; they ranged from the Great Plains to the Pacific coast and from the Canadian border to the Mexican border. *(See Figure 1.)* Mountain men, early explorers, trappers, hunters, pioneers, gold diggers, and others wrote of their encounters with grizzly bears in Idaho. Native

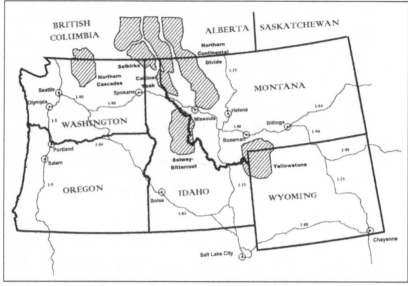

Figure 1. Historic range and densities have been greatly reduced over the past 150 years, although they are greater now than when grizzly bears were listed in 1975. Current grizzly bear population estimates in recovery areas are: Selkirks, 30-50; Cabinet-Yaak, 50-60; northern Continental Divide, 1,000; North Cascades, 1-6; and Yellowstone, 700. (Wayne Kasworm, USFWS, pers. com 2019.)

Americans living in Idaho—the Kootenai, Flatheads, Nez Perce, Shoshone, Bannock, and others—all held the grizzly bear as a sacred and revered animal that was often used as a totem. The Nez Perce Museum in Lapwai has a grizzly bear claw necklace on display.

Some of the earliest explorer accounts came from the journals of Lewis and Clark. The party ran into many grizzly bears on their way up the Missouri River in Montana. At that time, grizzly bears roamed the Great Plains and had highly carnivorous diets of bison carcasses and elk as well as high-quality forbs growing along the river bottom. The Corps of Discovery had heard about the grizzly bear in advance of their exploration and were looking forward to the encounter. They were quite proud of their Kentucky long-rifles, and being good marksmen, they felt perfectly capable of handling any animal they confronted.

Back in 1805, Webster had not yet created a dictionary. Consequently, Lewis, Clark, and the entire Corps of Discovery members spelled many words phonetically, but they still got the message across. On April 29, 1805, after killing a young grizzly, Lewis bragged in his journal that "the Indians may well fear this anamal equiped as they generally are with their bows and arrows or indifferent fuzees, but in the hands of skillfull riflemen they are by no means as formidable or dangerous as they have been represented."

Just a few days later, on May 5, William Clark and George Droulliard killed an enormous grizzly bear with some effort. Clark described it as, "…a verry large and a turrible looking animal, which we found verry hard to kill we Shot ten Balls into him before we killed him, & 5 of those Balls through his lights." Lewis estimated the weight of the bear at 500-600 pounds, about twice the size of the average black bear. He noted that after the bear was shot "he swam more than half the distance across the river to a sandbar & it was at least twenty minutes before he died; he did not attempt to attack, but fled and made the most tremendous roaring from the moment he was shot." Once the bear finally died, they butchered it for meat, bear oil, and its thick furry skin. Sobered by the size and ferocity of the bear, Lewis wrote, "I find that the curiossity of our party is pretty well satisfyed with rispect to this anamal."

Figure 2. Illustration from Sergeant Patrick Gass' journal after the Lewis & Clark Expedition, c. 1807.

Captain Clark and his men shooting Bears.   Page 95

They passed through Idaho on their way to the West Coast that fall and almost starved during the dangerous snowy crossing of the Bitterroots. When they returned to Idaho in the spring of 1806, snow in the mountains was still too deep to pass. Fully aware of the treacherous crossing that almost killed them the previous fall, they camped in the upper Clearwater River near current-day Kamiah and waited for snow to leave the Bitterroot Mountains. There, they encountered multiple bears and shot many, but they were confused as to the species.

One day they gathered up the multiple colored hides and asked the Nez Perce Indians to help them identify the different species, of which they thought there were many because of the various colors of the fur. The Nez Perce separated the hides out into two piles. One pile was the smaller black bear they were familiar with from the eastern United States. Confusion came from the fact that the western black bear came in multiple colors, from blonde to chocolate to black. The black bear, however, all had the smaller, shorter claws. The Indians told the party that these bears were more docile, climbed trees, and were easy to kill; they called them *Yack-kah*. The other bear, the "white bear" or *Hoh-host*, had longer claws, a silver tint to the hide, and was much harder to kill and more aggressive. They said killing them was equivalent to killing a warrior. The Nez Perce dictionary actually indicates the term for grizzly bear is *Xaxat*.

Based on their journals, we were able to determine that during their stay in the Bitterroot area of Idaho, the Corps of Discovery killed five grizzly bears. They stated these bears were not as ferocious as the bears they found in the plains of Montana.

The Bitterroots teemed with spring, summer, and fall Chinook salmon, sockeye salmon, steelhead trout, and many other species of fish that grizzly bears and Indians alike relied upon for their protein. Salmon spawned in the high rivers and streams and swam as many as

900 miles from the Pacific Ocean to complete their life cycle in Idaho. Grizzly and black bears were found congregated along waterfalls, shallow waters in high mountain streams, and other confined places that improved their fishing success and where resources were plentiful.

Another interesting quote by Lewis on May 15, 1806, says, "the most striking differences between this species of bear and the common black bear are the former are larger, have longer tallons and tusks, prey more on other animals, do not lie so long nor so closely to winter quarters, and will not climb a tree tho' ever so heardly pressed. The variegated bear I believe to be the same here with those on the Missouri but they are not so ferocious as those perhaps from the circumstance of their being compelled from the scarcity of game in this quarter to live more on roots and of course not so much in the habit of seizing and devouring living animals. The bear here are far from being as passive as the common black bear they have attacked and fought our hunters already but not so fiercely as those of the Missouri. There are some of the common black bear in this neighbourhood."[1]

Other early hunters included William Wright, who wrote about his early 1900's hunting expeditions in a book entitled, "The grizzly bear." [2] He stated that in August and September, "dog" salmon spawned in the tributaries of the Clearwater River, and there he watched many grizzlies fishing for salmon. Wright killed multiple grizzly bears while they were fishing, including two in one day. He said many had gathered to feast at that time.

Another time, he and his hunting partner killed a female and two cubs near present-day Kamiah, with a "modern" firearm known as the .30-40 Krag, one of the first smokeless military firearms developed in 1895 and used during the Spanish American war. He spoke of how impressed he was with the takedown power of this modern rifle. Being a good storyteller, he also wrote about once having hand-to-hand combat along the Middle Fork of the Clearwater River with a grizzly, eventually killing it with the help of his dogs and a hunting knife. He also wrote about being chased by a grizzly bear into Kelly Creek near the North Fork of the Clearwater, when his gun jammed and he had to escape by hiding under a logjam on the river.

Bud Moore wrote a book entitled, *The Lochsa Story: Land Ethics in the Bitterroot Mountains.*[3] He wrote of the trappers and hunters who killed off many bears; one of those he wrote about was Wes Fale, who trapped several grizzly bears around his cabin at Big Sand Lake. Bud lived in the Bitterroots in the early 1900s and worked as a sheepherder as a young boy.

Sheep followed the massive Great Burn of 1910 that destroyed millions of acres of old-growth timber and killed many firefighters and people living in the mountains. Grasslands and shrub fields replaced the forests, making for ideal conditions for sheep and their herders. There were still many predators remaining in the Bitterroots at that time, including coyotes, wolves, cougars, black bears, and grizzly bears.

Bud recalled his childhood when, as a young boy of 12 in 1931, he was hired to watch a flock of sheep up near Spruce Creek near the Idaho-Montana border. His father was a bit worried and came up to check on him at just the right time—there was a grizzly bear near the flock of sheep. During that same time, they also noticed several bear hides hanging from fences and trees, from animals shot by the herders, "and some of those were grizzly bear."

Bud became a mountain man and trapper in the Lochsa River country, was a marine during WWII, and later was hired by the U.S. Forest Service (USFS) as the District Ranger in Powell. During his tenure there, he found a grizzly bear track that had been hardened in the mud; in his book he stated it was "as if the mountains were trying to preserve the passing of the last grizzly bear." That was in 1946, and we credited Bud with recording the last verified evidence of a grizzly bear for the next 60 years.

He was also credited with having killed the last grizzly in 1956 at Colt Killed Creek near Elk Summit in the Bitterroot Mountains near the border of Idaho and Montana. That date and event had been special to me because that was the year I was born, and it took place in the patrol district of my first permanent job as a game warden. Bud denied that ever happened, but he did recall killing a large black bear near the cabin that someone later said was a grizzly. He laughed about it, saying that he never bothered to correct the account. In some publications you will still see that factual error.

Bud was a character and continued to be a mountain man until his dying days. In his 70s, he was still snowshoeing into the Bob Marshall Wilderness in Montana to run his trapline—alone. He would often spend the nights under a blowdown he lit on fire and sleep with a wool blanket to stay warm. He was a wiry old dude who cut his own timber, following a closely scripted management plan, and milled it on his property in the Swan Valley in western Montana. He was always an advocate for returning grizzly bears into the Bitterroots and mourned the passing of the great bear.

He wrote a chapter in his book about grizzly bears, and I always considered him a naturalist and one of the last true Bitterroot Mountain Men from that era. I spoke with him a few times and once told him that if we ever brought grizzly bears back to the Bitterroots, we would make sure he was there to help release them. He always liked that thought. Unfortunately, Bud died in 2010 at the ripe old age of 91, before any reintroductions occurred. He never did get to help release any bears. But his desire and hope for grizzly recovery helped provide perspective and background for new-age land managers and a few of us biologists as well.

In 1985 and 1986, IDFG hired Dr. Wayne Melquist to search historical accounts and hike around the Bitterroots looking for grizzly bear sign. He wrote a report that included photos of a possible grizzly bear track.[4] During that time, in 1984 and 1986, I had been hired to hike the Bitterroots looking for wolf sign. I spent one summer and one winter exploring the Bitterroot Wilderness and Frank Church-River of No Return Wilderness areas. Timm Kaminski, Jerome Hansen, Don Young, and I partnered up at different times to ski, snowshoe, and backpack hundreds of miles of backcountry, trying to find wolves. Having recently worked in Glacier National Park as a bear management ranger, I also instinctively looked for grizzly bear sign.

In 1991 and 1992, we hired a few technicians to place trail cameras in promising habitat in the Bitterroots that might have a grizzly or two. Those locations were based on historical observations, accounts from locals, outfitters, USFS personnel, my neighboring conservation officer Gene Eastman, and reports that we had received. Greg Servheen, with funding from the USFWS, ran the project as a biologist in the Lewiston office. While in Powell, I helped identify sites and checked on the technicians to make sure they were okay but also made suggestions about likely camera sites. After two seasons in the Bitterroots, they did not find any evidence of grizzly bears. Additionally, hunters killed hundreds of black bears in that area over the years and someone would have likely either killed a grizzly or reported seeing one on their bait sites, if in fact they were there. But those studies helped lay some of the groundwork for what would later become the proposal for the Bitterroot Chapter of the Grizzly Bear Recovery Plan. If grizzly bears were not present or were present in very low numbers, they would have to be reintroduced to meet recovery goals.

CHAPTER 5

BB GROWS

FOR A WHILE AFTER HE LOST HIS SISTER, BB stayed close to his mother. This was partly because he didn't want to be separated from her again and partly because his mother became overly protective, if that is even possible for a mother grizzly.

BB learned everything he could from his mother. He learned to walk with his nose into the wind whenever possible to sniff for food and danger. His mother was ever searching for food, so she taught him what plants were good foods and which ones he should avoid. She taught him what to eat when the berries weren't quite ripe, where to find the first ripened berries, and what to eat after the berries were no longer available. It didn't take long for him to learn which berries were good and which ones made him sick.

He also learned that ripping old dead logs apart provided insect larvae and ants—which, by the way, had a very nice sour flavor. He learned how to dig roots, bulbs, and corms from glacier lily and spring beauty. And he found wild onion tops and bulbs quite tasty. He learned that vegetation ripened first at lower elevations and southern exposures and that they had to climb in elevation to find fresh forbs later in the year.

He learned that even though vegetation filled him up, meat was really what he liked best. Ground squirrels and marmots were a delicacy when his mother would dig them up. She rolled large boulders in order to get a small morsel. Often, while she was digging for squirrels or roots, insects would become exposed and BB loved licking them up.

It was late that summer before his mother finally cut him off from her milk, which was earlier than some other nursing females. That had been his favorite meal, and he whined about it for several days. He even dreamed of nursing while making little suckling sounds while asleep. He eventually forgot about it, though, with so many other things to eat, especially huckleberries. And he also felt a bit more independent, not being so reliant on his mother for food.

A grizzly's diet is 80-90% vegetation, but their digestive system is an adapted carnivore gut. Because they don't have a multi-chambered stomach (called a rumen), they can't digest vegetation as well as a deer or elk can. Instead, they evolved from a strict carnivore diet and have an elongated gut that gives the body more time to remove nutrients from the vegetation. Still, when you see what came out the back end, you can usually tell what went in the front end. A grizzly scat during berry season often looks like the inside of a berry pie, fresh out of the oven.

When grizzlies find a good field of glacier lilies to dig in, they often turn over acres of dirt to find the bulbs. Thus, they become not only a cultivator, but when they defecate, they also plant and fertilize seeds. When they defecate in these areas, they are leaving the seeds of many plants they have eaten, including berries. Globe huckleberry is one of their favorites in north Idaho and western Montana, and a grizzly bear will plant huckleberries all across the high country while they search for more to eat.

Huckleberries and bears are a team and rely on each other for reproduction and survival. The same goes for many plant and animal species. They are connected like a string weaving in and out of the tapestry of a mountain ecosystem. Once you lose a species, it may take a while for the others to catch on and adapt, but they all lose or gain something in the process. Once one is lost, other species must adapt and evolve or weaken and die. Some species that were suppressed by the lost species may increase dramatically. This change up and down the line is called trophic cascade.

In other words, all species affect something else, and when a species dies, it tweaks the system. There are winners and there are losers, but the ecosystems change along with species' composition. The beauty of the Endangered Species Act (ESA) is that it not only attempts to prevent species from going extinct, but it tries to recover the species and the habitat on which they depend. Losing grizzly bears or any species is unacceptable to the ESA or those who embrace the law; an ecosystem may never fully recover from the loss, so we must do what we can to prevent the loss or recover the species. And history has proven time and again that just because you love something doesn't mean you won't lose it. As Aldo Leopold wrote: "To keep every cog and wheel is the first precaution of intelligent tinkering."

BB and his mother gained plenty of weight in July, August, and September, when the berries were out in full strength. BB would eat a gallon or two a day, while his mother ate more than twice that. The high sugar content quickly converted to fat and BB got about as round as he was long. Eventually, after several weeks, the berries became fewer and days became shorter. Then, suddenly, the woods were full of humans.

At first BB's mother became more alert as she smelled their presence and heard vehicles driving on roads down the valley. BB heard elk bugling for the first time, and it scared him. He soon learned what was making the noise and became less frightened. His mother would often approach the sounds from downwind to investigate. Sometimes they would find where elk had been fighting, with the ground all torn up and the rank smell of elk urine everywhere. Other times they smelled humans and melted off into the forest.

After a few weeks, they heard loud noises—rifle shots—that immediately alerted his mother. She was very cautious around these noises and smells, but when darkness came, she would sometimes approach and investigate where the shots had been fired. Once again, her cunning proved valuable, as one night she was able to track a wounded elk until she found it under a blow-down. She and BB gorged on it until there was little left.

His mother's nervous behavior during this time of year made BB uneasy as well. The smells of humans were particularly alarming to his mother and, consequently, to him.

The nights were frosty, and early fall had turned into late fall. Then one morning, there was snow on the ground. For a few days it had rained, but now the temperatures were dropping. It had already snowed and melted, but this felt different. BB noticed that there were fewer and fewer birds singing and flitting about in the trees. Geese were flying overhead in large flocks. As foods became scarcer, he and his mother spent more time sleeping and less time foraging. Finally, with BB in tow, she headed to the highest parts of the Selkirk mountain range.

The second winter of BB's life was different from the first. He and his mother found a den site not far from their previous winter's location. She dug furiously into the hillside near some trees but soon hit a large rock she could not move or dig around. So she moved a few hundred yards to below the ridgeline and tried again.

Snow was accumulating, but she dug steadily until a tunnel appeared, then a bowl. BB did what he could but pretty much just watched and tried to stay out of the way of the flying dirt and debris.

For several hours she worked, throwing dirt outside until a mound appeared at the entrance. It was nearly nightfall when she came out to gather bear grass from under tree wells where snow had not yet accumulated. She ripped clumps out with her teeth and packed them into the den. Soon she moved into the den and invited BB in. BB was wet and cold from the snow on his back and eagerly entered the small entrance into the bowl. It was a tight squeeze. The female seemed content and was tired. For the time being, this was good enough, and they soon fell asleep.

The next morning, BB's mother pushed him out while she finished excavating and making some last-minute adjustments. The snow was still falling, and BB was groggy and wet from sitting in snow that was already a foot deep. He was very happy when he was allowed to go back inside. He was tired and didn't fidget too long before he heard his mother's breathing change and slow down. Shortly after that, BB felt more tired and groggy than he could remember ever feeling, and could no longer keep his eyes open. He soon fell into his deep winter sleep, safe and warm with his mother.

CHAPTER 6

THE RECOVERY EFFORT GETS UNDERWAY IN THE BITTERROOTS

THE ENDANGERED SPECIES ACT requires that species on the List of Threatened and Endangered Species (those species that are either threatened or endangered of becoming extinct) must be recovered. In order to recover a species on the list, the U.S. Fish and Wildlife Service (USFWS) has determined that each species needs a plan to chart a path toward eventual recovery and delisting. For grizzly bears, the first recovery plan was finalized in 1982. The Grizzly Bear Recovery Plan (Plan) identified the Bitterroot Ecosystem (BE) as an Evaluation Area, or "area in need of more research"; biologists needed a clearer understanding of the adequacy of habitat in the BE and whether or not grizzly bears still existed there. The USFWS developed the Plan with help from partner agency biologists and university researchers. The Plan had several chapters, one for each ecosystem where grizzly bears existed and needed to be recovered: Yellowstone, Northern Continental Divide, Selkirk, and Cabinet-Yaak ecosystems. The North Cascades and Bitterroot Ecosystems were in need of further evaluation.

The BE needed further evaluation prior to becoming an actual recovery area. This would require more detailed analysis of habitat and a review of the population status to actually decide if a separate chapter in the Plan would be written for the BE recovery or if it would be removed from the recovery efforts altogether. This evaluation (and eventual recovery) would require extensive efforts by partner agencies. This was the start of the Bitterroot Ecosystem Recovery Chapter (Chapter).

Everyone involved in the recovery effort realized where many of the obstacles and roadblocks would be, even before we began to engage the public in an official capacity. There had already been studies conducted on habitat conditions, and we knew that much of the prime habitat in the Bitterroot Ecosystem (BE) lay outside of designated Wilderness. These national forests provided livelihoods for many Idaho and Montana forest workers and yielded timber products for consumers across the United States. It was also a public land recreational mecca that provided hiking, fishing, camping, horseback riding, and some of the best elk hunting in the West.

We knew that some people were deathly afraid of reintroducing grizzly bears, not only because of their fierce nature but also because of the land-use restrictions (both perceived and real) that might accompany them. We knew that local, state, and national politics would play a huge role. We knew that wolves were being reintroduced and that all the baggage accompanying them would also weigh down grizzly bear recovery. And we knew that for grizzly bears to be recovered they would need more champions than detractors. We needed local support that would lead to political strength. All of these obstacles created challenges that the USFWS and partner agencies would need to resolve if bears were ever going to be recovered in the Bitterroots.

The Habitat Controversy

When grizzly bears were listed under the Endangered Species Act (ESA) in 1975, the Bitterroot Ecosystem was an area that scientists and managers believed might still hold a few grizzly bears. The Recovery

Plan of 1982 stated that more research was needed to confirm whether bears still existed there and whether the habitat would still support a recovered population of bears.

Salmon and steelhead were eliminated from many of their former spawning grounds in the Bitterroots when the Clearwater River Dam was built in the 1920s. The summer and fall Chinook, steelhead, sockeye, and Coho in particular were believed to be important for grizzly bear survival. Indeed, many early reports of grizzly bears in the Bitterroot revolved around salmon fishing areas. Also, seed from the whitebark pine, another important grizzly bear food in late summer, was eliminated during the whitebark pine blister-rust epidemic. Some surmised that these two blows to the habitat would reduce the quality and make it uninhabitable for grizzly bears.

Between 1979 and 1991, four separate grizzly bear habitat studies and assessments were conducted in the Bitterroots prior to writing the Bitterroot Chapter.[1,2,3,4] Each one indicated that habitat contained within the Bitterroot Ecosystem was of sufficient quality and quantity to sustain a grizzly bear population. Sadly, these studies were still not considered adequate by many skeptics and those opposed to recovery. But they were ultimately considered adequate for the Interagency Grizzly Bear Committee (IGBC) to authorize proceeding with recovery in the area.

[NOTE: The IGBC was established in 1983 and was a committee of high-ranking federal managers, including three USFS Regional Foresters, one National Park Service (NPS) Regional Director, the Regional Director of the USFWS, the Montana State Director for the U.S. Bureau of Land Management (BLM), and state Fish and Game Directors or others appointed by the state governors of Idaho, Montana, Wyoming, and Washington.

Their direction was to oversee grizzly bear recovery. They were advised by the USFWS Grizzly Recovery Coordinator. Other invitees included Bureau of Indian Affairs Directors and representatives from the Canadian provinces of British Columbia and Alberta. Recently, IGBC has been updated to include two regional directors for the USFWS and two for the NPS.]

The IGBC declared the Bitterroot Evaluation area an official Recovery Area in December 1991. The Recovery Area initially consisted of a 3.4-million-acre swath of contiguous federal land that extended from the Salmon River in central Idaho, north to the headwaters of the St. Joe River. It included the east slope of the Bitterroot Mountains in Montana and the Selway River, Lochsa River, and North Fork of the Clearwater River drainages in Idaho. The Recovery Area was designated as Wilderness or roadless areas being studied for Wilderness, and much of it was National Forest land, which was prime timber country.

After having spent two summers working in Yellowstone and five summers in Glacier National Park, including conducting extensive grizzly bear habitat analysis in Glacier for my M.S. thesis research, I knew what constituted good bear habitat. I had traveled many miles in the Bitterroots during the 1980s and 1990s looking for wolf sign, then as a game warden monitoring wildlife and looking for poachers, and later as a regional biologist monitoring game and habitat in the region. All that time on horseback and on foot, as well as by vehicle and helicopter, gave me a grizzly's perspective of the habitat. I concurred with the scientific reports, because many of the places I roamed reminded me of both the Yellowstone and the Northern Continental Divide Ecosystems. Also, black bears crawled all through the country in very high densities and found plenty to eat. IDFG estimated black bear densities in the area at about one per square mile.

Except for the sheer volume needed to support a larger body size, bear biologists know that there are few differences in food habits between black and grizzly bears. However, grizzly bears can exploit more foods because their longer claws and muscle-filled shoulder mass enhance their ability to excavate. That, in turn, also allows them to exploit more open habitat in the prairies and in alpine vegetation with fewer trees.

Because the habitat they used as they evolved was often in more open areas, they could not use trees to help them escape from other bears or predators. This may have led to their more aggressive personalities. Their real weight gains typically resulted from consuming berries in Glacier, as well as ungulate meat and trout in Yellowstone, all of which were plentiful in the Bitterroots.

Even though grizzly bears are typically larger than black bears and need more calories, grizzly (brown) bears are found in many areas of the world where poor foods are limiting population size and growth rates. Poor habitat quality results in a slightly smaller grizzly bear, with lower reproductive rates and lower population densities. Bear size and population density are almost totally based on food availability and quality. Many 500-pound black bears are found where foods are plentiful, and many 250-pound grizzly bears are found where foods are less diverse or rich. The biggest grizzly bears in the world are found in areas where runs of multiple species of Pacific salmon occur in rivers and streams where bears can catch them.

The initial Bitterroot recovery area was large enough and had sufficient diversity of foods to sustain a grizzly bear population, but we hadn't yet figured out how many bears the habitat could sustain. Part of the area had a drier climate similar to the Yellowstone Ecosystem in the southern portions near the Salmon River, whereas the higher elevations were dominated by lodgepole pine, subalpine fir, and spruce. Farther north, however, the moisture changed to a more maritime-influenced climate, with high rainfall and the presence of western red cedar at lower elevations. In this climate, the trees grew larger, the undergrowth thickened with dense stands of berry shrubs that included globe huckleberry, and the overall habitat for bears improved.

Farther north, outside of the Wilderness boundaries, the timber industry and the economy were dependent on a free flow of timber from federal lands in order to sustain a timber-based economy. The relatively small towns of Kooskia, Kamiah, Orofino, Pierce, Weippe, and Elk City in north-central Idaho all were dependent on logging as a critical part of their economy. These communities all bordered the proposed recovery area in Idaho.

Of Fear and Men

Agency biologists knew that the largest opposition for grizzly recovery would likely come from citizens who were afraid of grizzly bears. Fear is something that is embedded in our *amygdala*, or "lizard brain" and which, for many people, overrides the frontal cortex (where logical decisions are made). Neurologists say the lizard brain is at the core of the brains of all complex vertebrates, including humans, and evolved as a beneficial part of the brain—the fear center. It plays a primary role in our memory, decision-making, and emotional responses, including fear, anxiety, and aggression. Fear of large carnivores is something that we all have left over from our caveman days and our early survival instincts.

Biologists understand these instincts and work hard to bring rational thought into these conversations; but statistics and rational thought don't mean much when the possibility looms of being ripped apart by a 500-pound beast. I knew that firsthand from working with grizzly bears for a number of years and having many close encounters in grizzly country. As a bear management ranger in Glacier National Park, I constantly discussed and explained grizzly bear behavior and biology to visitors from California to New York. In Glacier, bears were always on my mind. Looking back, as a young man from Maine, I think working with bears may have been my way of proving my masculinity to myself. In my view, there wasn't a beast in North America more dangerous than a grizzly bear.

My life's goal was to study grizzly bears, and I couldn't fathom not working with them and furthering our knowledge of them. I had worked with bears for years and in 1984 was struggling to pull funding together for a graduate study. The USFWS Coop Unit at the University of Montana knew of my funding struggles and offered me a fully funded ground squirrel study. Moving from grizzlies to ground squirrels would have been a magnitude change from what I wanted for myself and what interested me, so even though I appreciated their offer, I declined.

Although it was a struggle, I finally did get my bear funding and M.S. study off the ground. I knew my own calling much better than the professors at UM possibly could. Grizzly bears controlled my thoughts and defined who I was at the time, but that didn't change the fact that they could injure or kill me as I studied them. All I had to do was look at a well-known bear biologist and professor from Utah State University to prove it.

Dr. Barrie Gilbert was studying grizzly bear behavior in Yellowstone in the late 1970s when he lost sight of his study animal. As he hurriedly moved closer to get a better view, he stumbled into the bedded female he had been following. She reacted defensively, sensing that Barrie's rapid approach was a threat. Barrie immediately knew the mistake he'd made, but it was too late to stop the attack. She quickly acted defensively to eliminate the perceived threat and in so doing ripped half his face leaving him blind in one eye and badly scarred forever.

Barrie did not blame the bear. He knew he had made the mistake and pleaded with the Park Service not to kill the female, as was often the protocol following an attack. The Park agreed the attack was normal defensive behavior and did not kill the bear.

To his credit, following the attack and recovery, Dr. Gilbert continued to study grizzly and brown bears in Canada and Alaska and oversaw many more graduate studies, particularly as they pertained to bear behavior. But his scarred face was a constant reminder to his students and the rest of us that we were studying a dangerous animal, and as soon as you forgot that, you could be unceremoniously reminded.

Being able to control my fear around bears gave me confidence and perspective. I learned and understood how fear tended to wane with time spent in proximity to bears. Walking hundreds of miles in high-density bear country without incident, I developed a low-level fear and alertness, much like driving a car in traffic. My experience taught me, though, that for most of us, our fear might peak if we encountered a bear, much like it does when driving a car on a narrow road and meeting a large rig driving too fast toward you. Low-level fear forces you to walk with your head up and your senses on alert. An encounter causes adrenaline. Hikers in bear country should practice what they would do under various encounter scenarios. Bear spray can help provide a fallback if Plan A doesn't work.

However, even in Glacier, encounters were not that common and were a miniscule part of what you occasionally experienced while enjoying the great wonders of bear country. Injuries were so rare they became statistical anomalies. Statistically, getting killed by a bear in Glacier was more rare than getting injured by a vehicle, falling off a cliff, drowning, or having a heart attack.[5] Most people don't know that, however, and don't care; it is still a risk. Humans like being king of the forest, top dog, and in control of their surroundings. It's comfortable and allows the amygdala to sleep.

We knew that bringing bears into someone's forest playground and messing with their sanitized comfort would be an uphill battle. Discounting someone's fear as irrational would likely backfire. Not understanding it would be a mistake. We had our work cut out for us.

We also knew that the timber industry would be highly skeptical and fearful for another reason and would oppose recovery as well. When an animal is listed under the ESA, any action on federal land has to go through a Section 7 consultation with the USFWS to determine if the action would be detrimental to recovery. On private land, even if an individual bear is not killed outright, actions that are detrimental to a species recovery might be considered a "taking" under Section 9. Timber was king in that country, and being sensitive to the industry's concerns was going to be a key to success.

Appeasing the timber companies would likely also appease much of the local citizenry. We believed that for grizzly bears to survive, local citizens had to largely support them. Grizzly bear mortality from the "SSS" (Shoot-Shovel-Shut up) contingency was all too likely, especially given a small population of unwanted bears. Forcing bears onto an unwilling public that decried an overreaching federal government was biologically different than doing so with wolves. Wolf reproductive rates could sustain high illegal mortality, but grizzly bear reproductive rates are some of the lowest in the animal kingdom. The loss of a reproductive female could be catastrophic to a recovering grizzly bear population.

We state biologists and conservation officers were all too aware of high poaching rates in these outpost communities, and some of the out-of-work lumberjacks could think it was their God-given duty to eradicate any grizzly bears forced upon them.

Historical Background of the Bitterroots
and Competing Philosophies of Land Use

Bitterroot recovery was happening at the same time as wolf recovery in Idaho and Yellowstone. Local citizens, industry, and state and local politicians were feeling railroaded by the federal government. The battles were likely more about who controlled the land and way of life than they were about wolves or grizzly bears. People saw their way of life fading as transplants from "back east" or the "left coast" moved into the West. Those newcomers saw the vast acreages of federal land as more than a resource for utility and commerce. They were challenging the Old West mentality and invoking a new philosophy of espousing natural processes such as predation, let-burn wildfires, and ecosystem management rather than maximizing timber or livestock production.

Following the Great Burn of 1910, the U.S. Forest Service's primary function changed. That conflagration burned 4,700 square miles in north Idaho and western Montana. The loss of timber resources was so great that Forest Service Chief Gifford Pinchot and the leadership of the Forest Service believed that suppressing wildfire was of utmost importance, thereby preserving wildlands and wildlife, as well as human life. Additionally, what burned was no longer available to the timber industry and the public.

Much of the habitat within the Great Burn took decades to recover, as the fire was so hot in some places that the soil was actually sterilized. Because the seeds of some trees could not regenerate in many areas, grass, forbs, and shrubs moved in, providing an open canopy ideal for grazing and browsing ungulates such as elk and deer and, of course, domestic sheep and cattle. By 1920, the Bitterroot Mountains had become important to the sheep industry, and thousands of sheep grazed in the wildlands of Idaho and Montana. With sheep came sheepherders.

The primary biomass of wild ungulates at the time consisted of mule deer and bighorn sheep. Elk were scarce, partly due to their low initial numbers when forests were thick and grasslands were minimal, and partly due to unregulated and commercial hunting at that time to supply mining camps, homesteaders, and logging camps with fresh meat. When sheep became prominent on the landscape, sheepmen killed predators on sight. Hunters, trappers, miners, and homesteaders, as well as government control efforts, all contributed to the elimination of grizzly bears and wolves. Bud Moore's account of seeing a grizzly bear track in the mud in 1946, near the Bitterroot divide, was considered by the USFWS to be the last grizzly bear in the area.

Meanwhile, habitat continued to change as time and natural succession went on. Eventually, as grasses and shrubs grew tall and decayed, soils recovered enough to provide some organic materials to allow trees to grow. IDFG closed elk hunting in the Bitterroot primitive area in the early 1900s. Elk were transplanted from Yellowstone into various parts of Idaho, and they took off over the following decades.[6] (Note: The Idaho Fish and Game Commission was established by a citizens' initiative in 1938 to create professional wildlife management and buffer it from the whims of politics).

Elk numbers increased in the Bitterroot area until after World War II. In 1948, massive winter kills occurred along the Selway and Lochsa rivers, greatly reducing the populations. The Selway-Bitterroot primitive area was designated federal Wilderness in 1964, but elk numbers didn't reach the highs of the 1940s again for decades.

Large carnivores such as cougars were still scarce, and because most westerners considered predators to be harmful in some way, black bears and cougars continued to be killed and poisoned into the 1970s. A few remnant Idaho grizzly bears survived in the Selkirk Mountains near the Canadian border and near Yellowstone; they were listed under the ESA by the USFWS in 1975. Following groundbreaking research on black bears and cougars in Idaho by Drs. John Beecham and Maurice Hornocker, licenses and tags were required to hunt them and hunting seasons were developed, allowing populations to grow.

During the Reagan years of the 1980s, timber production in Idaho and the West soared. Mills boomed and local communities developed a sense of identity and self-worth. Timber production had been a primary base of the north Idaho economy for generations and was peaking in the 1980s. Changes in the landscape and area economics, however, took decades.

By the early 1990s, the elk numbers in the area had peaked again and the elk habitat—or what was left of it—was badly overgrazed. We knew at the time that elk could not be sustained at such high levels for long. But with the timber harvest of the 1980s, the resulting deforestation, and the return of shrubs and grass to the landscape, elk numbers could be sustained … for a while. Eventually, carrying capacity would decline and so would elk. Forest fires were being controlled, and timber harvest was being heavily scrutinized. Timber harvest was dramatically reduced on the Clearwater and Nez Perce Forests; thus, elk habitat and carrying capacity waned.

When elk numbers peaked in the early 1990s, so did obligate predators such as cougars. Cougars and black bears were thought by many to be responsible for declining elk numbers in north-central Idaho. So research was initiated by IDFG, and researchers found that 54 percent of elk calves that died were being killed by black bears before they were two weeks old. Cougars killed 36 percent of the remaining calves that died before they reached six months of age.[7] Then in 1995 and 1996, wolves were reintroduced into Idaho, and elk hunters found a new predator to blame.

Because of declining habitat conditions, increasing predator numbers, and a couple of very harsh winters thrown in, elk numbers were declining dramatically in north-central Idaho. By the late 1990s and early 2000s, IDFG biologists recognized a serious decline and began restricting hunting. As could be expected, many hunters blamed predators and still do to this day. Most biologists, however, understood that the changes were much more complex than that. For instance, we likely lost 30-40% of that elk population during the harsh winter of 1996-97, when the habitat had turned from predominantly grassland/ brushland to predominantly mid-seral forests.[8] Elk numbers still have not rebounded and, as of 2019, are at a fraction of their former highs.

I spent 14 years as a conservation officer and biologist in the Clearwater Region, reviewing hundreds of timber sales for the Idaho Department of Lands and the U.S. Forest Service. It was my job to recommend mitigating measures to reduce timber sales' impacts on wildlife. During that process, I learned a lot about timber harvest planning and forest management from professional foresters. I also took a continuing education class on Landscape Planning at the University of Montana to better prepare myself for timber sale evaluations. What I learned from experience and education was that there is a significant difference between the impacts of timber harvest and forest fires on habitat and the ecosystem.

Fires tended to remove large blocks of standing trees in a somewhat random fashion but retained standing snags. Usually grasses and shrubs replaced trees when the canopies were opened up. This natural process of succession takes decades for a forest to replace itself, thus creating a mosaic of forest types and age classes across a burned landscape.

Timber harvest, on the other hand, typically required roads and mechanical manipulation of the forest. Removing trees in large blocks (*clearcuts*) provided the easiest, most efficient, and most econ-omical harvest of trees. Also, clearcut management required replanting of trees within a couple of years. However, in the process, herbicide suppression of browse species that competed with seedling trees reduced the availability of browse for game.

The reforestation of clearcuts occurred within a decade or two following harvest; after a fire, however, natural regeneration often took several decades. Fires burned live and dead material and returned minerals such as nitrogen and carbon to the soils. As a result, the first plants to grow following a fire were rich in nutrients and very attractive to big game. The remains from clearcuts, on the other hand, were cleaned up and put into burn piles, after which the area was replanted and fertilized. Many of the young seedlings were also attractive to game, much to the consternation of foresters. Brush and grass were temporary and short-lived in clearcuts but lasted decades longer in many burned areas. In addition, burned snags provided shade for seedlings and habitat for countless bird and mammal species.

But the differences are clear. Forest fires have occurred for millennia: that natural process has resulted in an evolution of plants and animals that best suit the landscapes and climates. Commercial timber harvest has only occurred on National Forest lands for about 150 years in Idaho. Although we are learning a lot about how to reduce and mitigate impacts of harvest on wildlife and the landscape, we are still a long way from making it beneficial to the ecosystem.

And while I believe there are still places where some types of timber harvest may be beneficial to certain species of wildlife and certain ecosystems and forest health, the primary reason for harvesting timber is to provide benefits to humans, period. We have to be okay with that because humans need timber resources. If you live in a wood-framed house or eat from a cereal box or use any kind of paper, you need wood products. Along the way, the forest and wildlife can obtain some benefits from timber harvest. But I personally take the rhetoric about timber harvest always being important for the health of the eco-system and reducing wildfires, etc., with a high dose of skepticism.

In some cases, timber harvest can dry out understories and leave large quantities of slash and debris. I've seen fires burn through harvested forests and stop dead when it hit old growth. Old-growth forests are cooler and wetter in certain systems and not as susceptible to frequent fires. Some of the old-growth cedar/hemlock forests in northern Idaho were several hundred years old, and the forest climate there was cool and wet and undergrowth was sparse. We used to call them the asbestos forests. Stand-replacing fires only occurred there every 300-400 years or more.

Opening those forests up to selective harvest and removing the "over-mature" timber, as foresters called it, has changed the character of the habitat forever. The forest dried out and filled with underbrush and young trees, which was good for some species but bad for others. Roads were graded into hillsides and topsoil was removed. Water and soil run-off into streams was increased. Dead and down materials were removed and slash burned to create a more commercial forest. Never again would 500-year-old cedar trees grow. They will be harvested in a manicured forest every 100-120 years for telephone poles and cedar fences. That is an incredible loss to ecological processes and the landscape, but America has accepted the losses to provide products for a modern society.

Anyone who has paid attention to the controversy realizes people will argue that having a younger more productive forest is better for the landscape, but they may have lost the perspective of what histori-cally was there. Again, any biologist will tell you that almost any forest or successional state is good for something. My opinion, however, is that the loss of old-growth forests will never be replaced, and therefore the species diversity and water quality will suffer, even though younger forests are essential.

But I am also an elk hunter and pragmatist and know the benefits of early successional and managed forests. And climate change will increase fire frequency and intensity and thus change all the old models and expectations for our forests anyway. So, the battles over how forests and wildlands are managed will continue to wage on, and politics and personal perspectives will continue to affect what happens on the ground.

Changing Political Support for Environmental Causes

In recent times, it seems that many conservative policies and administrations support resource extraction industries over environmental concerns. Liberal administrations typically support a more balanced approach between industrial use of resources and environmental causes that are often at the expense of resource extraction. But citizens of both parties, seemingly in contrast to their politicians, care about their public lands.

In the 1960s and 1970s, environmental laws made huge advances under both Republican and Democratic administrations. People of all political persuasions were fed up with rivers that were so polluted they caught on fire and air that was too thick with fumes to breathe. We were appalled that chemicals used to kill insects caused bald eagles' and other birds' eggs to become too brittle to hatch. Rachel Carson wrote the book, *A Silent Spring,* that forecast a spring without the "songs of birds" as they died off from our chemicals.

During that time, litter was everywhere on highways and back roads. Television commercials evoked our emotions as a Native American stood by a roadway while someone tossed a pile of trash at his feet and the camera zoomed in on a tear rolling down his face.

Sunday nights were about Disney and *Bambi, Larry the Lonesome Cougar,* and *Grizzly Adams. Mutual of Omaha's Wild Kingdom* had

Marlin Perkins and Big Jim traveling the world, learning about and saving wildlife. *National Geographic* showed the Craighead brothers studying grizzly bears in Yellowstone and Jacques Cousteau exploring our diminished oceans. Wildlife and wise resource management became a concern as wildlife populations declined and species went extinct.

A best-selling nonfiction book entitled, *The Population Bomb,* written by Paul Ehrlich in 1968, explored our dark future caused by pressures associated with ever-increasing global populations. Then, the Apollo 8 astronauts circled the moon on December 21, 1968, and took a photo of the small blue orb in the distance that was our planet, our everything. All the humans and animals that had ever lived and died did so on that tiny globe. And we realized that we were on a very small and deteriorating life-support system. Fear developed that we were losing our health and our ability to survive on our only planet.

At the same time, communal hope and desire developed to make America a shining symbol of environmental health and return the planet to a sustainable and healthy state. Thus, the environmental movement was created, and along with it, a new wave of scientists was initiated into the professional world of wildlife management.

The human race was concerned; we needed to act immediately—and together. A sense of hope and immediacy sent young people like me to college to learn about wildlife and the environment so we could protect and nourish it. Our wildlife management classes taught us about the iconic wildlife professional and author Aldo Leopold and his "Land Ethic," a philosophy that was based in science and ethical standards.

Leopold lauded the philosophy that the land was to be used wisely, and it fit my philosophy perfectly. Throughout my career, I espoused one of my favorite quotes from his famous book, *The Sand County Almanac*: "A thing is right when it tends to preserve the integrity, stability, and beauty of the biotic community. It is wrong if it tends otherwise." I never interpreted that as a purely preservationist philosophy. To me it was a "wise-use" philosophy rather than a "no-use" one. On the other hand, wise use at times meant no commercial or industrial use. In the vast American West, there was room for both.

People who weren't alive then don't realize how far we have come in a few decades and the dangers of slipping back. Times have changed, and much of it can be traced to which political party sided with which divisive issues in order to get votes. Sagebrush rebellion tactics and advocates and "war on the West" rhetoric gained momentum when timber harvest, mining, and grazing began to wane.

Once a stronghold of labor-union Democrats, north Idaho began to favor Republican candidates because of national policies that were impacting timber and mining resources. Ronald Reagan began calling government the enemy and, by doing so, further reduced the public trust of public agencies. He selected James Watt as his Secretary of the Interior, and resource management became much more extractive oriented. Bipartisan efforts to heal the planet and create a sustainable future began to devolve into an us-versus-them argument. The pendulum swung to the right during those years and changed the West and how people perceived environmental concerns.

However, during the Clinton administration, the pendulum swung to the left once again, replacing timber-harvest objectives with wildlife and ecosystem management objectives. The spotted owl recovery effort stymied harvest of the few remaining old-growth forest areas on the west coast. Loggers became unemployed as National Forests reduced timber harvest and mills shut down.

Adding insult to injury, after decades of planning, wolf reintroduction was controversially taking place. The pendulum had swung far enough that environmentalists and agencies moved their plans forward on wolf and grizzly bear recovery, knowing that, not only did the Endangered Species Act require them to do so, but the courts, the Administration, and much of the public supported it as well.

Still, agency stalwarts were well aware that politics played as much a role in environmental debate as any policy or law. The battle lines were drawn between the extractive industry with their Old West values and a burgeoning New West population (for a good discussion on Old West and New West, see Culver, 2003, Dax, 2015). [9, 10]

Conservation-minded wildlife management professionals tried to do their jobs while balancing the old and the new philosophies. Many agency biologists felt that recovering and managing grizzly bears and other species was our calling and motivation.

Some environmentalists suggested recovery might help make amends for many of society's past mistakes. Perhaps it would correct some of our errors and reset the balance of nature. It would show that society cared more about doing what's right for the "land ethic" vs. doing what's financially beneficial at the expense of the environment.

Some environmental groups, however, began seeing the public mistrust of government and industry as a way to encourage membership. They too attacked the government and filed frequent lawsuits because efforts to recover a species weren't sufficiently restrictive to be good enough for them. They would then laud how they were able to stop something horrible from happening, and, oh, by the way, please send more money. They often became wildlife agency adversaries while claiming to be friends of wildlife. They managed to split alliances and focus on fundraising and "biological purity" at the expense of political compromise that could make the recovery of a species work on the ground.

It took decades to learn from our mistakes, and we found that some of our mistakes in managing our resources were catastrophic. Unfortunately, that did not prevent us from making more of them. The value system of the resource extraction industries, though important in developing the West and the economy of the past century, were no longer aligning with the changing attitudes and needs of a modernizing society.

As resources became scarcer and sharing them required more compromise, the winner-takes-all attitude resurfaced. Outdoor recreation on public lands for the millions of New Westerners, plus the annual influx of millions of tourists, were directly competing with the livelihoods of declining numbers of Old Westerners who depended on an extractive industry for survival. And thus, a conflict of not only desires but also a way of life and control of the land, was on display at our public meetings and during our efforts to reintroduce grizzly bears into the Bitterroots.

CHAPTER 7

BB GETS AN EDUCATION

Life and death in nature are the truisms unwashed by morals and ethics created by human society.

THE SECOND WINTER went by more quickly for both BB and his mother. BB slept through most of it. He was not in any rush to head out until March rolled around and the days got longer. His mother woke up a time or two and pushed out the den entrance to see how spring was progressing. BB followed her outside and walked around the den for a little bit, stretching his weakened muscles. His mother's nose tested the air for the smell of spring— the faint scent of growing grass, forbs, and blossoms wafting upward from the lower elevations. BB imitated his mother, smelling the same air and trying to understand the cues.

About a week after they made their first excursion outside the den, a heavy storm blew in and a couple more feet of snow piled up. They again slept as much as possible, but their bodies were starting to slowly wake up. Frequent trips outside allowed their bodies to gradually return to an active state. The heavy snow was followed by warm weather, and water dripped into the den. BB was definitely restless, and his mother was having difficulty keeping him quiet in the small confines of the den. BB was scrambling laps around and over his mother to burn off energy. Finally, they headed out, this time for good.

Spring came a little earlier than the previous year, but there was already green showing in the lower elevations and on south-facing slopes. BB's mother headed over the ridgeline and down the south side of the mountain, looking in familiar areas for early vegetative growth. She didn't find any carcasses in the avalanche chutes as she had the previous year, so she relied on vegetation and insects for their first meals.

She slowly moved laterally across the mountains, making her way from green patch to green patch until, after several days, she approached the river bottom. There, vegetation was growing best, especially out in the open where the sun could warm the soil. Cow parsnip was already a foot tall and tasty, and other forbs and grasses sprouted with their spring vigor and nutrition.

The two bears foraged and slept in the confines of the canyon, constantly aware they were in a travel corridor for all wildlife, including other grizzly bears. Vigilant and aware of danger, BB's mother moved upslope to the same basin where they had spent several weeks the previous year. There they found early vegetative growth and safer surroundings. They spent weeks foraging undisturbed, as the rapidly growing spring vegetation provided ample nourishment for the pair of grizzlies.

BB felt an absence as he played without his sister. His mother graciously put up with his constant irritation and demands of her time from her only child. She focused on his rearing and training and taught him all of her survival skills. Like a sponge, he absorbed them all. He knew when he did well, and he knew what the swat of his mother's front paw felt like. He tried to avoid those. His strength grew along with his bulk, and having one-on-one time with his mother improved his skills and knowledge quickly.

Though black bear hunting was allowed in Idaho, baiting bears was not allowed in the northern-most part of the state. IDFG decided it would be best for the safety of grizzly bears and hunters alike if baiting were not allowed in Big Game Unit 1, where BB lived. BB grew up without the knowledge of bear baiting, but he learned about bear hunters by watching his mother and smelling and hearing humans in the spring and fall. They found occasional carcasses of black bears, from which hunters had removed the hides and skulls but left most of the meat. Bear meat was very fat and provided BB and his mother with lots of calories and nutrients.

They avoided other grizzly bears and humans as much as possible whenever they smelled their presence. However, human scents sometimes were associated with food, such as wounded or dead elk, deer, and bear. Every now and again, BB and his mother would come across a human campsite along a creek bottom or old road they were following. Sometimes they smelled interesting foods and found tidbits in the fire pit or where someone had buried trash or dumped bacon grease. Once again, BB learned a potentially dangerous lesson that there could be food close to humans. Because of this, BB did not always understand his mother's fear of the human scent, but he respected it and avoided it whenever he could.

BB's mother focused almost exclusively on natural foods, away from humans. She found and killed an occasional newborn elk calf or deer fawn, which were very tasty and provided good nutrition but very little actual meat. She wasn't an active calf hunter like some grizzlies and only occasionally happened upon a hiding calf cached by a wary and often frantic mother that had been feeding close by.

BB especially liked berry season, when he didn't have to move much at all to fill his ever-growing belly. Early in the season, his mother would wander over large areas looking for the first ripening patches of huckleberries but fed on chokecherries, strawberries, and serviceberries before the huckleberries ripened. From late July through the first of September, prime huckleberry patches provided the small family with everything they needed.

BB was growing fast and was now half as tall as his mother but still weighed quite a bit less. His long gangly legs and big feet showed his potential but as of yet unfulfilled size. This was the second year of BB's life, and he was starting to feel his independence, much like an adolescent boy. He would wander away from his mother on occasion, more secure in his ability to find foods and to catch up to her by using his nose. He never strayed too far—just far enough to test her patience. He would occasionally feel the tough love of a mother grizzly's right hook if he didn't come when called or did something else she didn't like. But most of the time he just tested himself.

There were not many grizzly bears on the U.S. side of the Selkirk Mountain range—perhaps between 30 and 40 bears. But a few places were prime feeding areas and more remote than others. BB and his mother lived in these remote sections of northern Idaho, avoiding regular contact with humans but increasing the likelihood of contact with other grizzly bears.

BB and his mother became friendly with another female and regularly spent time close to her. The female was older than BB's mother, but otherwise they shared similar coloration, physical traits, and even behaviors. The other female was BB's mother's mother— BB's grandmother. Although they didn't spend a lot of time together, they were often in the same prime berry patches in August.

The older female also had a cub that was the same age as BB, and when they got together in the same patch of berries, they often found themselves playing. The females allowed this, especially at this time of year when food was plentiful. Other bears also moved through the area, feeding on berries. The presence of two females seemed to be more of a deterrence than one, and they had few problems with the other bears. Also, the females were well known residents—especially the older female, who was larger than BB's mother and was respected in the bear community. As long as BB was with these females, he was quite safe from older males—they simply just avoided them.

Eventually, the days shortened and the long afternoon shadows of the autumn sun splintered the forest into shards of light and dark, summer and fall, growth and decay. Leaves began losing their chlorophyll and painted the landscape with dapples of reds and yellows, deep maroons, and rusty golds, contrasted against the cobalt blue skies, before they finally lost their grasp and floated to the earth in their final act. Hunting season and the cycle of birth and death, predator and prey, hunter and hunted began.

With every birth pulse in the spring comes a death pulse in the fall and winter—the beating heart of the natural world. Should we as modern man forget our roles in nature's life-and-death struggles, then we divorce ourselves from creation itself. There is no judgment in nature when a bear eats a deer fawn or a cougar strangles an elk calf. Death by predation is an important element in the survival of deer and elk as a species. Life and death in nature are the truisms unwashed by morals and ethics created by human society. Humans are predators too. The genetic makeup of every human on earth can be traced back to the successful hunter or warrior who became a successful breeder and sustainer of his offspring. It is not about choice, it is about our evolution and selection, fulfilling what we were meant to be. How we choose to express or suppress those innate genetic behavioral traits is our choice, but the traits are linked to our genome—the desire to be a predator.

Late autumn quickly approached, and the small family had survived another year and another hunting season without mishap. Luckily, they once again found a carcass from a hunter's wounding loss, after the last berries had dried up or fallen, and they were able to put on even more weight before entering their den.

BB was not quite two years old, but as he and his mother prepared to enter their third winter together, he now weighed almost 200 pounds and was beginning to look impressive. His belly was large and round, and his ribs were no longer noticeable. His long legs were about the only thing that still made him look like a youngster—that and his big ears and narrower face. It would be a year or two before his head developed a broader skull and a grizzly's signature dish shape and his legs became more proportional to his body. But his shoulders had a well-developed grizzly hump, and his claws were long and white. His hair was still quite dark, even after the long summer sun tried to bleach his back into blonde. Little silver tips were visible on his hairs, giving his rippling fur a shine in the late fall light. Standing in certain light or shadows he looked dark brown, and standing in the sun he looked a lighter, grizzled gray, with streaks of blonde.

When BB and his mother began their ascent up the mountain in the snows of late autumn, BB was beginning to feel like a big bear. He could now turn over large rocks and rip logs. He could also help his mother find a good den location and could even help dig the bowl. The den was bigger than last year's but still barely big enough for both of them to stand and move. When they entered the den that fall of 2005, BB was almost two. He didn't realize that when spring came around, things were going to be much different.

CHAPTER 8

———

CREATING THE BITTERROOT CHAPTER OF THE GRIZZLY BEAR RECOVERY PLAN

Moving Forward

THE FIRST MEETING of our biological working group took place in February 1992.

Federal agencies can no longer make many unilateral decisions. Federal rules and laws such as the National Environmental Policy Act (NEPA) require public input. It was not only a requirement; it was a good idea politically. Our goal was to write a plan that was biologically sound for recovery and acceptable enough to the public and politicians so that, even if they could not support it, they would at least be able to tolerate grizzly recovery.

So in February 1992, following direction from the Interagency Grizzly Bear Committee (IGBC), we formed a biological working group (*Appendix A*). At the time, there were a dozen or so active members, mostly biologists from the USFWS, USFS, and the states of Idaho and Montana, as well as Tribal biologists. We discussed our tasks and timelines and were overwhelmed by what lay ahead.

Biologists knew that despite all the biological work and writing to be done, reaching out to the public in a constructive manner would be our biggest and most important task. Our role, as required under the Endangered Species Act (ESA), was to develop the best biological recommendation for how to recover grizzly bears in the Bitterroot Ecosystem.

By August, we had created a Citizens' Involvement Group (CIG), which consisted of representatives from various organizations, groups, and interested individuals from Idaho and Montana (*Appendix A*). The CIG provided input and ideas to our working group and remained informed on the progress of the Chapter, including reviewing it and suggesting changes. They were tasked with passing along updates and information to their various constituents, members, neighbors, and friends.

The CIG was an outspoken group of environmentalists, local politicians, logging and mining group representatives, outdoor recreationists, hunters, and others with an interest in how grizzly bear recovery might impact their lives. Timber interests, however, took center stage. But the issue of safety, with having grizzly bears near these communities, was the underlying concern of most attendees, even among some supporters.

Needless to say, our CIG meetings were pretty exciting. Our first few meetings were mostly circus-like events that embodied an atmosphere of mistrust and myths, followed by attempts at clarification. It was a steep learning curve for the public, as well as for agency biologists, on how to create trust and understanding among diverse groups of citizens and scientists—especially with grizzly recovery happening on the heels of, and at the same time as, wolf recovery. These were arguably two of the most controversial species we could possibly impose on Idaho and Montana citizens and those espousing Old West philosophies. It was an uphill battle, but we had hopes and glimmers of success.

More people began attending our meetings, and we struggled to keep the size controllable and productive. Finding cool heads and negotiators was important, and Forest Service employees were often trained as mediators. Forest Service biologists, however, usually worked anonymously in the relative safety of their offices. They worked on timber sales and provided input and planning on roads and timber harvest mitigation. They dwelled on Forest Plans, Environmental Assessments, and Environmental Impact Statements. My perception was that they usually didn't like to rock the boat and that they worked well in small groups but at the time had more difficulty working in the chaos of large group dynamics.

Although I worked with many outstanding biologists and other staffers in the Forest Service, their agency leadership followed the multiple-use mandate to conduct as much analysis of all potential impacts as was needed to prevent injunctions and lawsuits. Lawsuits and resultant policies often caused either delays or prevention of actions on the ground.

Idaho Governor Cecil Andrus was a logger from Orofino. However, he claimed his election in 1970 was a result of his opposition to an open-pit mine at the base of Castle Peak, the highest peak in the White Cloud Mountains of central Idaho. Idahoans were opposed to the mine, once the potential impacts to the pristine nature of the area were documented by environmentalists, photographers, and journalists. The mine was never built, and the area was eventually designated a Wilderness Area. Andrus later served as Secretary of the Interior under President Carter and then returned to Idaho and was elected Governor again after his federal service.

Even though Governor Andrus, as a lifetime outdoorsman and a Democrat, was fully supportive of his Fish and Game Commission and the Department, he despised wolf reintroduction and thought grizzly bear transplants into Idaho were a crazy idea. He would cringe at anything we said in the news that was at all supportive of either one.

But, he pretty much left us to ourselves, unlike the Republican governors to follow.

The legislature, however, was another beast altogether. The GOP majority was so lopsided that Idaho basically became a one-party system after Governor Andrus left. The politics and control of state agencies became a political battle, and IDFG had always been a "burr under the saddle" of Idaho's agriculture- and industry-first politics. Subsequent Republican governors attempted to fundamentally change how Fish and Game ran its business.

The U.S. Fish and Wildlife Service was filled with biologists who wanted to make a difference but often got caught up in agency paperwork. The different branches of the Service had different responsibilities, from managing wildlife refuges to Section 7 consultations, research, and recovery. But I always thought the real action was with the species coordinators and field research and management staff.

Dr. Chris Servheen was the grizzly recovery coordinator and had been selected for the position in 1982. He was a close friend of mine before and during graduate school. We hunted together in eastern Montana, along with other friends. We drank beer together, and I even worked for him, trapping grizzly bears in British Columbia for Dr. Bruce McLellan's long-term grizzly bear study.

Chris was on my graduate committee, and I respected him. He possessed a wealth of grizzly bear knowledge, and never once in my life did I think he wasn't doing his best for grizzly bears. We forged a professional relationship during my 30 years with IDFG. He and I didn't always see eye-to-eye on everything, but then, who does? Other USFWS biologists working with us on the Recovery Chapter at the time included wildlife biologist Ann Vandehey and two outstanding Montana bear biologists and close friends, Tim Their and Wayne Kasworm.

Early in the Chapter writing, Wayne Wakkinen, the Idaho state biologist working on the Selkirk grizzly bear recovery effort, was assigned to chair our working group. He was known to be slow to rattle and was a calming influence for the group; he was a good selection to help lead the biological and CIG groups forward.

Wayne Melquist was the Idaho Wildlife Bureau program coordinator in charge of the state nongame program. He was responsible for grizzly bears statewide and for reporting back to HQ and Director Conley on our progress at regular intervals; he also participated in meetings when he could. Melquist had also conducted a study and authored a report on historical grizzly bear observations in the recovery area in 1985. He was the Interagency Grizzly Bear Committee (IGBC) participant and staff for the IDFG Director at that time.

Because most of the Recovery Area was within the boundaries of Idaho, and the IDFG Clearwater Region in particular, Herb Pollard, the IDFG Regional Supervisor, and I had most of the responsibilities; we therefore took on leadership roles and increased workloads, which neither of us minded. The Forest Service provided biologists from the Forests within the Recovery Area boundaries and Region 1 headquarters, and the USFWS provided staff from their Montana and Boise offices. Jay Gore and Rich Howard were the USFWS representatives from Boise and participated in many meetings.

The working group was active during the summer and fall of 1992 and developed a draft Chapter for public review by August 1993. Meanwhile, against our wishes, the Idaho Legislature decided to get involved and developed a bill to block IDFG's involvement in grizzly recovery, similar to what had been done on wolf recovery (remember that wolf recovery was underway at that time, and they were already talking about reintroductions happening within a couple of years).

Representative Chuck Cuddy and Senator Margarite McLaughlin, both from the timber-based community of Orofino, sponsored the bill.

However, Director Conley was adamant that removing IDFG from the Bitterroot effort would eliminate the State's ability to steer the recovery efforts, and I agreed. Removing IDFG from the process would be like taking your best players out of the game, then yelling from the sidelines and complaining that you lost. The Nez Perce Tribe was more than willing to take over and partner with the USFWS if the state pulled out, similar to what they had done with wolves.

The bill was modified, and though it did not block IDFG involvement, it did create a Grizzly Bear Legislative Oversight Committee (LOC) that consisted of a representative from both the Senate and House Resource Committees, a University of Idaho wildlife professor, a woolgrower, a representative from the logging and mining industries, a cattle representative, and an outdoor recreation representative. They were to make sure our group of scientists and citizens didn't get too far out ahead of the politicians and industry.

Surprisingly, I actually enjoyed working with the Oversight Committee members at times and was particularly impressed with their Chairman, Idaho State Senator Laird Noh (chairman of the Senate Resource Committee), a moderate Republican with a level head. Although a woolgrower from eastern Idaho, the man was affable and open to biology and science—a true statesman who was always looking for a way forward and a middle ground. That type of politician is increasingly rare in today's society. Dr. Jim Peek a wildlife professor from the University of Idaho was another great statesman and member of the committee, who continued being the cool head, despite numerous members' "hair-on-fire" moments. He was able to use humor and science to educate and moderate some of the opinions of his fellow LOC members.

Before the LOC was formed, the governor and our Fish and Game Commission were both speaking out against grizzly bear reintroductions, and Herb Pollard wanted to know what we were doing about that. I responded in a March 1993 memo that we felt it was our job to study and report the biology, fulfill the ESA requirements, and let the politics run its course afterwards. We avoided politically sensitive topics such as designating management and recovery area boundaries that were wrought with controversy. Herb and other supervisors were feeling, and rightfully so, that our communications could be improved. They were concerned we were moving ahead of them and the political rumblings going on in Boise.

Initially, the Bitterroot Ecosystem (BE) was part of the Northwest Ecosystems Subcommittee of the IGBC, along with the Selkirks in northern Idaho and Washington's North Cascades. In July of 1993, however, the IGBC split the NW Ecosystems Subcommittee into three separate subcommittees—the Bitterroot (BESC), Selkirk, and North Cascade Ecosystem subcommittees. These subcommittees were to oversee the process in each ecosystem and report back to the IGBC.

Herb Pollard was the first chair of the BESC, and I was his right hand. Meetings were open to the public, although we tried to limit involvement to CIG members in order to avoid spending so much of the meeting reviewing previous issues and repeating business already completed. Government oversight and citizens' involvement were necessary at every step, and nobody wanted to be left out. Our every move was watched and debated at meetings and in the press.

Public meetings and comments were always colorful, if not always helpful. Public input from the CIG was critical in developing the Chapter, including some very good proposals from different groups. One of the first proposals was called the ROOTS proposal (Resource Organization on Timber Supply). ROOTS members were representing private timber companies and sawmill owners and were concerned that grizzly bear recovery meant reduced access to timber on federal, state, and even private land. They were very outspoken with their concerns about road closures, Section 7 consultation (a required ESA provision for reviewing any action on federal land that might jeopardize listed species), and other government oversight issues. Many simply did not trust the federal government. Core members of the group we interacted with included Dan Johnson and Phil Church of ROOTS, Seth Diamond of Intermountain Forest Products (Seth later died in a plane crash in July 1996), and mill owner Bill Mulligan.

We were encouraged when ROOTS made a reasonable proposal for us to review. Rather than oppose recovery, they suggested that if recovery was going to happen, it should occur primarily within wilderness boundaries. Part of their proposal was that the Frank Church River of No Return Wilderness south of the Salmon River should eventually be added and included in the review and recovery efforts. Also, and most importantly, they suggested that the prime logging (and grizzly bear) habitat north of the Lochsa River should be excluded. This original proposal also included various other tenets, but it was a clear change in direction for the industry representatives. They wanted to steer where recovery would occur instead of just opposing it altogether.

When we had put together our first draft of the Chapter in early 1993, we asked for public input on the primary issues and tenets of the work accomplished to date. We were somewhat concerned by the way our CIG meetings were turning into public rallies, with both sides trying to sway the direction of the Chapter by increasing sheer numbers present. We had to cancel a planned February meeting due to the way membership was being inflated, as different groups encouraged their members to show up in force to dominate discussions.

Rumors ran rampant. Someone even posed as a Fish and Game employee and made calls as an "official" pollster. Apparently, they told local citizens that IDFG planned on releasing bears into the area and an important meeting was being held on Saturday. We worried that things were getting out of control and our meeting room wouldn't hold that many people. To avoid a potential public relations disaster, we canceled.

By June, we had received dozens of letters from CIG representatives and members of the public, many expressing disappointment about our meeting cancellation. One faction, including local community timber interests such as "Save Elk City" and some logging contractors, supported the ROOTS proposal. However, several letters came from environmental groups supporting a different option. Hank Fischer, the regional representative for Defenders of Wildlife (DOW), wrote a letter stating that we should expand the Recovery Area boundaries to the north and south, including habitat that would connect grizzly bear ecosystems. He opposed eliminating sections of National Forests that were in prime timber harvest areas or other sites for potential conflicts in the Bitterroot Valley. He supported keeping the recovery area very large, to include spring range on the Montana side.

This position statement was indicative of environmentalists' position at the time. We also received letters from Wild Forever, a coalition composed of the Greater Yellowstone Coalition, Sierra Club, the Wilderness Society, the Audubon Society, and the Idaho Conservation League, all of which supported Fischer's views.

At a following CIG meeting, Hank Fischer and Tom France, regional director and attorney for The National Wildlife Federation (NWF), began to discuss a compromise with ROOTS members. They were as impressed as we were with the ROOTS approach. With the addition of two powerful environmental groups (NWF and DOW), the proposal began to take on a life of its own. Much to our working group's amazement, over the next few months and years, the ROOTS proposal developed wings. It began to be pushed as the primary proposal, circumventing much of what we thought at the time was the more common agency-centric and more biological approach to recovery efforts.

At the same time, Hank Fischer was now moving away from his earlier stance of recovery area expansion. Instead, he moved toward the ROOTS compromise of wilderness-only recovery, which some of his environmental group associates would later call a sell-out. Fischer's and France's strong support for the ROOTS proposal was based on practicality and their vision for a new collaborative approach to resource issues. They believed they could convince other environmental groups to support this proposal based on its merits and potential for acceptance by a broader coalition. Additionally, it could prove to be a shining example of environmental groups and industry collaborating to resolve complex resource issues. Many of us working on the Chapter were hoping for the same thing, because the ongoing disagreements between industry and environmentalists were making us all weary.

The ROOTS proposal's primary tenets were:

1) Conduct experimental non-essential (see below) recovery in wilderness only and eliminate prime timber country to the north from restrictions.

2) Develop a Citizens' Management Committee (CMC) to oversee recovery decisions (the CMC was not in the original ROOTS proposal but came along later).

3) Include no further logging, road building, mining, or environmental restrictions beyond what currently existed in Forest Plans.

The ROOTS representatives met with politicians and met regularly with Chris Servheen and with the Working Group on occasion.

The proposal jumped ahead of our efforts and, rightly or wrongly, began to headline the discussions. Some politicians gave it a reluctant green light to proceed, thus encouraging us to believe it had legs.

The recently created Legislative Oversight Committee (LOC) scheduled public meetings in Orofino and Grangeville that summer. In addition to hearing from the public and interest groups, the LOC wanted to tour the recovery area, particularly the northern section. Consequently, we chartered an aircraft and flew the members around the North Fork of the Clearwater to the Bitterroot divide. This gave them a better feel for the controversial boundary discussions and gave us a chance to show the high-quality habitat for bears. Instead, what they saw was high-quality potential for timber harvest.

The input the LOC received at the open houses in Orofino and Grangeville in the next few days was 99 percent anti-bear. They took these public comments, including the ROOTS proposal, and made recommendations to our Working Group, IGBC, and the legislature. Those recommendations were:

> 1) Although reintroduction is not supported (by the LOC and thus the legislature), if introduced, it should be as an experimental non-essential population under the ESA and should only be in the Selway-Bitterroot Wilderness.
>
> 2) Establish a communications program to keep the public informed.
>
> 3) Adjust boundaries to avoid conflicts.
>
> 4) Return bears that wander outside core areas.
>
> 5) Make no special concessions for grizzly bears beyond current National Forest wildlife standards outside the recovery area.

To make reintroducing controversial species more acceptable, the ESA was amended in 1983, adding Section 10, which allowed for reintroducing "experimental" populations. Section 10(j) further stated an "experimental non-essential" population could be reintroduced into an area that did not already have an existing population of the species and would allow the USFWS to develop special rules that could reduce animosity toward the species.

Section 10(j) had successfully been used for wolf recovery planning. Special rules for wolves allowed killing of wolves that attacked livestock and allowed state agencies to kill wolves that impacted ungulate populations, to name a few.

Thus, Section 10(j) special rules were believed by many to be the best route forward to reduce impacts of grizzly bears on local livelihoods. In the final BE Recovery Chapter that was finally accepted and published by the USFWS, one of the special rules we described was the Citizens' Management Committee proposal that was supported by ROOTS and our CIG.

The working group and BESC reviewed the LOC recommendations and found most were acceptable and similar to ongoing discussions with the CIG. Our working group had to capitulate somewhat to the political powers and leadership preferences in hopes that compromise would ultimately result in victory for bears—and the public. We state employees realized the LOC had enormous influence with the governor and legislature and thus the IDFG Commission and likely our congressional representatives. We also knew the USFWS tentatively supported the ROOTS coalition proposals and preferred the idea of a compromised tolerance rather than a scorched-earth recovery.

As agency managers, we were very skeptical of the Citizens' Management Committee idea that would lead the recovery under the ROOTS proposal but wanted to see how that played out. Herb, Wayne,

Director Conley, and I were aware of our limitations in the process. But we felt we could impact it more readily if we had support from the legislature and governor, particularly if it originated from those industry representatives often opposed to wildlife causes.

Clearly, not everyone on the state side was on the same page, but we hoped to convince others in the group that the proposals, although not ideal, were a way forward to influence recovery. And IDFG needed to stay involved to help steer the ship and make sure the state maintained a leadership role. Montana Governor Racicot, a true supporter of collaboration and grizzly bears, was also one of the few politicians to show early signs of support for the ROOTS proposal. Only lip service, without solid support, was provided by most of our Idaho politicians, who were seemingly intrigued by the collaboration efforts but not grizzly bears. Despite continuing lobbying efforts by Dan Johnson, Seth Diamond, and others, political support was sparse. However, we were still hopeful that the new approach might change some attitudes.

As our Draft Chapter was nearing acceptance by IGBC in December 1993, there was real movement away from a purely biological approach with government oversight. In addition to the typical Chapter sections that outlined the nitty-gritty biological information, the experimental non-essential approach and CMC proposal were highlighted as possibilities for promoting recovery.

Meanwhile, we witnessed new and possibly disastrous battle lines being formed: environmentalist vs. environmentalist and biological purity vs. sleeping with the enemy. When wolf recovery was being discussed, all the environmental groups wanted reintroductions and were pitted against industry and Old West interests who opposed it. It was strength against strength and good vs. evil in the eyes of both sides. However, when the ROOTS coalition developed, we had hoped that most environmental groups would support a new and innovative approach to collaborative resource management. The USFWS was banking on it and putting their faith in two regional environmental group representatives, Tom France and Hank Fischer, to deliver the goods.

If the strength and power of environmentalism was going to overcome industry and Old West philosophies, environmental groups had to act together. France and Fischer would have to perform a miracle to get all the environmental groups on their side. Dan Johnson, Seth Diamond, and industry supporters of the ROOTS proposal would also have to perform miracles getting the Old West industry stalwarts and politicians to support grizzly reintroductions—no matter what kind of approach was used.

I was sure if the politicians began lining up against reintroductions and the ROOTS approach, the ROOTS coalition would fold like a house of cards and the industry reps would leave Fischer and France dangling in the wind. But until then, they were solid in their beliefs that this approach could work. The Clinton Administration, however, would be put at odds with industry AND their environmental supporters unless the sides came together. These political struggles were going to decide the fate of all our work over the next few years.

Kick the Can Down the Road

Still, the boundary description and any changes to the Recovery Area were primary sticking points among all interested parties. We kicked the can down the road and decided boundaries were to be reviewed and delineated when writing the Environmental Impact Statement—if the IGBC and the USFWS decided to move forward.

The recovery area boundaries and where bears might be recovered, in my mind, were likely still the most important aspect of how, or if, recovery would occur. This would be the test within and among coalitions. I knew the described recovery boundaries within the original review area varied in quality from north to south and east to west. All the National Forests, states, the LOC, ROOTS, and environmental groups had offered their recommendations to either remove sections or add other areas to avoid conflicts or enhance habitat. National Forest biologists contributed within the Working Group, and Forest Supervisors worked with the BESC to make their concerns known and included.

The habitat information we used to develop the Chapter was for the area within the original boundaries. The boundaries did not include any new areas added to the south or subtracted from the north, and no boundaries were shifted because of concerns, legitimate or otherwise. Though the proposal to expand southerly within the Frank Church Wilderness was appealing on the surface, we knew that the additional acreage was not as valuable to bears as that which would be lost to the north. Indeed, the Salmon Forest Supervisor stated he thought the Salmon River and Frank Church Wilderness within their Forest was not suitable for grizzly bears and should be excluded.[1] Forest Supervisor Burns would later become an important player in how IDFG responded to the recovery effort.

Linkage corridors to the north that connected the BE with the Selkirk and Cabinet-Yaak Recovery Areas and with the Northern Continental Divide Ecosystem (NCDE) were also important for any natural migration to occur. Although no evidence yet existed that grizzly bears had ever moved between recovery areas, connectivity was still a concern for many biologists in order to allow for natural recovery as an option. Enhanced linkages and corridors were also a concern for the USFWS in other ecosystems.

But if we were to move forward with the compromise proposal, linkages would have to be left out. And unfortunately, the highest-quality habitat to connect ecosystems to the north was that which ROOTS and the LOC were proposing to remove. For the foreseeable future, Chris Servheen was quite sure that if bears were to move between ecosystems, they would probably need to be transplanted. Of all the radio-collared bears monitored over the previous 20 years, none had moved between ecosystems.

This was a concern for me, because I had used the good habitat quality in the north part of the BE to develop the population recovery goal; in my estimate, that area offered the best habitat for the most bears in the Recovery Area. That apparently was not yet fully understood by all or perhaps was being fractiously disregarded by those pushing the ROOTS proposal. I had traveled many days in that country and had found that the huckleberries were thick along the western slopes of the northern Bitterroots; that was also the location

Looking into Upper Kelly Creek habitat, near the Bitterroot Ecosystem's Montana border.

of the best-quality grizzly reports I had seen. I believed strongly that this area would be the first place a grizzly would show up on its own and be verified, and I am on record many times stating that. That was why we spent so much time looking for bears there.

Population Recovery Goal

During the development of the Chapter, we had to estimate what a population recovery goal would be. Any population number we developed would need to be scientifically driven and would be immediately challenged, not only by other scientists, but also by environmental groups, locals, industry, and politicians. A recovery goal is necessary for delisting purposes, but it also gives biologists a goal under which to develop interim and recovery objectives. We needed to develop bear management units, objectives for numbers of females with young, distribution, mortality limits, timelines, and a myriad of other statistical and biological monitoring objectives. The original habitat analysis simply indicated that a population of 200-400 bears could survive there, but we needed to be more specific. We needed to develop a biologically defensible population goal.

Therefore, I developed the first goal, based on what we had for data and knowledge of grizzly bears in the Northwest. I divided the habitat into high-, moderate-, and low-quality forage, based on the vegetation, moisture, and geography, as well as potential human-conflict areas, and mapped potential spring range and quality food sites.

Using that information, I divided the evaluation area into approximately three equal parts: high-, moderate-, and low-quality habitat sections and concluded that the population at full recovery could be about one bear per 20 square miles within the Bitterroot Recovery Area.

This analysis, though rough and in need of more detail, estimated that the total population could be about 280 bears.

Although that seemed like a lot of bears, it was a projection 100 years into the future, which was our estimated time for recovery, given known reproductive rates, and was based on habitat we had in 1991. We would have to revisit the technique in more detail in an Environmental Impact Statement (EIS), following any boundary changes, and further analyze the population potential of the habitat.

In general, the climate in the northern part of the Recovery Area was moist and was dominated by cedar/hemlock climax forests and by shrubs and grasslands that had evolved from fires and timber harvest. The farther south you went in the BE, the more similar the climate and vegetation was to Yellowstone's. One reason the Selway-Bitterroot was designated federal Wilderness was because of its rocky, rugged terrain, which wasn't as productive for logging and agriculture. Congress was obviously not giving up much development potential. However, black bears, elk, deer, and many other species of wildlife found the wilderness to be very good habitat. (The scourge of exotic vegetation and toxic weeds had not yet taken over the wilderness in the early 1990s. That was yet to come.)

By establishing this population goal, we were able to develop bear management units, estimate how many females with cubs needed to be counted annually, and think about distribution of bears, mortality limits, etc. At the time, population biologists and ecological scientists had decided that a population of 70-100 bears would be considered a Minimum Viable Population (MVP) if they were well distributed, connected, and had successful annual reproduction. On the other hand, the population goal of 280 was what we believed the habitat could support in the Bitterroot Ecosystem—a habitat-based goal, which was higher than the MVP. Even so, geneticists and practitioners of bear management in the modern era knew the difference between theory and reality; the reality is that one bear is one too many if people don't want them there, no matter how great the habitat.

You Want How Many Bears Where?

The average citizen undoubtedly envisioned that a goal of 280 bears meant that the government likely had trailers full of hungry bears they were going to dump into the Wilderness, including all those problem bears from Yellowstone and Glacier National Parks. The Chapter did not initially explain how bears would be recovered—only that they would be. We told the CIG that if bears were to be moved into the Bitterroots following an EIS, it would be similar to how it was done in the Cabinet-Yaak Ecosystem. In reality, the USFWS found it hard to locate a surplus of two young bears in three years that fit the criteria. These criteria required that bears be young and therefore less likely to return to the capture site, mostly female, not known to have been in any conflicts, and be healthy.

It would take many decades for any population of bears to become established, let alone reach recovery levels. However, scientists always need a number for plans and management goals, and the public and politicians want a number to argue over. Some folks think that a single bear is too many because it will change everything they think and do. Others think nature should dominate and the bears should have their place, like it was when Lewis and Clark passed through.

However, once the ESA was signed into law in 1973, federal agencies were mandated to develop recovery plans for all the species on the list. One of the common complaints we received about reintroduction of wolves and grizzlies was, "Why? We don't need them, so why?" The simple reason is that it was a federal mandate, as required by law. We were doing our job, to the best of our abilities, to recover bears under the ESA. However, even with the force of the ESA, which was one of the most powerful pieces of legislation ever created, it was clear that no scientific recovery effort could move forward without adequate political and public support.

The wolf recovery program had forged ahead of the bear recovery effort and muddied the waters along the way. Wolves had been reintroduced into Yellowstone and Central Idaho in 1995 and 1996. Reintroductions happened with support from a strong coalition of environmental groups, political backing from the Clinton Administration, and—based on numerous national surveys—strong public support. Local people felt they were being inundated by an overzealous federal agency, Bill Clinton's liberal administration, and a steady progression away from a resource-based economy. The world was changing too rapidly for some.

The grizzly recovery effort was not being helped by politicians either. Even Idaho Governor Cecil Andrus, the former Secretary of the Interior under Jimmy Carter, who helped create all those national conservation areas in Alaska, was opposed to bringing grizzly bears into Idaho. Idaho's entire congressional delegation was opposed. The state legislature was opposed. County commissioners were opposed. Yet, there were a few of us in the state government that were walking the political tightrope between recovery and politics, between doing our jobs and possibly losing our jobs. We knew that grizzly recovery was required under the ESA, and we also believed that, morally and ethically, it was the right thing to do. However, morals and ethics of wildlife biologists differ from those of politicians and the ethos of the Old West industrial infrastructure of Idaho and Montana.

Those were exciting times and clearly not without risk for those of us on the bottom of the totem pole!

Interestingly, however, of all the issues we encountered in the development of the Chapter, the one that plagued us most frequently was the issue of boundaries. It seemed that discussions had moved mostly into where they should be, as opposed to if they should be there, and that, at least, was a step forward!

We finished the draft Chapter on time in December 1993 and provided the public an opportunity to comment on it again. One of our primary goals was to increase public outreach and communication, so we developed brochures to answer questions that were raised during the CIG meetings. The Chapter was mostly a biological document that was based on similar Chapters for other Recovery Areas like Yellowstone, NCDE, Selkirks, and Cabinet-Yaak. But no preferred alternative or description about how recovery would occur was included.

To move forward with recovery, an EIS would need to be completed. An EIS would identify a preferred alternative for recovery, define the Recovery Area and any boundary changes, study impacts of bear recovery, analyze habitat quality, and review all primary issues identified during the development of the Chapter.

The decision whether or not to move forward with an EIS was a huge one. It had to consider funding, personnel and staffing, political support, biological need, and a myriad of other things that had to fall into place. It would take years to develop and would require biologists, agencies, and supporting publics to dedicate themselves to it. The decision to move forward, however, rested with the IGBC, the Secretary of the Interior, and other high-ranking officials within the state and federal agencies, not to mention all the politicians who had an oar in the water. Clearly, the decision would not be based on science alone.

CHAPTER 9

ALONE

Off in the distance, birth was replacing death, and the emergence of many dormant plants and animals had begun.

THE WINTER WAS LONG enough to test BB and his mother's ability to get along in tight quarters. Though his mother was still 100 pounds heavier and definitely still in charge, BB let his discomfort be known, and would occasionally complain. The first part of the winter was all about their "light hibernation"—not quite true hibernation, but a deep restful dormancy that allowed them to pass the cold winter months without a shiver.

The latter part of the winter into early spring was a bit different. BB was more restless than his mother and wanted to get out of the den much earlier than his mother did. He would dig at the entrance and poke his head out into a white snow, realizing it was still too early for leaving the protections of their den. He would crawl back in and, in a fitful sleep, dream about the wonders that lay ahead when they could finally escape the little hole.

Finally, one bright day while sitting outside the den, he could smell the sweet smells of spring, as the sun-warmed air pushed fragrances upslope toward the den. He was excited and coaxed his mother out. She sat groggily at the entrance sniffing the air, yawning, stretching, and testing her weakened muscles. Things were changing around the den now. Winter was finally releasing its grasp, and the sounds of collapsing snow and gurgling water were everywhere. Mountain chickadees were chirping and flitting about excitedly. Large flocks of ducks and geese could be seen heading north toward their summer grounds. Off in the distance, birth was replacing death, and the emergence of many dormant plants and animals had begun. It was spring, and BB knew it. He was very excited!

After a few short excursions, the female finally decided it was time to go. BB could hardly hold his enthusiasm in check. He bounded ahead of his mother and made his way up slope to the ridgetop; then, not waiting, he made his way down the other side. His muscles had weakened considerably over the winter, and even though he had lost a lot of weight, his enthusiasm pushed him forward. He worked his way back up toward his mother as she slowly moved across the slope downhill. She stopped occasionally and sat back on her haunches while BB waited for her.

BB was now breaking their trail but would check over his shoulder to make sure he was on the right path and she was still following. His mother would stop and investigate a log or rock that was now exposed by the melting snow and then move on. Once, she stared at a pika that was chirping loudly at her from a boulder field, and BB ran up to it to try and catch it. He moved a few boulders, but the cocky little pika scurried through the boulder field, chirping at BB like a squirrel would a backyard dog, and then disappeared just out of reach.

Finally, BB gave up and pursued the much-easier-to-catch grasses and forbs. Grass was the first food BB and his mother had tasted in almost six months. Soon, they found forbs growing along a sunny draw that had melted back a few weeks prior. Downward they moved, until green was more prevalent than white, to where spring had finally taken up residence. There, they rested and fed.

Within the next few weeks, changes seemed to be occurring between BB and his mother. BB was not sure what was going on but he tried not to think about it. His mother seemed to be shorter tempered than usual, and a strange distance seemed to be growing between them. He would try to nuzzle up to her in the evenings or when napping during the day, and she wouldn't be as nurturing. Sometimes she would lick his face and play with him, but quite often she acted like he wasn't there. BB tried to impress her by digging up a ground squirrel or a midden that would provide some food for her. He even found a deer fawn one day that was hiding in thick cover and pounced on it, killing it instantly. He began feeding on it as his mother approached, and he backed off as she fed. Unlike before, she did not leave much for him to eat. Still, they were a family unit, and he stuck close to her. The less attention she paid to him, the more he tried to play with her, but she mostly just ignored him.

It was already early June, and BB was in his third spring. BB's mother was starting to be more interested in the smells of other bears. She was also starting to smell differently herself. It was a strange smell to BB, one he hadn't smelled before, and it was strangely exciting to him as well. One day, he curiously sniffed his mother's rear end where those wonderful scents were emanating from, and she roared at him, spinning around and swatting him hard. He fell back, confused.

His confusion was soon heightened when other smells appeared—the smells of a male grizzly. At first, he didn't pay too much attention to it because in the past his mother would move away, taking him with her. This time, however, she seemed interested and didn't move off. Instead she squatted and peed. BB could smell her urine and it was that same strong smell again; it excited him and he didn't know why.

Suddenly, BB heard a branch snap and looked over in the direction of a large male grizzly that was slowly approaching. BB rushed off to the edge of the clearing, expecting his mother to follow, but she didn't. The large male approached the female, stiff-legged, with an exaggerated walk, showing off his size and strength. The male was almost three times BB's size. BB didn't understand what was happening, but he was frightened and confused. Why wasn't his mother doing something? Why was she just standing there? Was she in danger?

BB slowly moved toward his mother again, not knowing what else to do. He had always moved toward her when danger was near. However, it was the wrong move this time. His mother turned on him immediately, and with a loud roar and gnashing teeth, she charged him. It wasn't a bluff charge; it was a full charge, and BB knew it. He had never seen his mother act like this, and it scared him. He ran off, looking over his shoulder as he ran. The big male followed but was still more interested in her than in him. BB stopped 50 yards ahead of his mother when she stopped. BB sat watching as his mother returned to the big male. Until now, his life had been all about the comfort and care of his mother—her protection. She had been his teacher, his nurse. What was happening?

BB didn't understand, and could not believe what was going on. So he tried again. He slowly moved back toward his mother and her suitor—again, the wrong move. This time his mother charged and connected, hitting BB hard and taking a chunk of hair and skin off his rear end. And the big male had had enough too. He charged and chased BB out of the clearing until BB got the message. BB didn't stop running until long after he heard the heavy breathing of the male fall off and disappear. He was hurt and scared—and now he was alone.

A heavy, empty feeling filled BB's body. His attachment to his mother was broken—final. He couldn't go back there, but he couldn't leave either. He just sat there, trying to figure out what to do next. His brain, though not fully developed, had been filled with enough knowledge and training to get a head start in life.

In the grizzly bear world, BB was now a teenager. However, he did not feel prepared for life without his mother. He was too big now to climb a tree; his claws were too long to get a grip on the bark. But he wanted to climb a tree like he had done when he lost his mother the last time. He was scared, and his instincts told him to hide. So, confused and dazed, BB pulled himself together and moved closer to the river and the thick alder patches that were there. He walked through the water and pulled himself up on a bank surrounded by thick alders and lay down. He licked his wounds and tried to come to grips with his situation. He felt safe there, and though he was not hungry, there was food, so he decided to stay put for a while.

CHAPTER 10

THE NEXT STEP:
THE DRAFT ENVIRONMENTAL IMPACT STATEMENT

The Grizzlies are Coming!

IN DECEMBER 1993, the Interagency Grizzly Bear Committee (IGBC) accepted the Bitterroot Recovery Chapter to amend the USFWS Grizzly Bear Recovery Plan. It had taken two years for our team to develop the Chapter, which was pretty remarkable, given the controversy.

But at this point, the IGBC needed to make a decision on whether or not to move forward with writing the Draft Environmental Impact Statement (DEIS). The DEIS was where all the impacts would be analyzed and all the important decisions would be made, thus defining the future of recovery efforts.

In July 1994, the IGBC met in Powell, the heart of the recovery area and my home when I was a Conservation Officer. All the top brass were present, along with representatives from our Working Group and the CIG. It was a big show of authority and special interests, and some of us were worried about what would come out of it.

The Bitterroot decision was on the agenda for day two. When I met with fellow biologists for breakfast that morning, Danny Davis, the Clearwater National Forest Biologist and member of the Working Group, told us he had spoken with his Forest Supervisor earlier and had learned that the mood among Forest Service leadership was to nix the DEIS. The Forest Service was reportedly nervous about the politics and potential impacts on their Forest Plans and timber harvest, but mostly about the costs and staffing associated with writing an EIS. Foresters responsible for recovery in the North Cascades, Yellowstone, and Northern Continental Divide Ecosystems (NCDE) did not want to see available funds spread too thinly with a new recovery area.

I began a slow simmer; we'd come this far—why would they stop the forward momentum now? The Forest Service dominated the IGBC with upper-level staff, and I feared they could easily overpower the vote and persuade the others if they so desired. I was worried and depressed, despite being surrounded by my familiar haunts and scenery.

The meeting was to be held on top of Beaver Ridge Lookout, overlooking the vast Bitterroot Ecosystem. It was a perfect vantage point to see the Bitterroot Mountains, valleys, lakes, and forests that looked much as they did when Lewis and Clark walked through 190 years prior. The group slowly assembled in a circle near the lookout, standing and facing each other, many with their arms folded across their chests. Chairman Ralph Morgenweck, Regional Director for the USFWS, called the meeting to order.

The discussion began as Regional Foresters and the Bureau of Land Management (BLM) Director spoke, one after the other, expressing their concern about starting another DEIS and recovery effort before Yellowstone and the NCDE had been delisted. They cited their already stressed budgets and staff and warned that they would not be able to provide much help. They didn't think the timing was right and felt it should be put on the back burner for now. The meeting was going as Dan Davis had predicted, and it was not looking good.

But those of us who understood the Forest Service and other federal agencies were not all that surprised.

I stood next to IDFG Director Conley, as he listened intently. Jerry was not a big man, but you would never know it by the way people listened to him and the authority he carried in that group. As the longest-serving member, he was highly respected by other members and was, in my opinion, the one person in that group who could be relied upon to do the right thing for wildlife.

I had a good relationship with Jerry, dating back to meetings we had both attended during the Chapter development. He had a soft spot for grizzly bears and a moral compass that supported recovery. His respect for me had increased when he found out my background in grizzly bears, and he looked to me for input. I leaned over and whispered to him that, although the Forest Service had helped a little with the Chapter, they wouldn't have to do anything on the DEIS. That would be all IDFG, USFWS, and perhaps Montana Department of Fish, Wildlife and Parks (MFWP). I told him we didn't need the Forest Service to complete the EIS, though their input and help would be welcomed.

Director Conley cleared his throat and spoke. The crowd silenced as the little man with a big voice told them it was imperative to move forward with the DEIS. He told them his staff would handle the workload and all they would have to do is provide input. He said emphatically that it was time to get off the fence and move this project forward.

Jerry's short but impactful speech made it impossible for the Forest Service to vote against it. They had no excuses if they didn't have to provide staffing or spend any money. They just had to get out of the way. I was never prouder of Jerry than I was at that moment. He changed the course of the Bitterroot recovery, at least for the time being. Following the speech, the IGBC voted unanimously to support developing a DEIS.

As we walked the short distance off the ridge to our trucks, Hal Salwasser, the Regional Forester in charge of the National Forests in most of the recovery area, sidled up to me and smiled. He asked me what I had said to Director Conley that invoked "the speech." I think Hal was supportive of the project because his heart was in the right place, but he did not want to overrule his Forest Supervisors. I told Hal the words were all Jerry's and all I said was IDFG could handle it ourselves. Hal smiled and nodded, and I think I made a new friend that day. He gave us a compliment then that I will never forget when he said, "I like guys who are good at their jobs." Hal decided after the meeting to provide his Regional I&E (Information & Education) specialist to help with the DEIS and instructed his staff to provide assistance as needed without impacting their ongoing priorities.

Within the next few weeks, the USFWS established an EIS team and disbanded the working group. For starters, Chris Servheen hired John Weaver as the USFWS EIS team leader. John had a background with wolf recovery, and had been the Forest Service's Grizzly Bear Habitat Coordinator in Region 1, headquartered in Missoula. He was a known entity, with qualifications that suited the position. Other team members included Wayne Kasworm, the USFWS Cabinet-Yaak bear biologist; Laird Robinson, USFS Region 1, I&E; Diane Daily, USFWS Missoula and also I&E for the IGBC; Curt Mack, Nez Perce Tribe; and myself. MFWP and the USFS occasionally provided input and participated at important junctures.

Our team continued to meet regularly with the Selway-Bitterroot Ecosystem Subcommittee to keep everyone informed and committed. The USFWS had obtained some funding for the team, and six months of my salary was covered. I was still a regional biologist with IDFG, but working on the DEIS became half of my job.

Team membership and involvement would change somewhat over time, but Servheen, Kasworm, Robinson, and I began and ended with the team, through completion of the Draft DEIS. Because most of the recovery area was within Idaho, IDFG and the State of Idaho had the most to gain or lose in this process. For that reason, I had the full support of Director Conley and my Regional Supervisor, Herb Pollard, to participate on the DEIS team.

Citizens' Involvement and Input

The USFWS continued public involvement throughout 1995, and they began the legal process required by the National Environmental Policy Act (NEPA).[1]

Ultimately, three preliminary alternatives were identified and published in the *Federal Register* and in a *Scoping of Issues and Alternatives* brochure, which was mailed to 1,100 people who were on our lists of interested public.

During the comment period, the USFWS held seven public open houses, and in total, more than 300 people attended. Scoping sessions were held in eight communities close to the proposed recovery area and across the region.[2] They received 3,300 comments that were summarized, published, and then distributed to media outlets, agencies, and EIS team members. The process moved forward in the public arena, and the team got to work.

However, some observers and participants wondered why a team of government scientists was taking so long to develop an EIS document and urged us to move the process forward more quickly. But the NEPA process cannot be rushed; if it is not done properly, it can cause delays in the courts. We had only been working on it for a few months, and already they were impatient; after all, it was not being done by a vast group of agency biologists and attorneys with only one project to address. The EIS team was a small group of individuals from different agencies scattered across hundreds of miles, tasked to summarize comments, review documents, and move them to the next person in line of authorizations. It is frustratingly slow, and all the while, outside people are trying to "help" or "delay" the process and political influence is rattling cages.

In today's world, if you want to find out about a project or want to find others who share your opinions and values, you can turn to the internet or watch cable TV. But in 1995, the internet was just beginning. Even then, though, you could do a search with your dial-up modem, which I actually did. In my search for grizzly bears, I got forty results; today, you would get more than eleven million results.

In order to at least try to get a clear view of public opinion in general and not just the opinion of those you talk to or who have an axe to grind, you need to conduct a statistically and technically accurate public survey. In 1995, almost nobody owned cell phones, so everyone was easy to contact via their landline.

Of course, there was always a danger that we were asking the public for too much input. We could have too many public meetings, hold too many hearings, and conduct too many surveys. Meetings gave us an opportunity to scope out issues and concerns with those who attended, but what did the rest of the public think?

We wanted to scientifically survey attitudes of the general public and not just those who showed up at meetings. So, we hired a Florida firm, Responsive Management, to conduct a public survey.[3] The vast majority of people who had an interest in the topic but did not have a stake in the issue needed to be counted.

The survey asked some initial background questions about a person's familiarity with the Bitterroots. It questioned 919 U.S. residents, 18 years or older (which, statistically, is a sufficient sample size), who were randomly called. Approximately one-third of them were local, one-third regional, and one third national.[4]

The primary polling question asked respondents their opinion of reintroducing grizzly bears to the Bitterroot Mountains. For those of us who lived in the communities being impacted, the results were startling: if you supported recovery you were pleased with the results; if you opposed recovery, you were likely dumbfounded. The survey showed that 62 percent of local, 74 percent of regional, and 77 percent of national respondents supported it.

Based on our turnout at meetings, we never would have guessed that so many locals supported it. But there it was. In any election, those results would be considered a landslide mandate, but this case was much different. The politicians we had elected felt differently. And they, not the public, made these decisions.

Not surprisingly, of those local respondents who did not want bear recovery, the number one reason given (48 percent) was that grizzlies were dangerous to humans. Surprisingly, of the 38 percent of locals who were opposed, only 7 percent, or 2.66 percent of the total local respondents, were worried about land-use restrictions. The remainder were concerned about safety and other issues.

These results put our efforts into perspective. We were giving 2.66 percent of local citizens in Idaho and Montana the majority of the compromises! This seemed to be proof that the "squeaky wheel" syndrome was true, and we were totally aware that in this case the squeaky wheel carried political power. We knew that despite overwhelming support, the survey was not a vote.

That did not seem like a fair approach to this issue. It had become purely political, and we began to see the reality of that more clearly. Local and state politicians knew who their supporters were and felt sure environmentalists from Missoula and other population centers had somehow been more heavily counted than the loggers from Weippe—and they were right because that's how random selection works. For instance, say you have 1,000 randomly distributed jellybeans in a jar; if 600 of them are white and 400 are black, your chance of drawing white beans is about 60 percent.

Statistically, loggers from Weippe and ranchers from Ravalli County were outnumbered by residents of the cities and others who did not have a financial stake in the effort. The majority of randomly selected respondents supported recovery and only feared occasionally running into a bear when hunting or hiking in the Bitterroots. However, loggers and ranchers believed that if bears were recovered, not only would it impact their livelihoods, but it would also compromise safety in these gateway communities. In other words, the closer you lived to the recovery area, the more likely you were to oppose reintroductions.

We, of course, received comments from some residents who feared grizzlies. Jay Gore was a well-liked and respected USFWS biologist from Boise who had worked on wolf and bear recovery in Idaho. In January 1992, while he was working in Washington, D.C., he had received a couple of threatening phone calls regarding grizzly bears. According to his report, the man used "strong, vulgar language" and said, "If Gore comes back to Idaho, he'll be sitting on a dead grizzly." He also proclaimed that grizzlies are "child killers." Jay also received a similar call from a man in Lewiston who said, "We don't need wolves or grizzlies 'cuz they are animals of devil worshippers." One letter Wayne Wakkinen received from a woman in Orofino claimed that people who supported grizzly bears had to be "condom users," which she apparently believed was sacrilegious.

But based on other letters we received, God was not just on the side of grizzly bear opponents. We also heard from supporters who were sure God was on their side. One gentleman quoted Kristina Gale-

Kumar, saying, "If we are loving and mindful of keeping God's laws, Heaven awaits us. If we are hateful and destructive, constantly breaking God's laws and destroying his creation, Hell awaits us." And, of course, Genesis 1:25 was quoted: "And God made the beast of the earth after his kind, and cattle after their kind, and every thing that creepeth upon the earth after his kind: and God saw that it was good."

Threats were often shelled out over the phone or otherwise anonymously, but those seldom really concerned us. We had grown to have tough skins. Back then, conspiracy theories were not blasted across the internet into your email or Facebook page, and real hatred was somewhat contained. Nonetheless, we knew that, even though these people were not likely to actually follow through on their threats to government employees, they might very easily dish out their anger anonymously on grizzly bears. That was our concern and one that underscored all our negotiations. The squeaky wheel could break the axle of recovery if it were not tended to.

Several groups of recreationists were involved in our discussions. The Backcountry Horsemen of Idaho was a conglomeration of all the Backcountry Horsemen (BCH) Chapters in the state. Don McPherson, the National Director at the time, was the local chapter president (later chaired by Steve Didier). Don was a retired Fish and Game Conservation Officer of the "old breed"; he had grown up in that country and was probably on a horse as soon as he could walk. He took his first extended horse pack trip in the Selway-Bitterroots at age 12 with his father.

Don was a local legend at IDFG because of his knowledge and prowess with horses. In fact, he helped me select my first two horses when I became an officer in Powell, and he trained me in the ways of horses. I rode several times with him as he introduced me to trails, horse sense, and his philosophy on all things. He had a story about every stump or turn in the trail, about people he'd "pinched" for violating laws, and about anything else you asked him about. Don was crusty and didn't mince his words.

Backcountry Horsemen supported natural recovery first, rather than reintroduction. But if they were to be reintroduced, they supported the experimental non-essential 10(j) option. And they supported reintroduction only if the population was based on a minimum viable population of 70-90 bears, there were no trail or road restrictions, and management was guided by Fish and Game.

Don and most horsemen were okay with grizzly bears, but they didn't want restrictions on where they could or couldn't go with their stock, and they didn't want them "thick as fleas."[5, 6] Many local horsemen didn't understand what changes they might have to endure, so they were naturally very concerned.

Outfitters were similarly concerned with restrictions on access and black bear hunting. Of course, the use of bait for hunting was common among outfitters in and adjacent to the wilderness. In areas with known grizzly bear populations, baiting was usually outlawed. Montana does not allow bear baiting anywhere in the state, and neither does Idaho in areas adjacent to Yellowstone or in the Selkirks. Outfitters were worried, and rightfully so.

Baiting in grizzly country is a bad idea, in my opinion, for a number of reasons:

> • First, when baits were being replenished at a site, it was easy to disturb a bear that was feeding there. If it happened to be a grizzly, a confrontation of some kind could turn out to be lethal for one or the other.

> • Second, grizzly bears that were attracted to a bait during twilight hours could be misidentified and killed.

• Third, if grizzlies are rewarded time and again with human foods at a bait site, they could become food-conditioned and be dangerous to backcountry hunters, campers, and hikers. At a minimum, they might seek out the baits as an alternative food source, increasing the likelihood of conflicts.

• And lastly, during early recovery years, most of the grizzly bears would be fitted with radio collars that identified their locations. Biologists might want to temporarily close certain areas to spring bear hunting if a female with cubs were known to be using the area.

All of these would be justifiable reasons to restrict outfitter and hunter access but, of course, would be difficult for some of them to tolerate. In 1995, there were more than a hundred land- and water-based outfitters licensed in the Selway-Bitterroot and Frank Church-River of No Return Wildernesses. They provided a business perspective many people forgot about when thinking of the wilderness. I had always believed that in some ways, outfitters would benefit from the presence of grizzly bears because people would want to hire them to safely hunt black bears or to either observe grizzlies or avoid conflicts with them while hiking or hunting. Apparently, outfitters didn't see it that way. They preferred business as usual and were worried about having further restrictions on their permits.

Outfitters and many supporters of baiting point to several reasons for maintaining bear baiting in grizzly country. One reason is that it would be less likely for a hunter to misidentify a grizzly if they had time to identify it close up over bait. They also point to a lack of data that supports the theory that baiting causes bears to become food-conditioned. Baiting is the most common harvest technique in Idaho, accounting for the majority of black bears harvested, and they argue that without it, many hunters could not harvest a bear. All these arguments have some validity, but they could be argued either way. Some compromises would have to be made in order to protect outfitters and harvest techniques and still support a recolonizing population of grizzly bears. Ignoring the dilemma will not work; outfitters, hunters, and grizzly bears will all be put at risk.

Meanwhile, educators were interested in helping to inform the public. Chuck Bartlebaugh, Director of the Center for Wildlife Education in Missoula, had a corner on grizzly bear and wildlife educational materials. He attended IGBC meetings and got support and funding to disseminate "bear aware" information throughout all the ecosystems. He was also instrumental in obtaining help from General Norman Schwarzkopf, who had successfully led the American battle against Saddam Hussein in the first Gulf War. The General was known as "The bear" because of his size and abilities and provided his name to support grizzly bear and other wildlife information and public awareness campaigns.

In addition, Brown Bear Resources and the Grizzly Discovery Center created a bear-teaching trunk to promote bear education within the various ecosystems. Defenders of Wildlife and the National Wildlife Federation (NWF) were also ramping up grizzly bear education efforts. The NWF hired Dr. Sterling Miller, a well-known and respected brown bear biologist, who had recently retired from Alaska Fish and Game. He was hired to work on Bitterroot grizzly recovery and promote some of the sanitation efforts for the recovery area.

We disseminated information in the form of Q&A brochures, newspaper articles, and other materials throughout development of the Chapter and DEIS. We wanted to address the misinformation we encountered at all our CIG and public meetings. It was a delicate process to avoid the biases of draft reviewers and still remain truthful.

Unfortunately, brochures have to be read, and anything produced by the government was often inherently perceived as biased and potentially untrustworthy.

The ROOTS coalition began making inroads immediately, once the EIS team was formed. Hank Fischer from Defenders of Wildlife and Tom France of The Wildlife Federation had a good relationship with Servheen and Laird. They all lived in Missoula and had frequent meetings and discussions. ROOTS was working the political spectrum trying to get folks excited about their compromise proposal and, at the same time, working on Servheen to convince him of their ideas.

The Clinton Administration was supportive of proceeding with the DEIS, though not yet supportive of reintroductions. Idaho's and Montana's Congressional delegations were visited by Servheen and others and were interested in seeing if a collaborative effort might succeed.

So, in January 1995, just prior to wolves being introduced, the DEIS was funded for the year. As a side note, around this same time, the Idaho Legislature removed IDFG from involvement with wolf recovery, thereby expecting that reintroduction, if not recovery, would fold without the Department's help. Instead, the Nez Perce Tribe contracted with the USFWS to conduct monitoring of wolves within the State of Idaho. The USFWS proceeded with reintroductions in 1995 and 1996, despite opposition from the governor, legislature, and many others.

In early 1995, the USFWS had high hopes of finalizing the DEIS by June of 1996. Funding was limited, and a compressed time schedule was being pushed by ROOTS and others. So, we started right away with writing the purpose and need and proposed action sections, hiring companies to conduct a public survey and economic analysis, getting the Notice of Intent (NOI) published in the *Federal Register*, and taking other necessary steps.

Unfortunately, along with all the normal delays associated with NEPA and ESA requirements, the Clinton-versus-Congress government shutdowns caused employees to be furloughed and also caused several more unplanned delays. But our immediate focus, and the only thing we had control over, was to complete a high-quality Draft EIS.

I began pulling together all the background and historical information I could. At the time, I was also working with professor Chris Wozencraft and his biology students at Lewis-Clark State College. I asked them to review the unedited version of the Lewis and Clark journals to figure out how many grizzly bears they had killed or encountered when in Idaho. I read several books that had been written about the area, including Bud Moore's "Lochsa Story" and William Wright's account of killing multiple grizzly bears in the Bitterroots. And I visited the Nez Perce Indian museum in Spalding, Idaho, to gain their cultural perspective of the great bear.

I was tasked with writing several sections on impacts and risks, but most importantly, I was given the task of combining and adjusting the LOC and ROOTS proposals to develop the preferred alternative. Through my research, I felt I discovered the area for the first time, even though I had lived and worked in it for many years. I now appreciated even more the Bitterroots and its wonderful history. And I became more convinced that recovery of grizzly bears was important.

We had important contributions by Rick Mace, John Firebaugh, and Arnold Dude from MFWP; Curt Mack, Nez Perce Tribe; and Laird Robinson, Tom Puchlerz, Sherry Munther, and other Region 1 USFS staff. We also contracted out to Chris Neher, University of Montana Bioeconomics specialist, to determine costs and benefits of recovery.

Of course, core team members Wayne Kasworm, Chris Servheen, and John Weaver from the USFWS were all looking at costs of translocating bears and conducting a biological assessment of the

10(j) rule, as well as other NEPA and writing oversight. Wayne Kasworm was later given the task of writing the other primary alternative, the Conservation Biology Alternative (CBA) proposal.

This was the first group of writers and analysts, and it's important to me to highlight the diversity and depth of those responsible for pulling the DEIS together. It wasn't done by a faceless bureaucrat in D.C. We were professionals who were most familiar with the situation, people, and land that would be impacted by grizzly bears. There were many, many more biologists and specialists who contributed greatly to the effort, and I included in Appendix A those who were recorded in meeting attendance sheets, minutes, and files. Obviously, this was a huge job, and there were many people involved over many months and years.

CHAPTER 11

BB ON THE MOVE

He was worried about every sound that he didn't recognize, but he was too afraid to investigate.

AFTER BEING REBUFFED BY HIS MOTHER, BB sat somewhat stunned for a long time, licking his light wounds. Eventually, he got up and moved a little, eating the lush grasses, sedges, and forbs near his temporary refuge in the alder patch. After a couple of days, BB began to feel better physically but not emotionally. The wounds were clean, and they hadn't penetrated too deeply. But he was very lonely. He missed his mother and her companionship. He missed not having to think about what to do next except eat and play. He missed her warmth and comfort and the knowledge that she was his protector. He felt very small and vulnerable. He was worried about every sound that he didn't recognize, but he was too afraid to investigate. So he just hid in the alder patch for days.

Finally, when his desire for activity outweighed his fear, BB decided to make a move. He started walking along the river bottom, feeding and investigating smells. At night he would bed down in a thick patch of alders or under a blow-down, where he felt protected. All the time, though, he kept moving. He didn't know where he was heading or why, but he continued to move away from the smells of other grizzly bears.

One day he practically bumped into an adult male black bear that was about his own size. They were both startled, but the black bear turned and ran first. BB stood his ground and was quite surprised that another bear would run from him! He still thought of himself as a vulnerable cub in need of his mother's protection; but after that encounter, he began to feel a bit better about himself.

BB weighed less than 200 pounds, but he was starting to look more like an adult and less like a cub. He was still rangy and lean, but he had big bones. He soon ran into another black bear, and that one ran from him too. By then, he was feeling more comfortable around black bears, and the smells of grizzly bears had all but disappeared.

BB eventually found some ripening berries, mostly service-berry and chokecherry—lots of them along the creek and river bottoms. He gorged himself on the berries and never saw another grizzly. Soon the huckleberries began to ripen, and he filled up on those as well. BB occasionally saw and smelled fishermen along the river. He crossed roads going west and roads going south. He climbed ridges and followed small drainages as they grew bigger. He passed clearcut forest openings, meadows, and even some houses, mostly at night, where he smelled strange animals; but he avoided them.

BB sometimes would bed down in what he thought was a quiet place away from people, only to be woken up by vehicles nearby or loud ATVs on the roads. When that happened, he always ran to hide and never stayed around people for very long. But he couldn't totally avoid them. They seemed to be everywhere. So he decided to change directions and move toward the rising sun to see what was there. He kept moving in that direction for days, passing drainages, roads, and houses. He found delicious apple trees and raspberry bushes and garbage cans filled with foods. Near homes, he saw strange grouse-sized birds that couldn't fly. But he mostly avoided all these things because he was frightened by humans and their barking dogs.

Finally, the humans became fewer as he climbed higher in elevation. Forests replaced fields, and although there were still roads, there appeared to be fewer of them and there weren't as many humans. BB found plenty of huckleberries in these mountains in the higher elevations, and his wanderings slowed. His belly needed filling, and this seemed like the place to do it.

Archery hunting season soon started, and vehicles began to move up into the mountains. BB became nocturnal to avoid these humans. He stayed in the thickest forest, away from roads. He would feed at night and sleep during the day, ever vigilant for wandering humans. He investigated smells that he thought might be food.

One night, he approached a campsite, following the unmistakable smell of elk meat and blood. Slowly he approached from downwind until he found an elk hanging between two trees. Legs were dangling, seemingly from mid-air. BB stood up and was able to reach a hindquarter and pull it down. He hauled it away in his mouth, like a dog would carry a newspaper. He finally stopped a few hundred yards from camp to begin eating and savoring his lucky find.

Early in the morning he heard noises that sounded like humans approaching. He slinked off into the darkness to watch and saw two humans approach his meat. BB was fighting anger and fear—anger that someone might take his food and his instinctive fear of humans. But they just stood there, looking at what was left of the elk leg, and then walked away. After a short while, BB followed the humans until he was sure they were gone. Then he scurried back to what was left of the leg and continued eating.

Later that night, BB went back to the campsite, expecting to find more meat. However, this time, the meat was not dangling from between the trees. He made a circle around the campsite, sniffing the air, and finally smelled the meat in one of the trucks. He stood up on his hind legs to look inside the truck bed and accidentally hit a shovel, toppling it over onto some empty beer cans. Suddenly, he heard people yelling and moving about making loud noises, so he ran off into the darkness; that time, he kept running and didn't come back.

BB's wanderings brought him near the Montana border in mid-October. The elevations slowly increased as he walked easterly toward the Bitterroot divide. Snow had fallen and melted already but was still visible on the peaks. BB was starting to feel like it was time to find a place to spend the winter. So he explored the high elevations along the border, looking for a ridge that reminded him of the ones he and his mother had denned in.

Hunters were still around, and he often found gut piles of the deer and elk they had killed. Sometimes he would simply smell them and move in to claim them from the other scavengers. Sometimes he would hear ravens and crows and would investigate, instinctively knowing they were attracted to kill sites. Sometimes, he would hear gunshots, wait until nightfall, and then track the smell of blood to a wounding loss. These tactics enabled him to continue gaining weight for a couple more weeks.

Suddenly, though, the woods became quiet. Hunting season was over in Idaho. Snow had begun to fall, and about a foot lay on the ground. Gradually, BB's days became occupied with longer naps when he wasn't feeding. There were still some mountain ash and elderberry bushes laden with berries; the orange and purple berries contrasted brightly against the white snow, and he gorged on those. The bright orange mountain ash was not his favorite by far, but they still provided some calories, despite their mealy, sour flavor.

BB moved along a ridgeline until he found where snow was blowing and accumulating on its eastern flank. Here he started to dig under the roots of an old dead whitebark pine. The soils were rocky and the first few inches were frozen, but he was able to dig under the tree and found plenty of earth he could move and roots he easily chewed off. He remembered how his mother had created an entrance and a bowl and tried to do something similar. After he had dug about three feet into the hillside, he hit a large rock that he couldn't move, so he had to make a right turn to dig around it. He continued digging until finally he had created a small entrance and bowl. He moved dirt out of the entrance and kept at it until he had a place big enough to lie down. Then he moved in for the night.

The next day, he continued digging and improving his winter quarters. This took him longer than he expected, and it was the third day before he was satisfied and pulled in bear grass for bedding. By now he was feeling tired. It was a groggy feeling that was a culmination of months of traveling, physical fatigue, and the change in his body that had been slowly happening over the last couple of weeks when food was becoming scarcer. BB had put on good weight, even in his travels. He entered the den weighing over 250 pounds, with a good layer of fat. He was a long way from his mother when he moved into the den for the winter, but she was still on his mind as his body started to make the changes for his long winter sleep. Slowly, BB dozed off in what was his first winter alone, far from other grizzly bears.

BB didn't know it, but he was in the northern reaches of the Bitterroot Mountains, the geological spine separating Montana from Idaho. It had been many years since a grizzly bear had ventured this far south in Idaho. BB had decided that he didn't much care for other grizzly bears or humans, and this new place suited him just fine for now. He had walked hundreds of miles in his travels, all over the Panhandle of Idaho. He had wandered far away from the Selkirk and

Cabinet Mountains and was now knocking on the door of a different ecosystem: The Bitterroot Ecosystem. BB slept peacefully that winter of 2006-2007, dreaming of his travels. He, of course, didn't realize that his journey of personal discovery was also making history.

CHAPTER 12

COMPETING PROPOSALS:
LEARNING POLITICS THE HARD WAY

*Passion and reason are not often good bedmates,
and the passion of environmentalists often
lays waste to practical solutions—
the perfect becomes the enemy of the good.*

ALONG WITH THE BOUNDARY ISSUES, a drumbeat of dissension was getting louder regarding habitat quality and the ROOTS proposal. Some of the primary science contributors and agency experts were wondering out loud what would become of the habitat quality if recovery were to only occur in the wilderness.

At one of our meetings in Missoula, we were discussing the habitat quality in the Bitterroots. When some agency people began questioning the habitat quality and its ability to support grizzly bears, I responded incredulously that, if we think the habitat in the Bitterroots is incapable of supporting a couple hundred grizzlies, then we need to stop what we are doing right now. No one said anything more that evening about that topic, but the discussion was far from over.

There was some wisdom with these concerns, however. I thought the original boundaries held adequate bear habitat for recovery and that adding the wilderness to the south only enhanced it. But by removing the habitat to the north from the core, a decline in what the recovery area could support was a huge concern, and environmentalists knew it. The group Wild Forever contributed to this concern by attending CIG meetings, writing letters, and making their habitat concerns known.

However, another group, The Alliance for the Wild Rockies, ended up taking on a larger role in development of the Draft EIS. They pulled together known environmental activist groups, as well as some well-known bear biologists and scientists, to develop a competing proposal to the ROOTS coalition proposal. It was called "The Conservation Biology Alternative for Grizzly Bear Population Restoration in the Greater Salmon-Selway Region of Central Idaho and Western Montana" or "The Conservation Biology Alternative" (CBA) for short. This effort was led by Mike Bader, a bearded environmentalist who wore plaid shirts, cargo shorts, and alternated between Birkenstocks and hiking boots.

Bader lived in Missoula, which had been the center of grizzly bear science for about 20 years. He was an outspoken advocate of natural recovery and enhanced habitat security. He had previously supported and helped to develop an ecosystem restoration and management proposal for the entire northern Rockies, and the Bitterroot grizzly bear project meshed with his ideas about how to save the region from development. That proposal was well written and researched and included much of the current knowledge about grizzly bear management—and the famous Dr. John Craighead had signed on to it.

Dr. Craighead had not only studied grizzlies with his twin brother, Frank, in Yellowstone for many years but had also led the USFWS Montana Cooperative Wildlife Research Unit at the University of Montana. Before retiring, he took on a new role as head of the Craighead Institute with his son Lance, advancing the use of satellite imagery and telemetry in wildlife research.

The CBA effort also included Dr. Chuck Jonkel, who had pioneered research of grizzly bears in the Northern Continental Divide Ecosystem from the mid-1970s until funding ran out. Jonkel mentored some of the finest bear biologists of our generation on his North Fork Grizzly project and as a University of Montana professor. He was an activist for grizzly bears and wildlife education and was loved by a generation of biologists. His son Jamie became a bear biologist and bear manager for the Montana Department of Fish, Wildlife and Parks (MFWP) in Missoula, and made many important contributions toward Bitterroot grizzly recovery over the years.

Others who contributed to the CBA effort included other University professors, geographic information system (GIS) specialists, population biologists, and economic specialists. The resulting document was professional and well written, and it defined a clear alternative to ROOTS.

However, in my view and the view of the team, neither approach was perfect. The ROOTS approach reduced the amount of quality habitat in the recovery area, reduced regulatory protections for grizzly bears, and handed policy decisions over to a group of citizens rather than scientists and experienced managers. It was very industry friendly and focused recovery efforts in wilderness and away from timber interests.

The CBA approach, on the other hand, was not at all industry friendly. It was very reliant on Endangered Species Act regulatory protections under fully threatened status and emphasized habitat protections, corridors, linkages, and road density restrictions. It enlarged the proposed recovery area and the protected habitat by thousands of square miles. It also proposed a Scientific Management

Committee to oversee recovery. And it provided options of augmenting the population, similar to the Cabinet-Yaak augmentation program. Bears would be released in the wilderness AND in the area to the north that was removed by the ROOTS proposal.

For the most part, I personally believed that in a perfect world the CBA approach was the best biological approach—if it could have been implemented. However, I felt the habitat additions, restoration, and linkage protections made it less likely to be acceptable to the public and politicians. The burden it placed on local economies and recreation made it less likely to be supported by locals. I believed that if people didn't want bears there, they wouldn't survive, even given the best habitat and linkage protections from industry. Animosity of a few could fuel illegal poisoning or shooting of grizzly bears, and that was a huge concern.

I think in hindsight, however, that the CBA approach could have been highlighted more as a comparison, and a more hybrid approach might possibly have been designed. In some ways, like the CBA folks, I felt ROOTS was too much of a giveaway to industry and to the local public's unreasonable concerns. But the CBA was overly restrictive, thus ignoring and alienating the local publics altogether. It created a real headache for the team, agencies, and especially the USFWS and Chris Servheen. It was also a stand that many of the CBA supporters took for wolf reintroductions—that the 10(j) alternative was not "good enough" to recover wolves. Clearly that argument has proven false.

I think Chris was tired of fighting with the timber industry about road densities and linkage corridors, and he really felt the ROOTS proposal stood a chance of getting local and political acceptance. He realized, however, that it relied heavily on Hank and Tom getting the CBA environmentalists and bear recovery supporters on their side. In addition, the ROOTS folks had to get recovery opponents, Old

West stalwarts, and politicians on their side. I think Chris believed the ROOTS alliance was innovative and just enough of a change from the way wolves had been reintroduced that it might stand a chance of acceptance by politicians who were on the losing end of wolf recovery. And he had outside help to move the project forward—a win-win situation.

I was very concerned that this would not happen—that the sides had already been fortified. The CBA felt France and Fischer had sold out in some fashion. They didn't want their proposal to be diminished or forgotten, and they pushed to have it included as an alternative in the DEIS, which the USFWS supported. The CBA felt that ethically and biologically they were right, and ROOTS felt their proposal was politically and practically more likely to be accepted. But, as Defenders of Wildlife president Rodger Schlickeisen asked, "Is our goal to make a statement, or is it to make a difference?"[1] Passion and reason are not often good bedmates, and the passion of environmentalists often lays waste to practical solutions—the perfect becomes the enemy of the good.

I worried that with the two sides so far apart and arguing, we would never get bears back. I was afraid industry and politicians would use the arguments to derail recovery. As Seth Diamond stated, "If bear biologists can't agree, then of course, citizens won't agree."[2] But the ROOTS coalition stayed strong, even when politicians began to waver. I remember talking to Bill Mulligan of ROOTS some time later when more politicians began opposing recovery. I told him I was surprised that they were still supporting the proposal, even when it looked like things were falling apart. To his credit, Bill said, "a promise is a promise, and we think this is the right way to go."

In mid-summer, the EIS team leader, John Weaver, decided to take a hike in the Bitterroots to look at habitat himself, so he drove up to the Montana/Idaho divide near the Twin Lakes trail head. It was a short distance from where Gordon Scaggs had written his M.S. thesis on grizzly bear habitat twenty years prior. He day-hiked along the Bitterroot spine, which was some of the rockiest, craggiest habitat in the Bitterroots, and returned proclaiming that the habitat was not good enough for grizzlies. I had taken my horses on that particular trail, and I would agree; that trail beat up my horses and was not good bear habitat, at least not until you moved down and out of the rocks and into some of the beautiful alpine lakes, meadows, and forests. But Weaver didn't do that.

Additionally, he had not been included in discussions between Fischer, France, and Servheen regarding the recovery effort and alternatives, and he confided in me that it really bothered him. As the team leader, he rightfully felt a responsibility to be involved at all decision points. However, Fischer and France apparently never spent much time talking with him or any of us other than Servheen. They attended many of the CIG and BESC meetings to persuade other participants of the merits of their proposal and to update us on their meetings with politicians, but I always felt they were telling us what to do. By so doing, in my opinion, they may have undermined the team somewhat by becoming the negotiators and ultimately failed to bring many others over to their side. To their credit, however, they knew the level of compromise the timber industry folks were willing to accommodate, and their bottom line was to get bears back into the ecosystem. There was never any doubt as to their motivation, and they relied on the bear biologists to tell them if they had gone too far. It was a give-and-take that relied on their talents and abilities much more than many of us were accustomed to or comfortable with; giving someone else negotiating power was tough on biologists and agency professionals who were used to making decisions.

The two of them had worked within the political circles and upper levels of government while the rest of us worked with the locals. I understood, though, that someone had to work at the upper levels, and it might as well be the nonprofits and industry representatives. We in government were restricted from lobbying, and most of us just tried to avoid politicians whenever we could. Still, there seemed to be a power struggle for leadership of the process.

Weaver came to Idaho that spring, and we went turkey hunting and discussed much of what was occurring with the DEIS. I felt a distance growing between him and the rest of us throughout the summer. He was becoming more of an antagonist with his habitat stance and concerns about the preferred alternative and thus became more isolated from the team and his supervisor. In October, Weaver resigned as the Bitterroot DEIS team leader, citing family concerns.

Although losing Weaver was a blow that could have caused another delay, Chris Servheen immediately reorganized the team. His reorganization included increased responsibilities for Wayne Kasworm and me. He also hired a writer/editor, Johnna Roy, who had been a biologist with the USFS on the Clearwater National Forest. She was familiar with the project and the area and would prove to be a very good editor and whip-cracker to keep us on schedule. The core team for the foreseeable future was set; there would be four of us, plus Laird, the I&E specialist.

Political Changes
IC 36-103(B) IDAHO FISH AND GAME CODE AND MISSION STATEMENT

"All wildlife, including all wild animals, wild birds, and fish, within the state of Idaho, is hereby declared to be the property of the state of Idaho. It shall be preserved, protected, perpetuated, and managed. It shall be only captured or taken at such times or places, under such conditions, or by such means, or in such manner, as will preserve, protect, and perpetuate such wildlife, and provide for the citizens of this state and, as by law permitted to others, continued supplies of such wildlife for hunting, fishing and trapping."

Meanwhile, Idaho politics were taking a hard turn to the right. Cecil Andrus fulfilled his last term as governor in January 1995 and was replaced by Phil Batt, a staunch conservative. Because IDFG's mission statement was to preserve, protect, perpetuate, and manage fish and wildlife, we often battled with industry and Old West stalwarts. And not surprisingly, we were often the whipping boy in the state legislature because of it.

Batt's first order of business was to attempt to replace the IDFG Commission with his own appointees. The 1938 state law and citizens' initiative that established the IDFG Commission was clear about how the commission appointments were to be staggered and how they had to be split evenly between political parties in order to reduce political interference from the governor or his party. That meant that Batt had to wait until commissioners' terms were up in order to appoint his henchmen.

We infuriated Batt when he was a legislator, and as governor, he spoke publicly of his desires for change at Fish and Game. This may have appealed to his industry supporters but ultimately led to an outcry from sportsmen. Sportsmen's groups across the state organized and vehemently protested Batt's attempted interference with the Department and staged multiple protests. He publicly backed down, but silently set about to forever change the IDFG Commission.

Batt decided he would change the commission by increasing the number of commissioners by one, thereby adding his mark with an additional appointee. Commissioners, though appointed by the governor, had to be confirmed by the state senate. Also, Batt and the commission found a loophole in the statute that established the commission. According to the statute, if a candidate identified as an Independent rather than a Democrat or Republican, then he was not counted in the party tally. However, we found over time that the Independents who were appointed were very conservative, and along with the Republicans, conservatives soon dominated the commission.

Batt selected several commissioners during his term who were clearly conflicted about what their role was. Like most of us at Fish and Game, I personally never cared what political party commissioners were affiliated with; I only wanted them to give wildlife the priority it deserved. We had previously had many good commissioners from both parties, as it should be. However, we soon had anti-predator, anti-grizzly bear, anti-wolf, pro-timber, pro-sheep and cattle, and pro-industry commissioners appointed.

One of Batt's appointments to the commission was Jeff Siddoway, a woolgrower from eastern Idaho and the husband of Cindy Siddoway, a member of the Legislative Oversight Committee. I had worked with Cindy, a level-headed contributor who I liked and respected. However, I had heard from folks who knew Jeff that he was likely to oppose the Department's position on predators, elk depredations, recreation access, and other impacts to hunting and recreation—things that impacted his livelihood as a woolgrower. We feared he wasn't a friend of Fish and Game.

Many people in the state were happy to see the changes Batt was making, but many others were worried about what it meant for the Department's mission and direction. One longtime supporter of Fish and Game opined, "the foxes are now in the henhouse." But, even though Director Conley could see the writing on the wall, he still had work to do.

Shortly after Governor Batt had selected Jeff Siddoway as a new Fish and Game Commissioner, I attended a team meeting in Powell. We were in a small, comfortable cabin behind the Lochsa Lodge, discussing the Citizens' Management Committee (CMC) portion of the ROOTS proposal. During our discussion, I raised my concern about whether Governor Batt would be likely to select CMC members who would support grizzly bear recovery—especially given his recent selections on the commission, including Jeff Siddoway. I laughed when I said it, but as soon as I said it, I knew it was a mistake. It came across as demeaning and arrogant. Even though trust had built up among the group, I worried that someone would repeat my comment outside of our group.

As I feared, soon after arriving back in Lewiston, I received a call from a ROOTS member, giving me a heads up that someone had told Siddoway of my comments. I then got a call from Siddoway, confronting me about it. Jeff said he had heard I had a problem with him being a commissioner. I hemmed and hawed and frankly don't remember everything I said, but I suppose it included at least a partial apology. Somehow, I think we ended the call being on OK terms, but I had received a shot across the bow and a lesson in politics. I was appropriately worried I had made another enemy on the commission. I was also worried I would soon have more enemies than friends among the commissioners, and that couldn't be a good thing. My predictions about Jeff, however, were quite accurate—he was not a friend of wildlife.

During the winter of 1996, we were deep into writing the draft EIS, and the public was on edge. On January 15, I was quoted extensively in an article about grizzly bears in the Idaho Statesman by AP writer Dan Gallagher. In the article, headlined, "Supporters Say Information Can Reduce Public Fears," I was quoted as saying, "The more people know, the less they have to fear." The article clearly branded me as a Bitterroot DEIS writer and grizzly bear supporter. The quote was somewhat innocuous and true to me but not to everyone, especially when Idaho and the commission had come out against grizzly bear reintroductions in the Bitterroot.

But the quotes didn't stop there. He also quoted me in contrast to what Senator Noh had said regarding the many precautions needed to avoid conflicts; I had grandly stated, "Grizzly fear is unreasonable; I've stepped between females with cubs. It's incredible what the bears have let me do." I was also quoted saying several other knucklehead things, all of which, unfortunately, I actually did say.

Apparently, during the next few days, something relating to the article happened in Boise because the Director called Herb Pollard and told him to get me and meet him at the airport for breakfast the following morning, January 23, at 7:15 sharp. Jerry was flying to Lewiston specifically to meet with Herb and me. "Breakfast with the Director" was a well-known euphemism for "pack your bags, you're reassigned to a fish hatchery in East Podunk."

I knew the politics were changing in Boise, and I was worried my publicity was not helping either the cause or the Director. I didn't sleep much that night, thinking that my short ten-year career with IDFG, doing what I loved, was coming to an end or at least an unwelcome change.

That morning, Herb and I were waiting at the airport at 7 a.m., and my nerves were getting to me. During breakfast Jerry gave me a lesson on how to deal with the press. He told me to only speak with the media when I knew what I wanted to say, say only what I had planned on saying, and occasionally give them a nice but non-sensitive quote; and he told me to never give up an opportunity to teach but not preach. What he didn't tell me to do was to stop talking to the press or to pack my bags. Then he got up, shook our hands, and left to fly back to Boise. I stared at Herb with a perplexed look and asked him, "So, am I still employed—and still working on the EIS?" He laughed and said, "I think so." That was Jerry. He could see some value in me and wanted to make me better at the job, not get rid of me for political reasons. And I appreciated him immensely for it. Not everyone who had "breakfast with the director" could count themselves as lucky.

We continued to work on the DEIS throughout the spring and summer of 1996 and were making good progress. We developed the background information and alternatives, and the meat was being put on the bones of the DEIS. It was an intense time, and I was never sure if or when I would get a call from Boise telling me to cease and desist. We had multiple meetings in Missoula, and Johnna and I would work on the project during the four-hour drive each way from Lewiston. Wayne, Chris, Johnna, and I would hammer out issues, write, and then return weeks later for the next session. Johnna was, by then, doing much of the heavy lifting and pulled what we were writing into a cohesive document. I was always amazed at what she accomplished between meetings.

Still, the habitat issue lingered. During one of our DEIS team meetings that Johnna and I thereafter called "The Blackboard Meeting," Chris Servheen asked us to revisit the habitat issue and the population goal. He looked at the habitat within the proposed recovery area and assumed it was all pretty similar or at least adequate. He felt that the wilderness acreages added to the south would offset habitat subtracted from the north. So I reminded him how I had arrived at the population goal of 280 bears.

I mapped habitat segments on the blackboard, based on the habitat studies available to us and on our knowledge of the area and bears. I had designated the northern third of the recovery area as the highest-quality habitat, able to support 163 bears, or roughly 58 percent of the goal. Although high-quality habitat occurred throughout the recovery area, the best was what ROOTS was proposing to leave out.

When that became clear to Chris, he was visibly upset. Apparently, I had previously been unclear as to how I had used habitat quality in my estimates. The preferred alternative removed what many believed was the best habitat from the core of the recovery area, and that was what had led to much of the concern among environmental groups and some biologists. I think Chris fully realized then what we had done, but at that point, we were too far down the path to turn around.

Kasworm, Johnna, and I were surprised we were revisiting this issue so late in the process. Unfortunately, in our preferred alternative, I felt we were trading away important grizzly habitat to retain timber interests. But Chris recovered quickly, and he calmly addressed the situation. He may not have fully understood the problem with the DEIS earlier, but he knew how to deal with it. The technique I used to develop the population goal would need to be calibrated using modern tools and taking into account the habitat included under the preferred alternative. We would find out how my "old school" technique and estimate would hold up to state-of-the-art scientific analysis. We would then know how important, or not, the habitat was that was being omitted from the proposal.

The process moved forward, now with a better understanding of the obstacles. Habitat quality was the sticking point for most concerned parties. But so was the formation and involvement of the Citizens' Management Committee (CMC). The Alliance felt strongly that the recovery should be led by scientists and managers rather than a group of potentially politically-motivated citizens selected by the governors of Idaho and Montana.

I shared their concern but also valued the need for deference to local citizen and industry input. The proposal was for the governors to select the CMC members—seven from Idaho and five from Montana—who represented industry, recreation, livestock, mining, outfitters, etc., and included one representative from IDFG and one from MFWP. They would review management proposals for the recovery area and make decisions on them. Day-to-day management would still be conducted by IDFG and MFWP. Over time, the CMC proposal would continue to be adjusted, all the way to the final EIS.

CHAPTER 13

BB REACHES THE BITTERROOTS

He could see far across the Bitterroot Mountains, and the high peaks were stark white, holding onto their winter cloak in defiance of the warming sun.

BB WAS NESTLED IN HIS DEN, which was located in the historic Great Burn area north and east of Murray, Idaho. In just two days during August of 1910, the Great Burn torched more than three million acres across western Montana, northern Idaho, and eastern Washington. The fire changed the landscape from a dense forest of old growth into millions of acres of burned logs and bare soils. However, through time, the land healed and became something different. Grasses, forbs, and brush eventually took hold and, in many places where forests reigned 100 years ago, huckleberry fields reign today and it has become some of the best grizzly bear habitat in Idaho.

BB's winter went by so rapidly he might as well have been in a cryogenic chamber. He moved occasionally to keep circulation to all parts of his body, but it was reflexive and mostly not conscious. His sleep cycles were not like those of a human. They were deeper and less interrupted by wake times. Having to never eat or drink or eliminate waste allows a body to reach a different level of rest and healing. So when it was time to awaken, he was not sure how long he had been sleeping. He only knew it was time to get up and check on conditions outside.

He slowly gained consciousness and began to become aware of his surroundings. A slight dripping could be heard, and light was showing through snow in his tunnel, which would normally be much darker. BB felt the urge to begin moving, slowly at first, but soon more eagerly. His heart rate in full slumber was very slow, but his body temperature was only a couple of degrees cooler than when fully awake.

In order to fully awaken, BB's body began to shiver, and his body temperature quickly rose to 99 degrees. Although still groggy and stiff, he pushed his way up the tunnel to peer out the entrance. It was a sunny day, so he dug through the snow and ventured out of the den to sit on the melting snow outside his winter home. He breathed in the early spring air and recognized a few faint smells of bare moist soil, sunshine on the pine needles, and finally, there it was—the smell of growing things wafting upslope in the warm afternoon breeze. He yawned and stretched. His muscles were very weak, having lost 25 percent of their bulk since fall. He had lost 100 pounds over the last six months, while he lived off his ample body fat.

BB's body functions would take some time before they were fully functional again, so he was in no hurry to leave his den. He sensed he might be pushing things a little, probably weeks earlier than when he had emerged from the den with his mother. But he was already growing restless. He decided he should go for a short walk to check things out before leaving the den for good. The movement would help strengthen and prepare his lethargic body.

BB's feet were tender from the long winter. His road-toughened footpads had sloughed off in the den, and only new soft pads now protected his feet. Walking on the crusty snow was okay at first but quickly became unpleasant. Every time he lumbered into a tree well and stepped on a pinecone, a quick jolt of pain shot up his leg, making him pause before continuing.

He slowly reached the ridgeline and peered over the backside into the warming sun. Far down the mountain he thought he could see more greenery and brown soil on the sunny southern slopes, but snow still commanded the mountains. He could see far across the Bitterroot Mountains, and the high peaks were stark white, holding onto their winter cloak in defiance of the warming sun. He knew that if he left now, food would be scarce, so he reluctantly headed back to the den. He left little pink spots in the snow where his pads had worn thin and bled a little. He crawled back into the den and lay awake for a while before dozing off. Maybe in a few more days he would leave; there was no hurry.

BB didn't know how long he had slept when a noise outside his den woke him. At first, the sound was a bit muffled, but soon he was alert enough to recognize the sounds of sniffing and padded feet at the entrance to his den. He froze as the adrenaline began flowing into his brain and his body temperature recovered. His heart was pumping blood forcefully now, and he was quickly and immediately aware of what was going on. Wolves! His remote hiding place had been found!

The wolves had crossed the mountain range and walked up the ridgeline over the crusty snow on their way to the next drainage. Elk in this part of Idaho had become increasingly scarce over the prior decade, and finding vulnerable elk that were winter weakened required lots of hunting. The pack hadn't eaten in days and were desperate for a meal. Suddenly on top of a ridge, they unexpectedly crossed BB's tracks and smelled blood. They instinctively followed the tracks to the den to investigate.

Wolves are no match for an adult bear, but a young, inexperienced bear could be taken down. A bear in a den, however, posed a different challenge. Wolves are a coursing animal; that is, they typically find prey and attempt to make them run, thereby opening them up to attack from the side and rear and reducing the potential for injury to the wolves. Wolves will weaken their prey by biting behind the front leg, in the Achilles tendon region on the hind leg, or sometimes in the gut, all in an attempt to weaken their prey until they can no longer flee. Wolves avoid attacking standing prey because they open themselves to injury from flailing front feet or antlers.

A bear's teeth and claws were formidable and deadly, and attacking a bear in a den was a desperate move that starvation provoked. However, they had a strategy that had previously worked on a young black bear in its den, and they had successfully made a kill. That bear had made a shallow excavation and his body was only a short distance under the surface. Their strategy was to dig him out and pester him by taking nips and bites. That worked well on a young bear with a poorly constructed den. Eventually, the bear had panicked and attempted to make a run for it up a nearby tree. The attack happened quickly before the bear climbed the tree; because of the potential for injury, it was serious business. A well-placed bite from a bear could injure or kill a wolf, so timing and agility were crucial.

These wolves didn't know about grizzly bears, however, as they had never encountered one this far south in the Bitterroots. Had they had experience with a grizzly, they likely never would have attempted what followed. A grizzly bear, even a young one, is a different beast. They can't climb trees; instead, they will stand and fight. In order for wolves to be successful with a grizzly bear, they would need to get a young grizzly bear to charge and maybe stumble, allowing them to attack and weaken the bear through multiple bites until it finally became too weak to fight.

On the other hand, BB had a little experience with wolves. They were fairly common in the Panhandle and occasionally provided him and his mother with some meat. His mother would sometimes try to steal food from one or maybe a pair of wolves but would avoid a pack. BB remembered the terrible day the wolf attacked him when he was a cub and his mother came to his rescue. He remembered how ferocious she was and how quickly she had killed the wolf. All these experiences coursed through his confused brain as the wolves' faces appeared at the entrance to his den, sniffing and growling.

The wolves began digging and widening the entrance and slowly made their way closer to BB. BB made a couple of half charges up the entrance, unsuccessfully trying to scare them away. His movements were slow and awkward due to the tight confines of his narrow den entrance. The wolves were within striking distance and were becoming desperate and impatient. Finally, one of the wolves began digging from the side. When BB was excavating his den last fall, he had to dig around a large rock, so part of the tunnel and bowl were very close to the surface. With only a foot or so of dirt enclosing that part of his den, this was its weakest point. Through the struggles, the large male wolf could hear the bear just under the surface and began digging. Soon BB's rear end was exposed, and the adult male wolf made his move by taking a huge bite, crushing flesh and ripping hide.

The pain shot through BB like a bullet, and he instinctively knew it was now or never. With incredible speed and fury, he rushed out of the den and attacked. The wolves anticipated his exit and split to both sides of him. There were six of them and one of him. The alpha male was surprised at BB's size and ferocity but didn't change his tactic. He attacked BB's backside again. BB spun to try and swat the male just as he jumped aside. Meanwhile, another wolf bit him on the other side, sinking his teeth deeply into BB's flank. BB's thick hair and under-fur protected him some, but the pain was still infuriating.

BB was not an experienced brawler, but his instincts were cunning. He fought back with another quick spin and swipe, this time connecting with one of the younger wolves that was attempting a lunge. The younger wolf yelped and rolled down the hill, then got up, limping, and slowly returned to the fight.

BB instinctively realized that his only chance was to place his back to the den and swing at or bite whatever came into range. Every time he had exposed his rear end, it got bit, so he stayed put and battled. Two of the wolves were particularly skilled at sparring with BB. They quickly came in for a bite but backed off before he could hit them.

This went on for over an hour as BB weakened. Hair and blood were splattered on the snow, and red was more prominent than white. BB knew he was losing the battle and was weakening fast; his head swung from side to side as he gasped for air and spat blood. The wolves could sense victory, and the alpha pair moved in for the kill.

BB noticed it first out of the corner of his eye. The most persistent female wolf was approaching from his right, slowly preparing to attack, but BB saw the big male sneaking in from the left. The male was waiting for the female to make her move before he would make his. Then, once BB was occupied with the female, the male would sever BB's hamstring and Achilles tendon and cause him to collapse. At that point, it would be over.

But BB somehow anticipated the move. Just as the female attacked, BB swiped at her with his right paw, then lowered his haunches in a swift pivoting motion to his left, meeting the male's attack head-on. His swipe had connected with the female, sending her flailing through space, while his spin allowed him to meet the male with open jaws. The wolf realized his mistake too late as BB bit down hard with a tearing, shaking motion on the wolf's neck. The alpha male was instantly killed, and the female was badly injured.

The pack backed off, slowly at first, then retreated to the ridge. The male lay at BB's feet while the other wolves began howling from a semi-circle behind him. They howled for some time before slowly moving off the ridge. The attack had been a horrible mistake. They had lost the fight, along with their pack leader, father, and mate. They needed to leave. Slowly, the alpha female limped off, leading her offspring away from the scene for good.

BB slowly returned to a normal breathing pattern as the adrenaline left his system. Pain replaced the anger and fear caused by the battle. He was bone weary and very sore from not only the exertion but the multiple bites, wounds, and bruises as well. BB ate some snow to relieve the dryness in his mouth. It was late in the day now, and he sat outside his den looking at the dead wolf at his feet. He thought it smelled bad, and he hated it. He decided to move over to a tree well below the den and lie down to lick his wounds. He didn't want to crawl back into his den now, as it felt unsafe and violated. The ground under the tree was dry and provided a place where he could lick his wounds. He knew the wolves were gone, but he still felt unsafe. Even so, he could no longer find the energy to move. There was fresh snow there that he could eat to relieve the burning in his throat. The cold snow made his wounds feel better too. He licked at them for a short while and then fell into a feverish sleep.

Bears have one of the best immune systems in the animal kingdom. This is probably another evolutionary adaptation that has allowed them to do battle with other bears and wolves, eat rotting carrion, and survive infections, salmonella, e-coli, and various other bacteria and viruses found in their daily lives. Bears' bones and amputations will heal and allow them to survive when most other animals would die. Three-legged bears are not uncommon in the wild. Bears often have many wounds and scars, but few of them die from common injuries.

BB's injuries, however, were numerous and severe. Wolf bites are full of bacteria and can cause serious infections. BB would surely recover from a bite or even a few bites, but the injuries he received in this fight, with the full influx of bacteria from the saliva of several wolves, was overwhelming. His immune system had not yet strengthened for the season. His white blood cell count was lower than it would be during the peak of summer, and his body temperature rose in a fever.

BB didn't know what was happening. He would shiver, then become very hot and then very cold. He wanted some water but just wanted to lie on the snow and sleep. He was delirious. He eventually wandered toward a small creek that was forming from the melted snow and lay down in it. He created a muddy wallow as he rolled in his delirium. Days went by while he went from bad to worse, his body doing valiant battle with the microbes coursing through his system.

Finally, more than a week after the fight, the fever broke and BB's ravaged body began to feel better. During his fever, even though he did not lick the wounds, they had begun to heal. There were no flies around yet to lay eggs, so the pus turned to crust and the weeping from the wounds slowly stopped. He began to heal. Nearly two weeks had passed since the day of the wolves, and he now felt well enough to try walking.

BB got up and limped from his wallow and day bed to some green grass that had started growing along the small creek. He ate a few mouthfuls, but it didn't taste very good. Food was scarce at that elevation, so he slowly limped his way downhill. He moved at an angle across slope as he tried to keep from slipping and falling on the snowfields. He investigated patches of dry ground for bits of food and occasionally found some. Ants coming out of dormancy, grubs, and some cow parsnip just emerging from the ground were all delicacies. He ate it all. His body told him he needed the nutrition, and his stomach was getting back into eating mode. The more he moved, the less stiff and sore he felt, but he stiffened up when he rested. Eventually, he found his way to a nice green area on a hillside above a creek that was fully exposed to the sun. He ate and slept for several days. He had survived a terrible ordeal and was getting better. He was acquiring important experience and survival skills and was gaining confidence along with his scars. He was becoming a real grizzly bear.

CHAPTER 14

IDAHO DEPARTMENT OF FISH AND GAME, POLITICS, AND THE DRAFT EIS

THE USFWS DIDN'T ONLY WORK on the Draft Environmental Impact Statement (DEIS) during this period. They were involved in extensive political activity by request and design. During 1996 and 1997, they met with and briefed dozens of politicians, committees, and other individuals and groups. They also met with the Interagency Grizzly Bear Committee (IGBC) to update them and maintain their support and, of course, met with the public. They didn't sit on their hands, but were actively involved in getting information to all interested political entities and to many people and groups who had already made up their minds. They often worked in very unfriendly circumstances, but still Servheen and others continued their efforts. At the same time, the ROOTS coalition also busied themselves by meeting with governors and state and federal politicians.

As time went on and more effort was made to meet with politicians, support began to wane even more. Those efforts were now being met with indifference, or worse, hostility. The team, however, continued to dig in and do the best we could. We tried to ignore the politicians who were being quoted in the newspapers and on television. In September 1996, we completed the first Draft of the EIS and

Servheen sent it to Washington, D.C., for review. At that time, Director Conley asked me to come to Boise and give the Idaho Fish & Game (IDFG) Commission an overview of the DEIS.

By then, the commission was becoming stacked with Batt appointees who did not support the reintroduction alternative in the DEIS. In fact, they had already developed a position statement of "no reintroduction, and natural recovery only" for grizzly bears. The team, of course, had developed proposals for recovery, one of which would be natural recovery; but the preferred alternative was reintroduction as an experimental non-essential population with Citizens' Management Committee (CMC) oversight.

The commission wanted to meet with me, and I assumed it was to make it clear what my marching orders were as we moved forward. Structurally at IDFG, the commission hires and supervises the director, but the director oversees IDFG staff. This was not always well understood by commissioners and would often need to be clarified by the director. However, that being said, the director could be pressured into doing things with staff that he may or may not wish to do.

Herb and I went to Boise for the meeting, and I had prepared a short presentation; I expected vigorous opposition, especially by John Burns, one of the new Batt appointees. Burns was a Forest Supervisor who had gained a negative reputation after he and other Targhee Forest Supervisors approved the clearcutting in the 1980s of partially beetle-killed lodgepole pine immediately adjacent to the boundaries of Yellowstone National Park. Photographs from the space shuttle showed the stark clearcut line along Yellowstone's western boundary.

Burns was later transferred to the Salmon National Forest and retired there. Our perception was that he resented restrictions to Forest Plans that were due to grizzly bears near Yellowstone. All actions on federal land had to be reviewed as potential impacts to grizzly bears under Section 7 of the Endangered Species Act (ESA). Road densities, security, and impacts to vegetation, all had to be analyzed considering grizzly bears as a threatened species. Consequently, as a former supervisor of the Salmon National Forest, he was quite familiar with the southern portion of the proposed Bitterroot recovery area, as well as potential restrictions and increased analysis required to meet timber harvest and multiple-use goals.

Dick Meiers, the chairman of the commission, was a holdover from the Andrus commission. He was one of our better commissioners and was liked and respected by almost everyone. It was not uncommon for commissioners to discuss agenda items with other commissioners and staff, and he gave us a "heads up" that John Burns said he knew "how to stop a reintroduction of bears into the Bitterroot."[1] Meiers didn't, however, know how he had planned on doing it. I had the feeling I was being invited to a weenie roast, and I was the weenie!

When I went before the commission, there were no public observers in the room—only a few IDFG staff, including Herb. Biologists from the field seldom gave presentations to the commission, and this was my first one. There was palpable animosity in the room, and the spotlight was uncomfortably on me; but Chairman Dick Meiers had a way of putting people at ease. Seeing me nervously standing there for the first time, he said, "If I were as big as you, I wouldn't be afraid of grizzly bears either!" That got a laugh and allowed me to relax a bit. However, I noticed commissioner Burns was not amused.

During the question-and-answer session, Burns was noticeably hostile and questioned how an IDFG employee could legitimately be involved with what was believed to be a reintroduction effort. Director Conley deflected the question and said they had discussed removing me from the team as soon as the USFWS made a decision about which alternative they were going to endorse.

Jerry knew my support for grizzly recovery was a possible liability but had kept me on the team to make sure Idaho's involvement and interests were maintained and to keep his promise to the USFWS. The commission clearly felt I might betray their new directives and, as a grizzly advocate, would insubordinately support reintroductions (that, of course, was the preferred alternative, which was ultimately selected by the USFWS). So I respectfully responded to the question by saying, "Mr. Chairman, Director Conley, Commissioner Burns, I am honored that you would think that I can tell the United States Government what to do."

Everyone except Burns laughed at that. They were then able to believe I was pretty much just a biologist providing the USFWS with Idaho information and perspective, as opposed to having influence over the final direction of the DEIS preferred alternative. That was mostly true. Although I was a grizzly bear supporter, I did my best to make sure that Idaho's interests were represented in the DEIS.

The commission had said that, although they opposed reintroductions, if they were to happen, then they supported 10(j), the experimental non-essential population option. I took that as a tacit admission that we couldn't prevent bears from coming, but they wanted to steer how they would come and, most importantly, how they would be managed. So that was how I proceeded. I had to be careful, but I knew, for the time being at least, Director Conley had my back. Everything would be available soon enough for the public and agencies to review and comment. I felt we had produced a very good document and was eager for everyone to see it.

Shortly before the DEIS was released for internal review, the Bitterroot Chapter of the Recovery Plan was finally signed and published and was included in the DEIS as an appendix.

By November 1996, the USFWS had cleared the DEIS for agency review. It contained more than 350 pages of extensive analyses for each alternative, tables of data, maps, reports, and further information in appendices. There were four alternatives:

1) Reintroduction of an experimental non-essential population (the proposal),
2) Natural recovery (no action alternative),
3) The no grizzly alternative, and
4) Reintroduction of a threatened population with full protection of the ESA.

Alternative 1 was a derivation of what the ROOTS coalition and the Legislative Oversight Committee (LOC) had been working on as the preferred alternative. It received most of the attention and had most of the tentative political support behind it. It had also been our main focus for the past two years. It included introducing 25 bears over a period of five years. Under Section 10(j), the bears would be given experimental status, and special rules would be written for their reintroduction.

Of those special rules, the most controversial one was the CMC, which would be composed of 15 members to be appointed by the Secretary of the Interior, after consultation with the Idaho and Montana governors and the Nez Perce Tribe. Seven would be appointed from Idaho, five from Montana, one from Agriculture, one from Interior, and one from the Nez Perce Tribe. IDFG would also have one member, as would the Montana Department of Fish, Wildlife and Parks (MFWP). The CMC would implement the Bitterroot Chapter and develop management plans and policies, and agencies would conduct day-to-day management.

I had always tried to make sure IDFG would be involved in advising and implementing management. I had envisioned myself or another IDFG bear biologist working with the CMC and agencies, trapping and moving bears, conducting outreach and managing day-to-day activities within the Bitterroot, similar to what agencies did in other ecosystems. However, there was much more that needed to happen first.

Also in *Alternative 1*, the habitat issue was dealt with, at least temporarily, by designating a very large experimental population area, which included most of central Idaho and part of western Montana (*See Figure 3*). The actual recovery area would consist of the Selway-Bitterroot Wilderness and the Frank Church-River of No Return Wilderness, which was where the ROOTS coalition wanted all reintroductions to occur. Bears within the recovery area would get management emphasis. Those moving outside the recovery area, but within the experimental area, would be accommodated through provisions in the special rule and actions recommended by the CMC and advisors.

A win for the timber and mining industries with this alternative was that no Section 7 consultation would be needed within the experimental area and that current wildlife and road-density guidelines would suffice. People could kill a grizzly in defense of themselves or others and could harass a bear that was attacking livestock, but no additional compromises would need to be made.

Figure 3. Comparison of the Bitterroot Grizzly Bear Recovery Area for Alternative 1, Experimental Area for 1A, and Bitterroot Grizzly Recovery Zones for Alternatives 2, 4, and 4A. (USFWS Final EIS, 2000).

If there were significant conflicts between grizzly bears and livestock within the experimental area, these would be resolved in favor of the livestock. Toxicants lethal to bears would continue to be illegal in the experimental area.

Notably, there was a fair amount of flexibility written into *Alternative 1*, and if you trusted the CMC and the current rules for other wildlife species, then you could support it. However, if you believed the CMC would involve too many industry and livestock people who did not have grizzly bear recovery as their primary goal, you would not support the alternative. And, although habitat within the wilderness was good, in many ways it was not as good for bears as the habitat outside wilderness.

Alternative 2 was the No-Action Alternative, the natural recovery alternative supported by the IDFG Commission and many politicians and members of the public. (*See Figure 3.*) Many people felt that, if a wolf or bear could move naturally from north Idaho or Montana, they deserved to live there, but that introducing them would be wrong. Land-use restrictions would be mandated for all activities that might impact grizzly bears. The stark contrasts between *Alternatives 1* and *2* were the impacts to land activities and the provision that no bears would be introduced under *Alternative 2*. In effect, we believed this was akin to being a no-bear alternative for many years to come.

Alternative 3 was the no-bear alternative. Its purpose was to actively prevent bears from naturally reestablishing themselves in the Bitterroot Ecosystem. Despite many people supporting this alternative, it was actually illegal. Because the ESA required the USFWS to recover all species on the list, it would have to be changed to allow this; there-fore, it was a non-starter. But the National Environmental Policy Act (NEPA) required that a full range of alternatives be analyzed, even if they are theoretically not legal.

Alternative 4 was the Conservation Biology Alternative supported by many of the environmental groups and scientists. *(See Figure 3.)* It required extensive habitat protection and enhancement to assist natural recovery. Primary management responsibility was with the USFWS and included active state participation by Idaho and Montana. To define management direction and needs, a ten-member Scientific Committee would be appointed by the Secretary of the Interior in cooperation with the National Academy of Sciences. If needed, grizzly bears would be introduced into the Selway-Bitterroot Wilderness and roadless areas north of the Lochsa River. They would be listed as fully threatened under the ESA. It could take more than a hundred years for bears to become established and reach recovery goals of 300-500. In the meantime, no logging or road building would be permitted in roadless lands within the recovery zone. Many existing roads would be reclaimed and closed. Black bear hunting with dogs and bait would be eliminated within the Wilderness, and hunter education would be undertaken.

These alternatives were all based on extensive public involvement. They were essentially created by the public, with a little tweaking from agency biologists and managers. The rest of the document was a comprehensive overview and analysis of environmental and human consequences of each of the alternatives. It included 20 appendices relating to habitat quality, historical information on the grizzly bears in the Bitterroots, public attitudes, cost estimates and economic impacts, assessment of risks to humans, and other important information. Now it was up to agencies to review it internally, and it was time for us to find out what they thought about our baby.

More Changes at Fish and Game
Meanwhile, another concern began to develop. Our long-time Director and our supporter in Boise, Jerry Conley, left the department

to become the Director of Missouri Fish and Game. Deputy Director Jerry Mallet took over as interim director while the commission interviewed replacements.

Governor Batt publicly opposed grizzly bear recovery, and the ROOTS coalition had failed to persuade him to support their proposal. We started to feel some pressure and chaos develop within the department, although Mallet tried to maintain consistency and continue what Conley had started.

The Director position was advertised, interviews were held, and one of the candidates was Herb Pollard. I hoped he would be selected because of what it would mean not only for grizzly bears, but for salmon recovery and other wildlife concerns as well. Unfortunately, it was not meant to be. The commission had their own views of what the department's direction should be, and they had made their selection: Steve Mealey, a former Boise National Forest Supervisor.

The internal DEIS had been sent to Washington, D.C. in September 1996 and had been released for internal agency and biological review in November, following Washington's comments. The USFWS gave it to agencies to review—all except for IDFG. We had been very involved in writing it, but the USFWS had concerns about giving it to IDFG, who would be directed to give it to Governor Batt's staff, with the danger they would subsequently release it to the public.[2] So they did not give it to Idaho until the other agencies had commented on it and were able to adjust the DEIS accordingly. They then gave a few hard copies of the draft to IDFG for review, with all of the new agency comments included. Herb Pollard, Wayne Wakkinen, Wayne Melquist, and I reviewed and commented on it internally.

Jerry Mallet, our interim director, reviewed our comments and directed Melquist to summarize them and write a response to the USFWS. Mallet forwarded the letter to the commission on January 7.

On January 12, John Burns replied:

> "I have some serious concerns about both the con-
> tent and tone of the draft letter. The commission position was
> expressed by formal motion a few months ago, so quoting the
> 1995 ambivalant (sic) position of the commission is no longer
> appropriate. Also, expressing an opinion that bears will be
> introduced in any case and that the Department wants to be
> supportive of that effort is likewise inappropriate. I believe
> it would be a good idea to give Steve [Mealey, the newly
> appointed director] a chance to work on the response
> personally with you and the staff. I think the commission
> also needs to see the advance draft of the EIS if we are to
> comment sensibly. If there is any confusion on the position
> of the commission we can clarify that at the meeting
> this week." Signed, John B.

Burns wanted us to oppose the proposal rather than just provide
biological input. Mallet could not forward our comments to USFWS
until the arrival of the new IDFG Director. Although Mealey had been
hired, he was not yet in place or up to speed on the issues. On January
24, Mealey notified the USFWS that we would not comment on the
draft. Servheen sent the DEIS to Washington, D.C., for final review in
February. The public and IDFG would soon get another shot at it.

Steve Mealey was hired in early January 1997 by the commission, with strong support from John Burns, and was about to upset
the cart at IDFG. Mealey, a retired Forest Supervisor on both the
Boise and Targhee National Forests, had a philosophy that was purely
Forest Service and seemingly similar to that of John Burns. He was all
about multiple use, getting along with everyone, and doing what was
politically favorable. Unfortunately, he had a strong desire to tell
outside groups what they wanted to hear and try to please everyone.
Interestingly, he had also conducted research on grizzly bear habitat

in Yellowstone in the late 1970s, so he had knowledge of bears and was close friends with John Burns. These two factors concerned me and others. I didn't know Mealey personally, but I knew of him, and unfortunately, he quickly became aware of me and the project.

Mealey toured around the state in early 1997 to talk to all IDFG Regional staff and many special interest groups and sportsmen's groups. It was clear he would try to change the culture at Fish and Game. He told us times had changed, that we had a new governor, and that we were going to get along with the legislature by being more open to industry and less militaristic about our mission goals.

Our staff was not at all receptive. My colleagues and I got up every morning and went to work to do battle for fish, wildlife, and the sportsmen and women who cherished them. For us, it wasn't just a job—it was a mission, a career, and a calling. During his visit to our office, the staff grilled Mealey, and his answers did nothing to quell concerns and fears. For the first time in our careers, we were worried the new director was not on our side, the side of fish and wildlife.

After a sportsman banquet later that evening, Mealey spoke privately with me about grizzly bears and the DEIS. I let him know that I was a grizzly bear advocate. I told him the team believed that if bears were going to be recovered, reintroductions would likely be required. I said that, in effect, the department's stand on natural recovery likely meant no recovery, though an occasional bear might show up every now and then and be fully protected.

So, basically, I took a deep breath and with all the confidence I could muster looked him in the eye and said, "So, you know I am a grizzly bear advocate, and I hope you don't ask me to say or do something I do not believe in." I also stated that he was probably surprised that I had not been fired by now. He paused, then said, "Steve, as long as I am director, I will not fire you." Temporarily relieved, I told him I would give him all the biological information I had and that I always felt that the more people know, the less they have to fear. I said he could rely on me to tell the truth, but that I did not want to get involved in the political card game currently underway.[3]

I remember feeling somewhat relieved, but I also knew that there were many ways our involvement could be negatively impacted without my being fired. I may have said more than I should have, but I knew I would rather be pulled off the team than be forced to do their bidding by throwing monkey wrenches into the cogwheels of recovery. I wanted him to feel I could be useful without compromising my beliefs. I knew, however, there was still a long way to go. I wondered if, when the going got tough, he would support my continued involvement, as Jerry Conley had, or if I would become collateral damage. For the time being, he did nothing to change my status and our involvement with the DEIS. That, however, would be short-lived.

A week or so later, Director Mealey called me down to Boise. He wanted me to clarify how the habitat in the Bitterroot was evaluated, quantified, and analyzed to determine the bear recovery goal.[4] I didn't know it at the time, but I later found out that John Weaver, the former EIS team leader, had called him and told him that the habitat quality under the proposal was not sufficient to support grizzly bears.[5] I knew John was upset, but I assumed he had tried to positively impact the recovery effort from the outside, rather than to provide ammunition to derail it.

I believed Mealey thought that was the angle he himself could bring to the discussion—to still support natural recovery (which in everyone's mind meant no grizzlies) but to deny reintroductions because of the poor habitat quality. He could then make the case that the preferred alternative (*Alternative 1*) was not sensitive to grizzly bear needs. Mealey decided to hold a meeting to gather information he needed to chart a path forward. He invited Bart Butterfield, author of two reports on Bitterroot habitat; Dave Mattson, a doctoral candidate at University of Idaho and Yellowstone grizzly bear biologist with good knowledge of habitat; Dr. Jim Peek, University of Idaho wildlife professor and member of the LOC; Dr. Steve Knick, previous Selkirk grizzly biologist; Wayne Melquist; Tom Reinecker, the wildlife chief; and myself.[6]

We were in a small meeting room, significantly and appropriately called the Grizzly Room because of the grizzly bear hide displayed on the wall. First, Bart Butterfield went over his reports and the Geographic Information Systems (GIS) maps of his habitat analysis. Next, I gave my presentation about the habitat, the technique I used to obtain the population goal of 280, and why I was confident the habitat in the original evaluation area was very adequate.

All during my presentation, Mealey interrupted me, asked questions, made comments, and stated concerns. As a result, I lost my train of thought and my well-practiced presentation was undoubtedly less impactful. To make matters worse, I developed a splitting headache, and I remember just wanting the torture to end. I somehow made it through the day, but I clearly remember thinking that Mealey had made up his mind before my presentation and nothing any of us had said made a difference. He had his marching orders. He obviously felt he now had enough ammunition to support his approach and the commission's position statement.

Soon thereafter, Director Mealey publicly opposed reintroductions and concluded that the Bitterroots could not support a viable population of bears, given the proposed ecosystem boundaries and revised recovery area under the preferred alternative. He said he would not sign the needed permit to allow bears to be reintroduced. This was just chest-pounding and carried no real weight because federal law supersedes state law; if the feds wanted to reintroduce bears, they could, with or without the director's permit. But the support we had from Director Conley was now gone. Mealey came out with guns blazing, and that bothered us and USFWS.

The Fish and Wildlife Service prepared the draft EIS and Special Rule and released them to the public on July 11, 1997, making them available for review until December 1, 1997. Our new director would now be able to make his mark, and as I had dreaded, he finally removed me from the EIS team, now that the draft had been submitted for public comment. It was something I had expected, but it was still upsetting to me, Chris Servheen, and the rest of the EIS team. My involvement gave them a connection to Idaho and provided some hope that IDFG would eventually support the proposal—not to mention that the workload I had carried would now be redistributed among the remaining team members. Around that time, Herb Pollard decided to retire from IDFG and took a job with the federal government in Portland, helping with salmon recovery. The Idaho backers were slowly dwindling. Only the feds in Idaho remained. Montana, however, was still at the table.

In August, Mealey wrote a letter to the editor that was published in several newspapers, outlining his opposition to the DEIS. He also told Melquist to get a new team together, including me, to write a review of the DEIS that he could send to the commission. We were to reject the four alternatives and provide our own, calling for natural recovery with a "true" citizen's management committee.

Mealey claimed a new habitat analysis was needed because the original analysis did not cover the recovery area of the preferred alternative. He also wanted assurance of funding and a few other items, but those were his primary concerns. One thing he hadn't anticipated with his letters and comments to the media opposing grizzly bears was that he galvanized the environmental groups to come together in condemnation of him and the commission. The environmental groups, despite their disparate proposals, all wanted recovery of some kind.

For this new IDFG team to write a letter that was so critical of what we had all been working on for years seemed totally crazy to me.

But in some ways, it was actually cathartic. While providing input, I was optimistically thinking it could be a real benefit to the USFWS. They could take the comments, conduct the appropriate analyses on the habitat issue, and finally put it to bed, one way or the other. By the end of September, Mealey had passed our letter to the commission. Chairman John Burns included our comments in a letter to Chris Servheen on October 2. That letter, however, was not the only one sent.

In October, public hearings and open houses were held in seven communities to gather public comment on the DEIS and proposed special rule. Press releases were published, and the DEIS was posted on the USFWS website. Ample opportunity was provided to comment on the proposal and other alternatives.

The public comment analysis would take from December 1997 until April 1998 to complete. More than 24,000 public comments were received. Additionally, 1,367 people attended the public hearings and 294 people testified. Of those who testified, 157 were supportive, 103 were opposed, and 34 were unknowns. However, of all the comments received by the USFWS, 70 percent were critical of the proposal, 18 percent were supportive of it, and 12 percent suggested modifications.

Many in the environmental community signed post cards and petitions, and they overwhelmingly supported *Alternative 4*, the Conservation Biology Alternative. Of those commenting on *Alternative 4*, 78 percent supported it, 6 percent were critical of it, and 16 percent suggested modifications. They supported it as the best alternative for many reasons, including the large recovery area and linkage zones with other ecosystems, full protection of grizzlies as a threatened species, and strong oversight by the scientific oversight committee. Those opposed to the alternative were mostly critical of the stringent protection of the habitat and the fear that it would increase illegal taking of grizzlies.

Alternative 1 supporters typically agreed with what the ROOTS coalition and USFWS had been espousing over the past several years—

that it was the best alternative for restoring the species and protecting jobs. On the other hand, some who opposed it questioned whether the CMC had too much or not enough authority. And some felt it was a capitulation to those ruled by greed, ignorance, and fear or that local control by governors would be a slow death sentence for grizzly bears.

Alternative 2, the natural recovery alternative that was similar to what IDFG supported, received very little interest or comment. This proposal was to let bears expand from the current range in north Idaho and western Montana. Strangely, this alternative could minimally meet the ESA requirements in a basic sense and be the least costly or management intensive because it would take so long for bears to find the Bitterroot and recolonize.

Alternative 3, the no-bear alternative, received the third most comments and support. There were interesting comments by many citizens on all sides of the issue, in addition to the postcards and petitions that offered more general support or opposition.

The alternatives to reintroduce grizzly bears received so much attention that the option of "no reintroduction" was overlooked. Most biologists, myself included, would declare this to simply be another no-bear alternative because any bear that made the journey to the Bitterroots would likely not survive for long, given the low level of protections. Black bear hunters, baiters, and in later years, wolf trappers, would very likely inadvertently take any bear that made the long and lonesome journey, thus setting back any recovery. There were a few comments supporting it, stating that the time frame would take so long that people would have time to get used to grizzly bears.

IDFG's comment was to accept natural recovery with a "real" citizens' management committee. The Bureau of Land Management and Forest Service were leaning toward this recovery alternative as well, but the USFWS was adamant that it had been eliminated because it was, in effect, a no-bear alternative and would be mired in lawsuits.

How had the agencies moved away from the proposal *(Alternative 1)* we had all worked on? At one point, they were supportive but over time withdrew support when political winds began blowing in the opposite direction. The IGBC as a body became ambivalent, given the constant concerns voiced by members, including IDFG, its once most committed supporter. Agencies are nothing if not practical and political.

It was now up the USFWS to determine where they wanted to go. The strength of Chris Servheen's convictions and support within the agency were very important. The law was still on their side, and courts had been supportive of the ESA. If the Director of USFWS and Secretary of the Interior supported it, recovery would happen. But they were not likely to support it without public and, at least some, political backing.

Also, President Clinton was in his second term as a lame-duck president, but agency heads were hoping to accomplish much in his last two years. They had already introduced wolves into Idaho and Yellowstone in spite of much political opposition, but the public and environmental groups had overwhelmingly supported the wolf reintroduction under the preferred alternative. The wolf recovery process had also taken a couple of decades to get as far as we had in just four or five years. President Clinton had developed a good reputation within the environmental community, but now, with the environmental groups not all being on the same page, the administration was hesitant to support it. Secretary Babbitt had been supportive of the EIS process, but now a decision to move forward with recovery was needed.

Senators Larry Craig and Dirk Kempthorne from Idaho, along with Representatives Chenoweth and Mike Crapo, who had initially been somewhat supportive of the ROOTS coalition approach of collaboration, were not seeing the support they had anticipated for the proposal. The fact that the Idaho governor and legislature, and now the public comments, were mostly opposed to the proposal, gave them the political backing they needed to oppose the Plan. Montana Senator Conrad Burns also opposed it and actually called citizens' management a "mask for federal power."[7]

As another sign of political hypocrisy, these same politicians had for years been stating the need for collaboration, compromise, and middle ground. This was exactly what they said they wanted, but they failed to support it because leverage was shifting to their side. Their constituents were worried about impacts of grizzly bears, no matter how they came, and politicians saw little to gain in a grand compromise. For them, compromise was only necessary to bring the other side to them, not the other way around.

CHAPTER 15

BB ENTERS THE BITTERROOT RECOVERY AREA

BB RECOVERED FROM HIS ORDEAL over the next few weeks and began moving again. In the lush habitat of the Coeur d'Alene National Forest, he found foods that increased his strength. His limp was mostly gone now as the scar tissue healed within the muscle, and the outer wounds were no longer visible.

Spring had stretched into early summer, and foods were on every slope as the snow receded for the year. BB found ground squirrel caches of corms and bulbs from spring beauty and glacier lily. He dug them up and plunged his nose into the holes to lick up the delicacies. The new glacier lilies were forming as the snow receded, but it would be a month before the flowers were storing their starches in the bulbs. Small seepy areas were providing lush foraging for cow parsnip, angelica, wild onion, horsetail, snails and worms. He tried digging out a few ground squirrels and was quick enough to actually catch one. This small delicacy made him feel hungry for meat and reminded him of some things his mother did. He decided to try hunting.

Bears are not effective predators from birth; it is a learned behavior. Mothers will teach their offspring, or they stumble upon deer or elk calves and learn on their own. They are called opportunistic predators for a reason. An obligate predator such as a cougar or a wolf needs to kill animals to survive. An opportunistic predator and omnivore like a bear survives mostly on vegetation, but when the opportunity arises to become a predator, they usually don't hesitate. Some bears are good and efficient predators, and some are awkward and clumsy. BB was the latter.

Males usually spend more time as predators because they require more protein to sustain their larger bulk. In turn, their large bulk allows them to become better predators and better able to protect their kills. Also, the better they are as predators, the larger they become and the more likely they are to beat other bears for mating rights, thus passing on their genes.

BB was not yet an adult, but he was already a bit bigger than most adult black bears. Adult male black bears in Idaho typically weigh about 180 pounds. BB was around 250. In the St. Joe area, black bears were his only competition. Although he learned about catching calf elk from his mother, he also learned from watching black bears.

One day BB was foraging along a stream that had recently been logged and burned. Brush had grown rather thick along the stream bank near the mostly overgrown logging road. The Forest Service had replanted the road with clover and grasses that provided good forage for BB and also for elk. Soon BB noticed a black bear a few hundred feet ahead of him, zigzagging through the brush field. Suddenly the bear stopped with his head up and then charged a location at the base of a shrub. At the same time, BB heard the muffled sounds of an elk calf bawling. A young cow elk paced nervously nearby, making half charges at the black bear. As soon as BB realized the bear had an elk calf and was killing it, he immediately charged, and the black bear released the calf and ran off. BB quickly came back to the maimed calf and finished it off, feasting ravenously. Although the calf only weighed 30 pounds or so, it provided high-quality food for that day.

The next day, BB decided to start looking for elk calves by coursing through the shrub field. BB zigzagged all through the clear-cut, with little luck. While foraging along the road in an adjacent cut, BB saw another cow elk. He approached her curiously, and rather than running away, she began trotting about trying to draw his attention. BB started zigzagging in the area where the cow had been, and before too long found a bedded newborn elk calf. He pounced on it, holding the calf down with his front feet and crushing the calf's skull with a single bite—another feast for another day.

Although he didn't understand it, BB had actually found an elk calving area during the peak of the calving season. For about two weeks around the first of June, elk calves were born all about the same time. Elk have developed a survival strategy called predator-swamping, where they breed and birth in synchrony, thus producing more calves than predators can eat in a short time. Bears will typically only eat one calf every day or so, when they can find them.

By the time calves are two weeks old, they are mobile enough to avoid most bears. But for the first two weeks of life, black and grizzly bears are effective predators on elk calves. Once calves are more mobile, cougars become the more dominant predators. Finally, once the calves are six months to a year old, wolves take over as the more dominant predator in some locations.[1] In Idaho, adult elk are pretty safe from predation; based on research, more than 90 percent survive each year. Cougars are still the primary predator of elk, even more so than wolves.[2] If a calf survives the gauntlet of predators, it stands a better chance of survival as an adult.

BB didn't know or care about any of that; he only cared about his survival and filling his belly. He became pretty good at finding calves. Some were already old enough to evade him, but he managed to kill a few more before mid-June. He had consumed a couple hundred pounds of meat and had gained considerable weight during a lean time of year. And berry season would soon be starting.

BB knew that chokecherries, serviceberry, and twinberries, along with wild strawberry and others, were the first to ripen in lower elevations. He searched as he wandered the new areas before him. Active logging had produced plenty of food, but also a network of roads. BB was wary of roads but kept heading south along the slopes of the Bitterroot crest, avoiding them as much as possible. Eventually, he came to I-90, the four-lane highway running from Missoula to Coeur d'Alene, and he turned back. The traffic and noise scared him, and he saw no way of crossing.

For a while, he followed the highway toward the east, within earshot of the large trucks but out of sight of the road. The road gained elevation, and so did BB. Though he had a desire to cross the road, he just kept walking along it, feeding and looking for a crossing. Eventually, he crossed into Montana, a few miles north of the highway, along the Coeur d'Alene River, and moved easterly and downslope away from the lingering snows on the Bitterroot crest. BB slowed and fed, roaming toward the southeast, through drainages, crossing a web of logging roads, and avoiding traffic and cabins when possible.

BB noticed everything around him. Of particular interest was a scent from an old spore a grizzly bear had deposited when it had passed before him. He spent some time investigating the scent of the now old spore, but was still able to determine that the droppings were months old. The scats had mostly deteriorated, but in each scat, remnants of DNA, hormones and pheromones, the bear's diet, the sex of the animal, and its relative size all remained as information available to the powerful nose of a grizzly. BB determined that the bear was a female and had likely been in heat when she defecated in this spot.

Until now, BB had mostly steered clear of grizzly bear-related scents. He was young and inexperienced and had felt intimidated by other bears. He wanted to find a place away from other bears, especially males. However, this scent, although old, seemed somehow encouraging and comforting. No need to fear the close proximity of the bear, but knowing that a bear of his own species had been here and maybe lived here encouraged him and somehow decreased his feelings of loneliness.

Bears typically look for other bears, especially during the breeding season. Although BB was now in his fourth year, he was still not considered of breeding age for a grizzly. However, hormones were beginning to flow through his body, and the thought of finding a female grizzly somehow comforted and excited him. When males are in full breeding condition, testosterone generated from their testes flows through their body and drives them in a constant battle between fierce confrontations and the desire to mate. The testosterone drive can be very powerful and can totally control the everyday actions of an adult male. Feeding becomes secondary to finding mates.

Grizzly bears are polygamists: males potentially breed with several females, and females will breed with multiple males. The breeding season lasts several weeks through the summer and can cause males to lose weight and incur injury during mating battles; however, this ultimately provides the opportunity for the strongest and healthiest males to pass on their genes to the next generation.

BB was not thinking or acting like an adult male. The strange desires starting to flow through his system were still not strong enough to drive his behaviors. He was still cautious and, although getting stronger daily and gaining confidence, was not looking for a fight. The thought of a female reminded him more of the comfort of his mother than of any hormonal drive for breeding. The last thing he wanted to do after having just barely healed from his wolf encounter was to get into a fight with another bear. However, a female bear in the area was a good thing in his mind, so he moved on, continuing to forage but also instinctively hoping to smell another female in his travels.

BB found ripening berries at lower elevations but also found more human activities down there. He became more nocturnal when around human buildings, as he slowly passed through under the cover of darkness. When he was in the mountains, away from humans, he foraged during the day. He still had the strong urge to continue moving east and south, but the highway noise scared him. He eventually hit the Clark Fork River and Highway 135 as he approached the town of Saint Regis, Montana. He felt cornered by the obstacles and moved west, resting in the timber until dark. At night, he began following a small river that provided him with cover.

The highway noise was less than usual that night, maybe because it was the Fourth of July holiday weekend. However, around sunset, there were suddenly other noises that sounded like guns going off everywhere around the little town. These sounds reminded him of hunters and lightning, but they were much scarier, with whistles and blasts of color in the air and humans yelling and screaming. BB stayed down in the river bottom but moved swiftly west and south, away from the town, until he reached the highway. The river flowed under a bridge on I-90, but his fear moved him quickly along the river away from the fireworks and under the highway. BB kept moving until the sounds of the explosions were far in the distance and he was able to finally slow down and rest.

BB was now on the south side of Highway 90 and was officially in the Bitterroot Recovery Area. He didn't know it, but that small act of crossing the highway was going to put him in the history books and into danger.

CHAPTER 16

THE FINAL EIS CONUNDRUM

ALTHOUGH PUBLIC COMMENTS under National Environmental Policy Act (NEPA) requirements were never intended to be a vote, agencies always look for strong support for their action alternative. Without political, and particularly biological, support for a recovery project, moving forward in any direction is fraught with obstacles. The USFWS could move forward with *Alternative 1* in the Final EIS, fixing the major problems identified by comments, or they could give up on the maligned proposal and try something different, like a variation of *Alternative 2 or Alternative 4.*

Following the public comment period, Servheen and the team were feeling discouraged about the results. The ROOTS coalition's promises of a grand new strategy that would be the new way to resolve resource conflicts never materialized in much support from the public or politicians. Fischer and France were never able to get environmental groups, other than their own, to support it. Industry was very tepid about it, and politicians were adamantly opposed.

Not only did the ROOTS coalition not bring many Old West stalwarts to the table, but during their 1997 session, the Idaho Legislature created House Joint Memorial 6 (HJM6). HJM6 specifically called for supporting Governor Batt's opposition to the proposal, as well as immediate suspension of the EIS and withdrawal of the Federal Notice of Intent regarding reintroduction of bears. It seemed the tide had turned and now almost no one was supporting the proposal—except the USFWS.

In April 1998, I attended an EIS team meeting in Missoula. Director Mealey had told me through channels that, although I was to remain involved with grizzly bears, I should remove myself from the team that was writing the Final EIS and not talk to the press. In several follow-up emails, my directions were still not all that clear.

It was clear to me, however, that Chris, Laird, Johnna, and Wayne Kasworm had to reinvigorate their efforts and move forward with the preferred alternative. They needed to conduct a quality habitat analysis and revisit the CMC approach by addressing IDFG's concerns on both counts. I told them I thought they could make it better and stronger and that at least the biological concerns would be reduced or eliminated. They were already on it.

Chris had contracted with two outstanding biologists, Dr. Mark Boyce and Dr. John Waller. Boyce was a well-known scientist and professor at the University of Alberta, who specialized in habitat modeling and population viability analysis. Dr. Waller was employed at the time at the University of Montana and later became head of Resource Management in Glacier National Park. He specialized in Geographic Information System (GIS) habitat analysis and mapping of grizzly bear habitat. Their assignment was to:

1) Complete the GIS database on the Bitterroot, using all available information and science,

2) Develop a statistical protocol for estimating a stable grizzly bear population size based on a state-of-the-art model called Resource Selection Function (RSF),

3) Develop RSF models for Yellowstone and the Northern Continental Divide Ecosystem (NCDE) to be used in completing a comparison model to predict bear use by season in the Bitterroot Ecosystem,

4) Refine risk assessment models to improve survival estimates,

5) Run a metapopulation analysis that would estimate probability of persistence, and

6) Develop maps on the distribution and availability of major foods within the recovery area.

In summary, the team was to use the best science available to define habitat quality, how many bears could live there, and what the likelihood was for them to survive there over the long term. These were primary biological concerns brought forth during the comment period that we all felt created potential problems with the proposal. Now the team could rely on outside experts to address these concerns in a peer-reviewed, scientific fashion.

Mealey had also directed Dr. Dale Toweill, another IDFG biologist and writer, to work with EIS team members to review the Boyce and Waller study. Dale had just completed an extensive study on forest succession and wildlife habitat on the Clearwater National Forest[1] and had extensive insight into habitat quality within the recovery area because of it.

One of the comments from Mealey and others indicated there was no proof that recovery in the Bitterroots was necessary for long-term survival of grizzly bears in the lower 48 states. So part of this effort was to do what is called a *metapopulation* analysis and probability of persistence. A metapopulation is a series of connected smaller local populations that create a larger regional population. Would the addition of the Bitterroots connect existing grizzly populations and provide greater likelihood of persistence should one population blink out? This modeling effort could help establish the importance of adding the Bitterroot to recovery areas in the West.

The report was to be completed and peer reviewed by September 30, a mere three months away. The draft Final EIS was pretty much completed except for the appendix on habitat analysis, so this provided the team with a short window to plan for reintroductions.

The Selway Bitterroot Subcommittee meetings continued allthrough the period. When Herb Pollard left in 1997, Cal Groen became the new IDFG Regional Supervisor. Cal was very politically sensitive and was worried about our involvement with the EIS. He had removed himself from the chairmanship of the Bitterroot Ecosystem Subcommittee (BESC) for fear of going against the commission's stance on recovery and Mealey's direct opposition to the Plan. He did, however, remain on the BESC, and I provided him with all the information he needed to stay abreast.

While my participation in the final EIS had been diminished for several months, Servheen requested that the department reappoint me to the team. Bob Ruesink, the director of field operations for the USFWS in their Boise office, had become the new BESC chairman and fully supported my reinstatement. Although I would continue working with Bob and the subcommittee, for the time being, my involvement with the EIS team would remain in the background.

Runaway Horses

The USFWS was still optimistically thinking recovery was going to happen and that they should plan for it. With IDFG on the sidelines, Servheen was worried our experts were not going to be allowed to assist in reintroductions. He knew, of course, I would help as much as possible, even if it was on my own time; but that was of little significance if IDFG was actively opposed.

In order to do their own reconnaissance of habitat and potential release sites, Chris and Johnna asked if I could guide them into potential release areas in the wilderness for a few days in August. I agreed and suggested I take three horses and pack into Fish Lake on the Clearwater National Forest. They could fly in and meet me there. I would pack most of their gear, while they hiked between camps. From Fish Lake we would pack into Lost Knife Meadows and then work our way down the west fork of Moose Creek to the guard station, where they could be picked up by airplane in a couple days. They would get to see some of the northern reaches of the Selway-Bitterroot Wilderness when berries were ripening and could observe the habitat along the way. My fiancé, Kara, was going to fly into Moose Creek, and before Chris and Johnna headed out, we were all going to enjoy a big meal Kara made for us. After that, Kara was looking forward to riding back with me to the trailhead.

I had borrowed a third horse from Roger Westfall, the Conservation Officer stationed at Kamiah. The horse was a gentle thoroughbred with backcountry experience and would work nicely for a second pack animal. After I loaded him in my trailer, I headed up Highway 12 toward Wilderness Gateway. I should have realized the load was wrong for my undersized Fish and Game half-ton pickup, but it was all I had.

At one point, the truck began to swerve dangerously into the other lane, and I almost had a head-on collision with a semi before I could pull over. When I opened the trailer door, the borrowed horse broke his halter as he backed out of the trailer before I could untie him. I had an uncontrolled borrowed horse on Highway 12 for a couple of minutes before I grabbed another halter and caught him.

I then unloaded and reloaded horses and gear, putting as much weight forward as possible and then starting my trip again. I should have seen it as an ill-fated omen for the rest of the trip, but I didn't believe in such things then.

I spent the night in Wilderness Gateway campground. In the morning I packed my gear and headed to Fish Lake, a 16-mile pack trip. There was a nice meadow with belly-tall grass just beyond the lake, where I turned my horses out and collected them with full bellies before dark. I had my horses fed and packed, and I was waiting at the airstrip the next morning before the airplane arrived with Chris and Johnna on board. I mantied their gear, and we headed to Lost Knife Meadows, which was situated in a bowl with good grass for the horses. Chris and Johnna hiked while I packed the 11 miles to the meadow.

We set camp and I turned out the horses. They were doing fine but came in for oats before I was ready for them, so I shooed them back to the meadow. The borrowed horse decided he had no reason to stick around if I wasn't going to give them oats, so he moved away into the trees, leading my horses with him. I realized I hadn't heard my horse bell for a while, and when I checked, the horses were nowhere in sight. I quickly took off after them but couldn't figure out where they had gone. When I finally picked up their tracks, I realized they were headed down the trail the way we'd come, with a good head start. I assumed they would spend the night in a meadow a few miles away, where I could catch them. But it was well after dark, and I was worried I might spook them further if I went after them in the dark, so I returned to camp. I slept a fitful night, worrying about my stock and the fate of our trip.

I awoke early the next morning and packed a daypack with some food and a bottle of water; because I didn't know how far they'd go, I also packed a sleeping bag. I only had my riding/packer boots on, which aren't really designed for long-distance hiking, but I set out anyway and left Chris and Johnna behind. I told them I should be back by dark but, if not, to head to the nearest trailhead at Warm Springs. I started tracking the horses, and the horse tracks just kept going. They weren't at the meadow—or any meadow—and they weren't at Fish Lake. So, I headed toward Horse Heaven Meadows, which is where I was pretty sure they'd be.

I had been out of water for hours in the 85-degree August heat, and my body was getting dehydrated and starting to shut down. I had walked 18 miles in riding boots and on one quart of water in the August heat when I decided I had to take a chance on the creek water. I hadn't carried my water filter but had used the space for lead ropes and oats instead. I hadn't seen any nice little springs in quite a while, so I guzzled water from the creek until I was satiated and then cooled myself down by dunking my head before continuing my hike.

The horses were not at Horse Heaven either, and it was still eight miles to the trailhead and getting dark. I decided to stay at the Forest Service cabin, which was 100 yards off the trail. I didn't have a key to the cabin, so I threw out my bag on the porch. I then radioed the local conservation officer to find out if the horses had made it to the trailhead. At about dark he radioed back to tell me they had made it there about two or three hours prior and that someone had turned them around and sent them back up the trail! I quickly ran the 100 yards to the trail and here came my boys, heading back to Lost Knife Meadows. I caught them just in time, before they walked past me. I stopped them with a few oats I had carried with me and put them in the Forest Service corral overnight.

Relieved, but still concerned about my comrades, I headed to the Wilderness Gateway trailhead the next morning. I led the horses and walked the eight miles because I was not a good bareback rider in the mountains, especially without a bridle set.

I got Roger Westfall to head back into Lost Knife from the Warm Springs trailhead with me to get the saddles and gear. Chris and Johnna had hiked out to Warm Springs and hitchhiked back to Missoula. I was able to contact Kara to tell her not to come to Moose Creek, greatly disappointing her. When I finally got back home, I started to get sick with giardia. I was feverish and very sick for a few days before heading to the clinic to get treated. I'm sure the water I drank from the creek was contaminated, but at the time I didn't care.

It was a trip to remember, and not for good reasons. Although we didn't realize it at the time, the trip was much like the Bitterroot recovery process; it started with excitement and anticipation, and after much work and effort, ended with a thud and a great deal of disappointment.

CHAPTER 17

BB FINDS HOME

Once it's controlled, fear becomes nothing more than the whetstone to one's senses and they become a sharpened tool that you learn to use.

THE HABITAT SOUTH OF THE HIGHWAY was much like what BB was familiar with. However, south-facing slopes were drier than in northern Idaho, and they were not as lush with forbs and berries. This was a disappointment for BB, and the heat in the lower elevations was overwhelming. So he instinctively moved up and over ridges that divided creeks, while moving southerly but also gaining elevation.

Over the next few weeks, BB explored basins and small alpine lakes along the Bitterroot crest, staying mostly on the east side of the divide in Montana. The higher elevations provided him with huckleberries and some respite from the heat. His favorite food was starting to ripen. Whenever he found a good berry patch, he might spend several hours there filling his belly before moving on. The country was lush and quiet, just the way he liked it. He was in the St. Joe National Forest anytime he moved over the crest into Idaho.

He would spend his nights along the divide, sleeping near the cool mountain lakes and upper treeless basins. His travels only slowed when he found food. The huckleberries soon began ripening at higher elevations, and he found them now without difficulty. Occasionally, he would encounter humans hiking or fishing near the lakes, and he avoided them by staying among the scrub alpine firs until dusk. He walked the upper basins of Fish Creek in Montana and followed the long gentle draw of Cache Creek, while moving up in elevation. This broad basin in upper Cache Creek was full of good foods, and he followed it up to the Bitterroot divide to a gentle saddle where the berries were more plentiful.

Here, at Cache Saddle, BB stood and looked at the vistas to the northwest and the wide-open basins where Indian paintbrush and other alpine flowers bloomed. He saw scree slopes cascading down to boulder fields, melding into meadows crowded by forests and then to huckleberry bushes that were now tinged a burgundy red after the first frost of early August. The sun was low on the horizon and painted the clouds orange and turned the mountains pink and then purple. The cool breeze that was common at the upper elevations slowly quieted, and silence overcame the scene.

BB took a deep breath and could smell the ripening huckleberries below him. A lone mosquito released by the dying breeze found BB's nose and broke the spell. After a few minutes taking in the scene, BB wiped the mosquito from his nose and decided to descend to the slopes below. He had stepped into the upper reaches of Kelly Creek, 170 air miles from his natal den where he was born four years ago. Even though he knew he had never been here before, it felt familiar; he knew he was done traveling now, because he had found home.

BB sniffed the air and ground as he slowly moved forward, deciphering the molecular scent clues of those that preceded him. The saddle was a crossing route for many species of animals moving back and forth between the states and through the mountains. He could see way into the distance from where he was, and all he could see was trees, mountains, and the shiny reflections of the setting sun on the water. He could see no roads and hear no humans or their machines. He began to move slowly downslope, looking for huckleberries.

There were lots of huckleberries in the upper reaches of Williams Creek and Kelly Creek. Kelly Creek is best known for blue-ribbon trout fishing and, during the late 1980s and early 1990s, was also home to one of the largest elk populations in Idaho and the West. Although forest cover had changed and the elk numbers had declined over the following decades, huckleberry shrubs were still plentiful on many hillsides and provided forage for many bears.

BB was the only grizzly bear in the drainage, but he encountered dozens of black bears. They were all foraging close to each other in the thick berry patches. BB would occasionally charge a black bear that was getting too close to him and his berries, and he soon became the "bear in charge." Every black bear, including large adults, gave way to him when he approached. His attitude was changing, and his confidence was improving. He no longer avoided other bears; they avoided him.

Huckleberries were ripening everywhere as the first frosts of the season touched the basin, and the bushes were starting to turn deep red. It was late August, and the nights were getting cooler in this high mountain basin. BB was putting on several pounds a day as the sugars and starches in the berries turned into fat. BB gorged himself. He loved his new home.

He quickly learned the trails, where the game moved, and where the berries were ripest and when. He found large downed logs that he ripped open for grubs and ants. He rolled over large rocks that had not been rolled by a grizzly bear in decades. He dug up dried fields of spring beauty and glacier lily to get at the high-starch bulbs

and corms in the higher areas of the basin, and he defecated large piles
of huckleberry dung in the overturned dirt. His digging acted like a
cultivator, and he was planting and depositing seeds and fertilizer with
each defecation. A new huckleberry bush would grow in that spot next
year. He was the farmer that had been missing from these hills for too
long. He dug for fat ground squirrels when one chirped close to him.
He expended lots of energy for the morsel the squirrel would provide,
but the meat tasted so good.

Upper Kelly Creek became BB's home. He scouted the hills for
future den sites and foods. He located old outfitter camps that had long
been abandoned after the elk had disappeared. He investigated scats to
determine if one might be that female he smelled and thought about on
occasion. He made tracks in mud that hadn't seen a grizzly bear since
1946. Kelly Creek seemed alive again as birds and coyotes quickly surrounded BB's dig sites to eat escaping insects and small mammals, and
his presence became known to all in the drainage. A grizzly bear had
returned to the Clearwater National Forest, unbeknownst to the U.S.
government or to Idahoans. BB had made himself known only to
other animals and the mountains, as grizzly bears tend to do.

BB would have scared many people if they had known he
lived there because people, for the most part, are frightened of things
they don't understand. They hear stories of grizzly bears killing and
eating humans, and those thoughts tend to dominate during the silent
moments before falling asleep in their sleeping bags in bear country.
A fear of predators was instilled in us as far back as prehistoric man,
and it served us well when we roamed with saber-toothed tigers and
cave bears. That fear provided us with motivation for developing
weapons, not only to protect ourselves but also to kill for food or
resources. Fear is a motivator. Walled cities were created out of fear.
Wild animals change their behavior out of fear of predators. Fear is a
healthy thing, even as uncomfortable as it is.

For many people, the mere presence of a grizzly bear in the forest is just too much for their fear emotion. They cannot understand the good in an animal that can kill you. For others, fear can be put into perspective. For them, it can be used to motivate but not dominate. It can be used to simply sharpen one's senses, alertness, or behaviors. Once it's controlled, fear becomes nothing more than the whetstone to one's senses and they become a sharpened tool that you learn to use. In nature, there is little difference between the hunter and the hunted; both have sharpened senses, and their behaviors are honed. Life and death happen every day, but the strong desire to survive is instilled in all of God's creations.

Humans have divorced themselves from nature; it has become something to conquer or to observe from a distance. For some, killing wild animals is a necessity; for others, it is a sport. For a few, it is a way to reinvent oneself, to emerge as owner of life-and-death struggles, to become a predator, testing one's strength, cunning, senses, and abilities to adapt and learn. To participate in the life-and-death struggles of your grandfather and his grandfather—to be a hunter—is to be a predator.

To be fearful is normal; to control it is evolution. Driving down a busy road can cause fear, with the constant bombardment of movements, speed, unknown motivations, and large projectiles coming at you. But with time and experience, those fears can be conquered. By the same token, if we spend time with grizzly bears, we can conquer our fear of them as we learn to understand them. They are simply earning a living on the land and want to be left alone. Once you understand their ways, they can be accommodated. They can be protective of their young, their food, or their personal space, but depending on the animal, that rarely happens. They are flexible when encountered and usually run away. They choose to avoid humans when possible—a trait that has allowed them to survive in the modern world.

BB was not an aggressive bear. He learned that his fear made him stronger and made him faster and more alert. But he was still learning how to cope with his fear, his curious behavior, and his unquenchable appetite. BB was still learning to be a bear when new scents came to his home.

BB smelled rotting meat and something else—something that smelled of food. He also smelled horses and humans. He was alert to the smell of humans, but the food smells enticed him. The smell was coming from low down in the drainage, near a split in the creek where the South Fork and Williams Fork separated. It wafted up to him as he lay in his daybed up slope. It was a very curious smell and one that he wanted to investigate, but not until dark.

After dark, BB wandered down toward the smells and circled downwind to determine what it was. Although the smell of humans was there, it was waning and the smell of food was strong. Once he determined humans were gone, he moved in. Slowly BB moved toward the smells emanating from on top of a house-sized rock. He walked around the rock until he found a leaning log with sawed-off branches that allowed him to climb onto the massive stone. He began tasting the foods and found them to be similar but not exactly like anything he had previously eaten. It was good and there was plenty of it. He gorged himself until it was gone, then moved away, back down the log and into the brush fields. He had eaten enough to satisfy his hunger for the time being, so he moved uphill away from the site and bedded down.

Early the next morning he began foraging for huckleberries. But late that evening he again noticed those smells coming from the same site. BB slowly worked his way down and, determining that the humans were gone, moved in to eat the food. Again, he gorged himself. This food was new and different, and he didn't understand why it was there, but he was not afraid of it. He had not grown up with bear baiting, and his mother had never taught him to avoid it. It was just a remarkable source of food that had shown up all of a sudden. However, deep in BB's instincts, there was this lingering fear that came with the scent of humans.

The State of Tennessee is home to thousands of black bears. Deer, bears, wild boar, and humans abound in the Blue Ridge Mountains. Hunters kill hundreds of bears every year in Tennessee. However, the Bitterroot Mountains of Idaho are nothing like the Blue Ridge Mountains of Tennessee. The Bitterroots are millions of years younger and much wilder. Vast roadless areas are available only to those who can hike with a full backpack or use pack animals. Commercial outfitters provide the knowledge and skill necessary so that out-of-state hunters may experience this great area. Nonresidents are the primary clients of these outfitters, and in north Idaho where elk numbers have declined, outfitters guide bear hunts when and where archery hunting for elk once was king.

This was the case when the Tennessee hunter who had always dreamed of hunting in the wilds of the West booked a trip with an Idaho outfitter. It was the Friday before Labor Day weekend when the outfitter met his client at the airport in Missoula. The outfitter's lodge was in the Bitterroot Valley, and that's where the client and other members of his party spent the evening, drinking some Tennessee Whiskey and swapping stories. The client was a 74-year old man who had never shot a black bear before. He told the outfitter that it would likely be his last chance to get one, and he'd done his homework before booking this trip.

The next morning, the guides loaded their gear in the back of the pickups, and everyone hopped into the trucks and began the four-hour trip along the highway and up a rutted and rocky Forest Service road over to the divide into Idaho. The horses and mules were already saddled at the trailhead, waiting for their loads. The guides packed the gear into panniers and mantied loads and balanced them using scales and arm lifts. The loads had to be within five or six pounds of each other to balance well on the backs of the mules. Wranglers were well practiced at balancing loads, and they could always fix an unbalanced load by removing a shovel or an ax from one side and placing it on the other if need be. Once the mules were loaded, the hunters mounted their horses for the five-hour trip down the rocky trail into hunting camp. The old hunter from Tennessee was feeling 20 years younger as he mounted his horse and followed the guide down the trail. He couldn't imagine the dark turn of events that would happen to him over the next few days.

CHAPTER 18

FINE-TUNING THE FINAL EIS

WHILE WORK CONTINUED ON THE EIS, other things were going on at IDFG and the State of Idaho. By 1998, we had seen big changes in elk numbers in the Clearwater Region and didn't know exactly why they were declining. We knew habitat conditions for elk were declining, and we had recently had high winter mortality. In addition, bears, lions, and now wolves were being cited as mortality factors. Whatever the causes, we were in the middle of making major shifts to our big game regulations to change how elk harvest was being conducted, and at the same time, grizzly bear recovery was being promoted. Sportsmen were feeling inundated with bad news.

Governor Batt had decided not to run for a second term, and Senator Dirk Kempthorne had decided to run in his place. Kempthorne, during his tenure in D.C., had tried unsuccessfully to change the Endangered Species Act (ESA) to include economic impacts prior to listing and recovery. His signature piece of successful legislation was the unfunded mandate law. This clearly made him a proponent of states' rights and empowering local governments. He, however, was not a fan of grizzly bears, and he had made that well known.

Kempthorne won the 1997 election in a landslide, so we knew there would not be any good news at the statehouse regarding recovery for the next four years. This was our window for reintroductions, and we had a new opponent. We were told that his staffers, when briefing him on grizzly bear recovery efforts, displayed several 8x10 photos of mauling victims and highlighted the danger to humans. He was quoted in the papers as asking why we would want to reintroduce these "large flesh-eating carnivores" into Idaho. Many of us mocked his redundant description but knew that he had experience and connections and could impact the EIS, and we were worried.

Changes were happening within IDFG as well. In 1999, Director Mealey was fired after a few years of tumultuous service. He had been reprimanded by the commission after a moment of indiscretion that occurred during a tour boat trip on Lake Coeur d'Alene following a commission meeting. Mealey had been goaded into showing his distaste for a statue along the shoreline by mooning the statue, to the amusement of John Burns and Jeff Siddoway. Some other members of the commission, including Don Clower, found the trio's distasteful display in public to be unrepresentative of the commission and embarrassing to the department. The tour boat owner was livid, and other members of the public on the boat were disgusted. And, of course, the news media loved it.

It was a moment of lowbrow humor that was not appreciated, and Mealey never fully recovered from the embarrassment. He had lost his standing with the commission, the public, and possibly with the governor as well. Although Mealey continued to serve for a while after that, the department needed a new director. Rod Sando, a previous Director of the Minnesota Department of Natural Resources, was hired. Sando was a likeable and respected resource professional but was not quite ready for the deep red politics of Idaho. His levelheaded approach to resource issues and his honest dealings with politicians, in stark contrast to Mealey, were more supportive of our mission statement but were not appreciated in the statehouse. The IDFG staff liked him, however.

In November, I met with the team in Missoula to review the habitat and metapopulation analysis completed by the modelers. Boyce and Waller presented their analysis that they later published in the journal, "Trends in Ecology and Evolution." They estimated the habitat could support 308-321 total grizzly bears within the Selway-Bitterroot, Frank Church-River of No Return Wilderness, and the north part of the original evaluation area. Within just the wilderness areas north and south, the area proposed for recovery in *Alternative 1*, the population estimate was 234-299. Our original population goal of 280 bears was for the Selway-Bitterroot and the non-wilderness area to the north.

So even though our population goals were similar, adding the Frank Church Wilderness portions to the recovery area for *Alternative 1* ended up being almost as important as the areas to the north outside of wilderness that were left out. This new high-tech analysis would now somewhat alleviate my concerns and those of Weaver, the folks supporting the Conservation Biology Alternative (CBA), Director Mealey, and others. Removing the non-wilderness areas that were contentious and at the heart of the ROOTS proposal did not have the dire implications so many of us had feared. That should have been good news for environmentalists and others; unfortunately it wasn't.

Criticism of the habitat potential continued, with critics citing their fear that the lack of salmon and steelhead, along with declining whitebark pine, would reduce or eliminate habitat quality over time. We were happy to point out that grizzly bears survived quite nicely in the Northern Continental Divide Ecosystem (NCDE) and most other places where salmon were not a food source and whitebark pine was no longer available. But we still had to address these concerns in the Final Environmental Impact Statement (FEIS).

Meanwhile, the Craighead Institute conducted research that looked at the habitat addressed in the three action alternatives. They found that throughout the wilderness there were good quantities of primary and secondary berries important for grizzly bears and there were good quantities of whitebark pine in the southern wilderness.

Bob Keane and Steve Arno of the USDA Intermountain Research Station indicated only 20 to 40 percent of the historical whitebark pine was remaining in the ecosystem due to blister rust.[1] However, due to natural disease resilience, they believed it would bottom out at 5 to 10 percent of historical levels and would eventually recover with resistant trees. Fires are a critical component in maintaining whitebark pine in the wilderness areas. Researchers found that in high-elevation areas where whitebark pine thrives, fire managers tend to allow fires to burn naturally as per policy, which provided a better long-term prognosis for regeneration. This would be a positive long-term result for grizzly bear foods.

Also, as required under Section 7 of the ESA, the National Marine Fisheries Service posted a Biological Opinion on the possible impacts that grizzly bear recovery in the Bitterroots would have on listed spring/summer chinook and steelhead. They found there would be little, if any, impact that could not be easily mitigated.

This was interesting to me because we had always wanted salmon and steelhead to come back in quantities large enough to not only supply commercial coastal fishermen and inland anglers with catchable numbers, but also provide grizzly bears with a supplemental food source. Some had tried to use salmon recovery as a reason not to allow grizzly bear recovery.

For the final EIS, the team also identified potential human-related attractant sites for bears in the recovery area. As part of identifying sanitation problem areas within the recovery area and adjacent lands, a decent road and access map was also created. This was a road map of potential problems for any form of recovery, including natural recovery, which provided agencies and private entities with information for improving the recovery area for long-term bear survival.

The habitat issue was somewhat settled, but the question still lingered: Was the addition of the Bitterroot Recovery Area important for the long-term recovery prospects of grizzly bears in the Northwest? Boyce had conducted the metapopulation analysis, looking particularly at the northern populations of the NCDE, the Cabinet/Yaak, and the Selkirk Recovery Areas. He concluded that, by adding the Bitterroot population, the likelihood of extinction would be reduced by 88 to 90 percent. Even though the overall risk of eradication was relatively low, given the conditions at the time of the analysis, the addition of the Bitterroots would improve the likelihood of persistence by almost 90 percent over the next hundred years, which is pretty significant in anyone's book.

Although the analysis was modeling population stability over a hundred years, it did not look at changes in climate that might impact habitat conditions. It merely indicated that under current conditions the likelihood of eradication was minimal. Therefore, due to the many unforeseen events that could occur during that time, this analysis indicated that the Bitterroot Recovery would be extremely important in overall survival of grizzly bears in the long term and was, therefore, a needed action.

Many of the science issues raised in the draft EIS comment period were addressed in the final EIS and in additional appendices. But one sticking point remained relating to the Citizens Management Committee (CMC). Opponents of the ROOTS proposal (*Alternative 1*) continued to pick apart the CMC. Supporters of the CMC approach did not believe the USFWS would relinquish authority to citizens. Opponents of the CMC thought there was too much authority given to local citizens who did not want grizzly bears in the first place.

The USFWS, therefore, amended the CMC by requiring that the governors' selections be accompanied by documentation of their qualifications related to natural resource issues and their commitment to collaborative decision making. The committee would include a cross section of viewpoints, thus making the CMC more balanced. Additionally, the Secretary would appoint two scientific advisors to the committee, and they would be required to use the best scientific information available to make decisions. Fish and Wildlife Service also got a Solicitor's opinion that the Secretary of the Interior could, in effect, provide the CMC with authority. As a failsafe to environmentalist's concerns, the USFWS also stated that the Secretary could take back authority if, after a six-month review of CMC decisions, they were deemed not amenable to recovery.

All these additions, and more, were intended to quell concerns of the scientific and environmental communities but gave more ammunition for industry and political opponents to oppose reintroductions. It was a no-win situation. Politicians and IDFG labeled the CMC as not being a real Citizens' Management Committee because of all the new restrictions. However, I, as well as many others, saw the additions as a positive approach. We felt that retaining scientific advisors and vetting CMC members for their ability to work together for bear recovery would still allow political, social, and local economic interests to help steer but not dictate bear recovery. This would address concerns many of us had raised. I felt the changes could lead to a new way of doing business in natural resource policymaking. In my opinion, the USFWS had done everything in its power to support the new approach without relinquishing the primary goal of grizzly recovery.

During the EIS process, the Alliance for the Wild Rockies had proclaimed that acceptance of the preferred alternative and the experimental non-essential population would be illegal if there were already bears within the Bitterroots. This, of course, was something that the EIS team and I in particular had spent a lot of time investigating over the previous decade. Wayne Melquist had written of possible grizzly bear sign or observations that had been unverified in the Bitterroot; he wrote a clarification of his comments in the report,[2] saying there was no verified evidence of grizzly bears there. In addition, Chris Servheen, Gregg Servheen, Dan Davis, and I had spent years following up on reported sightings, in addition to helping with extensive remote camera studies and conducting our own efforts. We just could not find any evidence of a single bear, to say nothing of a population. We did not, however, have a good definition of a "population" of grizzly bears to support the requirements for reintroduction under the experimental population designation. Therefore, Chris Servheen queried 54 well-known bear biologists and asked what they would consider to be a "population" of bears, not to be confused with a minimum viable population or a recovered population. He received comments back from 37 biologists who agreed with the definition of a population of bears for the purposes of the Final EIS:

> *A grizzly bear population is defined by verified evidence within the previous six years, consisting of photos within the area, verified tracks and/or sightings by reputable scientists or agency personnel, of at least two different female grizzly bears with young or one female seen with different litters in two different years in an area geographically distinct from other grizzly bear populations. Verifiable evidence of females with young, to be geographically distinct (>10 miles) from the nearest non-experimental population recovery zone boundary.*

This was based in part on the definition used in the wolf recovery effort that had so far passed USFWS and legal muster. The CBA folks, however, were quite certain they could find grizzly bear evidence, possibly even a population of bears, in the recovery area. Their opinion was based in no small part on the determination of

Mike Bader and Dr. Chuck Jonkel. So, in 1999, they set about creating what they called the "Great Grizzly Search."

A team of dedicated students and interested citizens volunteered with the Alliance to scour the Bitterroots in search of grizzly bears. But first they needed training. Servheen was asked to participate and provide information on what would constitute verified evidence, and I was asked to provide my experience searching for grizzlies in the Bitterroot and be the primary contact for Idaho. Other biologists, including Dr. Jonkel and his son Jamie, were present as well. I did not want to be discouraging, but I relayed that I had looked at reports and sightings, walked trails on foot and horseback for years, and helped with a couple of intensive camera studies and had yet to see any sign of a grizzly bears. I told them that, after a while, it weighs on you and your enthusiasm wanes. That, however, did not discourage them.

We then defined what would constitute verifiable evidence of grizzly bears. The team had enlisted Dr. Lisette Waites, a University of Idaho DNA specialist, to identify any hair or other DNA collected. She agreed to identify hair to species, but only after specialists had ruled out black bear or other species. Servheen had decided that we should cooperate with this effort, if for no other reason than to keep the volunteers from flooding the University and media with false information.

By spring of 2000, the volunteers were out in the field in force. Although their enthusiasm was high, having found large scats and gray hairs over the spring and summer, they had not been able to verify any grizzly bears. They had a casual approach to evidence security that we wanted them to improve. We could not accept evidence that was loosely handled, with no chain-of-evidence record. We had to ensure that scientific evidence and collection methods were clean. That was not always easy with a group of volunteers whose enthusiasm exceeded their training. They never did provide grizzly bear evidence, despite finding large scats and having hairs analyzed by the University. Eventually, after three years of effort, the great grizzly search died when their funding finally dried up.

In May 1999, the Interagency Grizzly Bear Committee (IGBC) met via conference call.[3] Ralph Morgenweck, the Regional Director of the USFWS, discussed the Draft FEIS. He said that they had no additional comments worthy of producing a second draft, so the Final EIS would be sent to D.C. in June. They hoped to get it back in July, allowing the IGBC to get a final shot at it before signing the Record of Decision (ROD) in August. That would prove to be an overly optimistic schedule.

There was broad agreement within IGBC that the final draft was technically sound. The question was not the EIS but, rather, the alternative selected. The USFS and Bureau of Land Management (BLM) still preferred *Alternative 2*, the natural recovery alternative (as did IDFG), which the USFWS had denied because it would take more than a hundred years to see recovery and thus would be litigated as a no-bear alternative. There was broad agreement that there was not enough staff or funding to tackle another introduction and that it would be best to prioritize actions among ecosystems. The USFWS agreed they did not want to drain resources from other areas and that new dollars would be needed before reintroduction could occur in the Bitterroot. They cautioned, however, that the FEIS and the ROD to reintroduce bears would need additional National Environmental Policy Act (NEPA) updates after three or four years, thus creating an additional expense and time-consuming effort. Even though no one seemed to think there would be bears available to move within the next few years, there were concerns about what a delay would mean.

Montana and Idaho thought the USFWS should show progress toward delisting Yellowstone and other recovery areas before thrusting bears into the Bitterroot, thus creating more controversy, spreading resources, etc. This was the same argument that was made back in 1994 by the BLM, USFS, and others over whether to even proceed with the EIS. All the work on the EIS over the past five years, collecting facts and public input, analyzing data, conducting research, allowing for the process to move forward, all that … and we were back at square one.

The big difference now was that retired Director Jerry Conley was no longer present and the politics in the Fish & Game Commission and governor's office had changed. New IDFG Director Sando was not about to move against the commission and the governor in his first few weeks in office, even if he actually thought we should have bears. He would have been overruled and deemed insubordinate by the commission, and his tenure would have been cut short. It appeared there was only one IGBC champion for moving forward, and that was the USFWS—in particular, Chris Servheen and Ralph Morgenweck.

Bob Ruesink, the USFWS field director from Boise and Bitterroot Ecosystem Subcommittee (BESC) chair, seeing how things were going, suggested it might be wise to give the CMC a try before bears were reintroduced, thus creating a glide path. Montana agreed but sidestepped the proposal by saying it should be tried first where there were already bears, rather than diverting money to Idaho. Interestingly, the CMC approach had received strong support from state and federal partners, thereby relinquishing their normal authority to a group of citizens. I was very skeptical of the initial CMC approach under the preferred alternative in the DEIS, but the changes made in the FEIS seemed like a very good partnership between the public, professional managers, and scientists. Ralph Morgenweck said he would see what they could do to accommodate points made. But could he get the USFWS in Washington, namely USFWS Director Jamie Clark and Interior Secretary Bruce Babbitt, to support it, given all the opposition?

This was a dagger in the heart of the EIS team and proponents of reintroductions. We were losing our forward momentum and our closest allies. Time was running out on the Clinton presidency. But the die was cast, and the FEIS was sent to the black hole in Washington, D.C.

Congressional cheerleaders Helen Chenoweth and Larry Craig joined an anti-grizzly coalition, despite having previously paid verbal homage to the ROOTS proposal. Congressman Mike Crapo dropped any of his tentative support of the coalition proposal and collaboration mantra when he read the tea leaves. Senator Burns from Montana joined with Larry Craig and introduced another budget rider that would prevent reintroduction in 2000, but President Clinton forced Republicans to drop all the environmental riders in the budget.

I never expected anything different from our congressional representatives. At that time, they could be relied on to fight environmental actions that confronted the old ways of life and natural resource extraction industries. Compromise was not in their vocabulary when victory, albeit hollow, was in their sights. Even Montana democrat Max Baucus failed to support it in the end. The only politician to hold his ground in his support for collaboration and the proposed approach was Montana Governor Marc Racicot, and for that, I commend him—a rare politician who kept his word.

The FEIS ground away in D.C., and I imagine it was being held up for various political, biological, and legal reasons. But, finally, and with great anticipation, the FEIS was released in March of 2000. Two new alternatives were introduced: *Alternative 1A* and *Alternative 4A*. *Alternative 1A* was restoration of grizzly bears as a nonessential experimental population with USFWS management oversight. This was similar to the wolf reintroduction EIS, where the experimental area was large and wolves could be reintroduced and recovered within the bounds of the experimental area, but in which a recovery area was not designated. This differed from *Alternative 1*, which held recovery within the boundaries of wilderness.

Under *1A*, resource extraction activities could occur without Section 7 consultation. Everything would be similar to *Alternative 1*, except there would be no CMC and management would be conducted by USFWS. Day-to-day management could be contracted with IDFG, the Nez Perce Tribe, Montana Fish, Wildlife and Parks, and the U.S. Forest Service. A minimum of 25 bears would be reintroduced.

My guess was that this alternative was a nod to environmental groups that were opposed to the CMC approach. This proposal was, in fact, a good one and likely would not have had so much opposition from environmentalists had it been originally proposed. But by now, sides had been formed, and all sides were vested and convinced they were right.

The other new alternative, *Alternative 4A*, differed from *Alternative 4* mostly by reducing habitat protection in the linkage and corridor areas surrounding the very large recovery area, making it slightly more appealing to industry. Grizzly bears would be reintroduced and listed as fully threatened; they would also be protected here, much as they were in other ecosystems. Land management activities could be reduced if grizzly bear restrictions were to be implemented.

Again, this alternative was a minor change from the original; however, it was more likely to be acceptable because of the reduced impacts in the linkage corridors, even though it would still be quite restrictive in the relatively large core areas. A science committee would oversee management by agencies.

The analysis of potential impacts in the FEIS identified them as relatively minor. The occurrence of injuries to humans would likely be similar to other wilderness areas with grizzly bears, such as Montana's

Bob Marshall Wilderness, which had one injury/death in 50 years. Impacts to economics for livestock producers would be about 10-40 cattle or sheep annually once bears were recovered. Timber and resource-use impacts were also analyzed and reported under each alternative. It was estimated that at recovered populations bears might kill 200-500 deer fawns or elk calves per year.

The total economic impact was estimated to be an annual increased benefit to the region of about 40 to 60 million dollars, at a cost of $400,000, with most of those costs coming from bear management and reintroductions. These numbers baffled many reviewers, but the analysis had been conducted by an independent firm familiar with these types of projections and analytics.

So, there it was: The Final EIS. It was an incredible product created by scientists, legal teams, industry and environmental specialists, local and national citizens, and agency personnel, and took six years to complete. As fairly as possible, it analyzed everything that the public and scientists identified as a potential issue.

Once it was released, the public had ample time to comment. From April to October, the USFWS reviewed 14,800 comments on the FEIS. Governor Kempthorne immediately threatened to sue them to stop the reintroduction, and comments showed little cohesive support for any of the alternatives, still split mostly between *Alternatives 1* and *4*, or totally opposed.

The ROD and Final Special Rule were being written for the preferred alternative. Agencies were fighting the clock, trying to get the rule and ROD completed while also awaiting the outcome of the presidential election. In the meantime, the USFWS formally requested that Governor Racicot, the Nez Perce Tribe, IDFG, MFWP, and Governor Kempthorne embrace the CMC by appointing members to the committee. However, Kempthorne did not select CMC members; instead, he declared he would place the National Guard at the state's borders to prevent any grizzly bears from coming to Idaho.

A tough presidential campaign was run between Vice President Al Gore, a well-known environmental advocate, and George W. Bush, ex-governor of Texas and son of former President George H.W. Bush. We knew the results of the election could change grizzly bear recovery efforts forever. Bush was a well-known Texas oil man, and his environmental policies were expected to be very pro-extraction and supportive of industry. Gore was expected to be very similar to Clinton and supportive of environmental protections over industry.

Although the election was held and votes tallied, no official winner was determined until mid-December. The State of Florida's election was challenged in the courts because of questions about poorly cast ballots, intent of the voters, dangling chads, and any number of issues. Eventually the Supreme Court ruled in a split decision in favor of Bush, who won by one electoral college vote but lost the popular vote nationally. Ultimately, fewer than 500 voters in Florida had changed grizzly bear recovery on the other side of the continent.

Despite or maybe because of the election, on November 17, 2000, the USFWS published the ROD and Final Special Rule. Those documents reflected the decision to reintroduce a non-essential experimental population of bears, managed by a Citizens' Management Committee, to the Bitterroot Ecosystem beginning in 2002, at the earliest. I was pleased at the moxie of the USFWS, doing what they said they were going to do and moving ahead with recovery despite the outcome of the election. There was a brief celebration among a small group of us, but dark clouds were on the horizon. Politics were hellbent on change, and we expected something else to happen at any time.

Despite waiting for the other shoe to drop, the BESC met in December to discuss implementing the ROD. We discussed the CMC and science advisor appointments to develop momentum to move forward. Senator Burns authored an Interior appropriations rider that would provide $100,000 for formation of the CMC, peer review of the Boyce and Waller habitat paper, outreach, and sanitation activities but prevented reintroductions of grizzly bears in 2001.

We were still trying to figure out where bears would come from, how the BESC would interact with the CMC, and other implementation concerns, so actual reintroductions were not planned for another year anyway. But at least we had a list of proposed actions for 2001 that would lead toward reintroductions, and we were excited about implementation. Still, we worried about the new Bush Administration and what Kempthorne might have up his sleeve, but we were hoping for the best.

The day before George Bush was inaugurated, Idaho filed a lawsuit alleging that reintroduction would threaten the safety of residents and visitors and that the decision infringed on state sovereignty. Governor Kempthorne had a relationship with George Bush from his days as governor and had supported him in the general election. When Bush got his cabinet together, he appointed Gale Norton as his first Secretary of the Interior.

Norton knew her way around the Interior Department. She had been assistant to the deputy secretary from 1985 to 1990 and had managed Interior Department lawyers. She had also been attorney general in Colorado. She quickly became known as Bush's leading advocate for expanding oil and gas exploration and was a known friend to industry. Kempthorne asked Secretary Norton for relief from the previous administration's push to reintroduce grizzly bears. It did not take long.

The USFWS was on solid ground with historical legal standing, had conducted NEPA judiciously with a full EIS and public input, and had even envisioned a Citizens' Management Committee to reduce animosity coming from states and industry. The preferred alternative was a new way of doing business, brought about by an unprecedented compromise between industry and environmental interests. Advocates hoped it might change the way natural resource policies were developed then and in the future.

Still, Norton turned her back on her predecessor's promise, moving against her Fish and Wildlife Service professionals and their coalition of supporters, and sacked the proposal.

On June 22, 2001, one day before my marriage to Kara, the USFWS published a Notice of Intent (NOI) in the *Federal Register* (FR) to reevaluate the ROD signed just seven months prior. This time, Norton withdrew the decision and replaced it with the "No-Action" alternative of natural recovery. She cited lack of state and local support and danger to residents. A new rule simultaneously published in the FR proposed to remove regulations established by the November FR notice, relating to the non-essential experimental proposal for the Bitterroot Ecosystem.

Although public comments were received for 60 days, none of us thought they would change Norton's mind. After eight years of scientific effort and public involvement and hundreds of thousands of dollars, the new Secretary of the Interior had dealt a death blow to recovery in her first few months in office—something many of us didn't even know was legal or possible.

I didn't hear of the new proposal until after I returned from my honeymoon in Glacier National Park and in Banff and Jasper National Parks in Canada. Kara and I had spent a week hiking in God's country, looking for grizzly bears, marveling at the scenery, and enjoying new beginnings in the northern Rockies. We were looking forward to the rest of our lives, and I had planned on being the Bitterroot grizzly bear biologist for years to come. I expected big changes with a new bride and job, but I had no idea how much change was coming.

When I got word of Norton's shift in policy, I felt like I got punched in the stomach. There were so many unanswered questions now. How could they even do what they did? Weren't they required to recover grizzly bears? This meant no bears for many years, if ever. Would there be legal challenges? Who would file a lawsuit, and who would support the November 2000 ROD?

All our work on the Recovery Chapter and EIS was to no avail. Everyone's energy and engagement and all those great ideas were gone. I was sure there was much celebration in the halls of the legislature and governor's office, but among my associates and me and many of the citizens we engaged with over the years, there was extreme disappointment. I felt lost and cheated, but I wasn't the only one.

In October 2001, the USFWS released a report on the 28,222 comments it received on Secretary Norton's NOI to reevaluate the ROD and propose the natural recovery alternative. Ninety-eight percent of the comments were opposed and wanted reintroduction to proceed. Even in Idaho, 93 percent of commenters supported reintroductions. Norton had done something Fischer and France could not. She got all the environmentalists and many forest industry stalwarts on the same page, albeit in opposition to her new rule.

Not too surprisingly, many of the resource agencies, including mine, were supportive of natural recovery, even though their biologists were not. The vast public support for reintroduction made no difference. But, with overwhelming comments in support of reintroductions, Norton could not defend her actions with a "lack of public support" mantra. The USFWS, however, held back and did not sign the Secretary's ROD; instead, they just did not fund the old one.

On the books, reintroduction under Section 10(j) was still the rule. The ROOTS group, especially Defenders of Wildlife and the National Wildlife Federation, considered their options. But there was little support for a lengthy legal battle with the new administration.

It seemed that lawyers for Interior knew where they stood, and most of the agencies were supportive of the natural recovery alternative because they could, in effect, just forget about it and focus on other battles. Lawsuits seemed fruitless in the aftermath of the decision, but there was some hope that perhaps reintroductions could be revisited in the future, maybe under a new administration. People were stunned and deflated, and again, I was devastated.

In the great battle between industry and environmentalists, or as some called it, the Old West versus the New West, the Old West survived once again. The battle over control of the land stayed with the Old West stalwart politicians and their industry supporters. If grizzly bears were going to get to the Bitterroot Ecosystem, they would have to do it on their own. And against all odds, like a tree sprouting from a crack in a rock, at least one bear was going to do just that.

CHAPTER 19

THE DARKNESS FINDS BB

Sometimes you can see death approaching like the shadows of the setting sun, moving across the valley and up the slope to where you stand.

ONCE AGAIN, BB was detecting the smell of rotting meat—the sudden recurrence of sustenance. He needed the calories, and his body craved them. His need for food peaked in September, but berries had mostly provided his calories. There was an occasional dead elk or deer and sometimes a bear carcass, but never a pile of food stashed so far from humans and their homes. This was something new, something different, something dangerous. But he had gorged twice now and was becoming more comfortable with this new source of food. Human smells and sounds came and left, and food was there when they were gone. As long as he waited until dark, he would be okay.

The lessons of his mother were playing in BB's head like the sounds of wind in the leaves, always there in the background, always playing their music to the events of the day. He couldn't hear his mother, but he felt her presence in everything he did—her lessons, her comfort, her protection, her care. He still thought of her often but less often as the days turned to weeks, months, and years since their parting. But today, as the shadows grew longer, he thought of her. What would she do? She was always cautious and always waited until dark. So far, this lesson had served him well. He would continue waiting until dark.

BB smelled other bears in the area, along with the smell of rotting meat. He smelled blood as well, but this blood was from a bear, not the meat. He smelled urine that was several hours old and was excreted from an alarmed and running bear, and it made him stop and listen. His nostrils flared as he lifted his nose in an arc from left to right, sniffing for humans.

He had heard the sound of a rifle the previous day and, as usual, had investigated after dark. That was when he found the blood trail from the other bear. It did not lead to a dead bear, but it was near the rotting meat. BB knew there was danger in this place, but darkness was his friend; it would protect him. He knew humans could not see well in the dark; he'd stood in the bushes near humans as they walked by him in the darkness.

BB heard the humans moving away as the secrecy of night descended. It was almost dark now, and BB was hungry. The food was there again; he could smell it. It was so good, unlike things he found in the wild. It was rotting meat but also fatty and sweet like honey; it tasted so good, and it was easy to get his fill.

The shadows were gone now, and twilight gave way to the hooded obscurity of darkness. He was sure the humans were gone. It would be safe, and he couldn't wait any longer; he was salivating at the thought of the feast that awaited. He moved in, slowly at first, in the dark cloak of the forest, until he saw the pile of scraps. Then he moved into the open to claim his prize.

BB was four years old, more than 300 pounds, and beginning to look like an adult grizzly. His fur was dark brown with silver tips, and his claws were long and white. His face was dish-shaped, as the curve of the skull and muscle formed a wide appearance, making his ears look small. BB was approaching his prime, and his fur was sleek and thick. His scars had healed long ago.

The survival skills he had learned over the years had kept him alive. But in the near dark, his shape was simply that of a bear, indistinguishable from a black bear, and the shadows of darkness made his fur look black. He looked big because he was. The sun had set 30 minutes prior, and the long shadow cast by the Bitterroot horizon had passed over BB, as if waving goodbye; but the half-moon was rising and cast a pale gray shadow of the night world over the bait and the massive rock it sat upon.

BB was a proud, fine grizzly bear who had covered hundreds of miles on his walkabout, crossing the paths of hundreds of humans and their danger to get to this safe place in the Bitterroots, the place he called home—his home. He was the only one of his kind here, but for now, all his needs were being met. He was the king of this place, the proud grizzly bear, the Bitterroot Bear!

None of us knows precisely when our death time comes and neither do animals, although the will to survive often helps them escape early death. Sometimes strength and speed, luck, a sixth sense, or even providence may allow an extra day, week, month, or maybe even years. Sometimes you can see death approaching like the shadows of the setting sun, moving across the valley and up the slope to where you stand. Sometimes it happens quickly, like the strike of a lightning bolt, when you never see or feel anything. And sometimes the pain of dying makes living no longer seem like a gift.

Animals have all the same circuitry in their bodies that humans do, but their understanding of their bodies and life and death is different. They don't understand that what they have learned isn't always true—that sometimes death tricks you. Sometimes truth isn't what you smell, see, or believe. Sometimes it's different. You may be doing what you believe is right and safe, but still it gets you. Maybe it's simply a matter of waiting another minute or two before moving, turning left instead of right. Death is not a lesson, but it can be the penalty of a decision. Life is not owed to anyone and can be snatched from you in an instant. Death is owed to us all and will be collected; no one will escape it—not paupers, not kings, and not grizzly bears.

He felt the pain before he heard the bark of the rifle and spun to meet the aggressor head on. But no one was there—only the pain. He stumbled off to the darkness of the forest on adrenaline but felt weakness rather than strength, fear rather than safety. He roared in anguish as he stumbled and thrashed; the burning heat on his side and back would not cease. He could not feel his legs, and they wouldn't respond when he wanted to run. He rolled to stop the heat and pain, but it would not relent. He dragged himself toward the creek and lay down briefly, then got up and stumbled forward a few more yards, then lay down again. His sight was fading now, and the pain was finally subsiding.

BB was thinking of his mother and wanting her more than ever, just to be there to take the pain away and lick his face, his wound. He wanted her comforting protection; she would know what to do. He thought of his sister and the wolves, of the great places he had seen, of the wonderful place he had found—the place he called home. He didn't understand what was happening to him, but it didn't matter. The fight was leaving him, and he was slowly slipping away on the September hillside. His blood flowed into the ground now, trickling into Kelly Creek, becoming part of the creek, the river, the mountains. His blood dripped until more of it was on the ground than in his body.

The first grizzly bear to make his home in the Bitterroot Mountains in more than 70 years was now fading into a memory on the fallen leaves. With his last breath, BB mustered a great and final death roar; and his mighty heart beat one last time.

*An unsettled darkness fell
as the low moan of the
evening's thermal winds,
the breath of the Bitterroot Mountains,
slowly caressed BB's hair and
gently passed over him like a
mother's kiss; and all was quiet.*

CHAPTER 20

THE DEATH OF RECOVERY AND THE BITTERROOT BEAR

FOLLOWING THE NORTON DECISION and lack of forward progress in recovery of grizzlies in the Bitterroot, the Bitterroot Ecosystem Subcommittee (BESC) met to regroup. Although we had weathered the shift and were still a functioning subcommittee, we were at a loss for direction. Chris Servheen provided an update, reminding us that, although Norton had proposed a change to natural recovery, the original plan and *Alternative 1* was still the Record of Decision (ROD) to reintroduce bears. However, there was no funding or USFWS support for proceeding with anything at that point. He thought we should move forward with a five-year action plan for "natural recovery" as our design for making progress on grizzly bear recovery in the Bitterroot.

At least this gave us direction and a new focus. But my status was about to change. In the fall of 2001, after the Norton decision, a job I had secretly coveted opened up in Boise. John Beecham, the long-time IDFG black bear expert had decided to retire. The part of his job I wanted was to be the statewide black bear and cougar manager. When it was advertised, I discussed with my new wife the possibility of moving to Boise, and she was wholly supportive. So I applied for the position and got the job. I figured I could now refocus my efforts in a new area and start fresh. It was pretty good timing.

Headquarters was changing as well. Rod Sando, the well-liked and talented Director, was short lived because of tensions between him and the legislature during his short tenure. His demise came when he supported writing citations to two individuals who had killed cougars around livestock and then bought hunting tags after the fact so they could keep them. It was a cut-and-dried violation, and Sando supported the officers overseeing the case. However, it would soon blossom into one of those weird clashes between the department and livestock producers and their supporters in the legislature. Sando was not supported by the new anti-predator commission and was encouraged to leave.

The wildlife bureau chief, Steve Huffaker, would become the new Director of Idaho Department of Fish and Game. Steve was a solid supporter of wildlife but also had the political savvy to work his way around the statehouse. This shift occurred as several retirements were happening at IDFG. It was a whole new wildlife bureau when I arrived. Wayne Melquist was acting chief, and my immediate supervisor was Dr. Jim Unsworth, who had been a principal research biologist for many years.

Shortly after I arrived in Boise in April 2002, Unsworth informed me that I would be the new wolf manager as well. We were working toward delisting wolves, as they had reached their population recovery goals; wolves would become big game under my responsibilities overseeing carnivores. I was stunned; and because I had some experience with wolves, I knew they would be more than a full-time job, thus reducing the time I could spend on bears and cougars. I objected, but Unsworth just shrugged and responded by saying, "you can handle it."

Shortly thereafter, Wayne Melquist, the longtime nongame supervisor and grizzly bear supporter, retired, and I requested that I be allowed to take over his grizzly bear duties within the nongame program. At the time, we were also discussing delisting the Yellowstone grizzly, and they too would become big game. Huffaker and Unsworth agreed, and I became the statewide large carnivore program manager, overseeing wolves, grizzlies, black bears, and cougars. I was the first person to ever hold the position we created, and I reveled in my new responsibilities.

I still attended all the Bitterroot Ecosystem Subcommittee (BESC) meetings. We met twice a year—once in the spring and once in the fall. Chairmanship of the committee would alternate between state and federal partners, and I helped each of them run the subcommittee and maintain continuity. Sterling Miller, with the National Wildlife Federation (NWF), acquired National Forest Foundation grants for sanitation in the Bitterroot Ecosystem (BE). We spent time identifying and prioritizing potential conflict sites within the BE, particularly in adjacent corridors. Over the next few years we would provide bear-resistant containers and find a garbage-collection agency that could handle them. We now had new equipment and sanitation improvements across the BE.

We still had issues with problem bears in hunting camps within the wilderness, however. I met with outfitter Travis Bullock and discussed providing him with bear-resistant panniers and coolers for his backcountry camps. Outfitters were simultaneously lobbying the IDFG Commission to extend bear-hunting season in the wilderness through the summer to reduce camp issues. The wildlife bureau resisted the effort, and I pushed for Bullock to be the field tester of this new equipment. With Sterling Miller's National Forest Foundation grants and NWF help, we were able to purchase several bear-resistant containers for wilderness outfitters to try. They liked them and thus stopped their push for extended black bear hunts.

We also pushed for them to place horse feed on platforms surrounded by electric fences to alleviate bear problems. I personally flew into Taylor Ranch and met with biologists and caretakers Jim and Holly Atkinson, who provided me with a horse to ride to Bullock's outfitter camp up Big Creek. We went over the bear-proof fencing and camp cleanliness issues, along with the changes in equipment. I wanted Bullock, who was an officer in the Idaho Outfitters and Guides Association, to be an ambassador for the cause, and he was willing to do so. Flying B Ranch and outfitter Joseph Peterson also tried the bear-resistant containers and purchased some of their own. The outfitters seemed to be on board.

We also engaged the Forest Service's Nine-Mile mule pack string to teach outfitters and backcountry horsemen how to camp in grizzly bear country. And we contacted and worked with famed outfitter Smoke Elser from Montana. We held training sessions and provided horsemen with ample opportunity to learn from the Montana experts who lived and worked in grizzly country. We hoped that anything we could do to reduce backcountry users' conflicts with black bears would, in the long run, support grizzly bear movement into the BE and eventual recovery.

We also followed up on numerous reported grizzly bear sightings. Jamie Jonkel was the bear manager working out of Missoula for Montana Fish, Wildlife and Parks and followed up on grizzly bear sign and actual collared bears near the BE. In 2001, a male grizzly moved into the Nine-Mile area and actually twice stepped south of I-90, briefly entering the Bitterroot before heading back north. Also, in 2002 a bear was located in the Nine-Mile area just north of I-90, the northern boundary of the BE. Jamie reported that several bears were moving within 60 miles of the BE into new habitat. In 2002, he tracked a grizzly from Rock Creek to the Bitterroot River below Stevensville before losing the track. It was headed toward the Bitterroot Mountains.

Fish and Game Director and new IGBC chairman Steve Huffaker told the BESC to "stay prepared, involved, and vigorous." There were bears knocking on the door to the Bitterroot much earlier than any of us had expected. Any bear stepping into the BE, according to the USFWS Solicitor, would be fully protected as threatened under the Endangered Species Act (ESA) and would trigger Section 7 consultation. This was not welcome news at the statehouse, but no one there was going to propose any changes and, instead, chose to ignore grizzlies altogether.

The IDFG was involved in trying to control predation impacts on elk in the northern portion of the BE, mainly in the Lochsa and North Fork of the Clearwater River portions of the Clearwater National Forest, as well as in the Selway-Bitterroot Wilderness. Research was illuminating the impacts of black bears and cougars on elk-calf predation. Therefore, IDFG was promoting increased take of black bears and cougars.

When I was a biologist in the region, I wrote the first predation-management plan for the department. We focused on increasing baiting of black bears, lengthening the seasons, and doubling the bag limit. We also asked sportsmen to focus on what we called the Lolo Elk Zone. At that time, wolves had not established themselves there. Within one year of intense pressure, we doubled the take of black bears and cougars but with little or no impact on overall calf survival.

The elk population continued to decline, and the winter of 1996-1997 did not help the situation. The snows came early, trapping elk at high elevations in October during hunting season, and didn't relent until late spring. Thousands of elk died of starvation. We esti-mated we lost about 30 percent of the Lolo Elk Zone population that winter. Antler hunters and hikers were finding skeletons of elk piled up in draws across the forest.

The commission wanted to maintain the intense pressure on predators to reduce predation impacts on the dwindling and weakened population. And then came the wolves. It took a couple of years before a pack was established, but by the year 2000, a pack called the Kelly

Creek pack had formed in the Lolo Zone. The commission and hunters found a new culprit to blame for the elk decline, ignoring the fact that our research showed that predation by bears and cougars, winter mortality, and changing habitat had already done the work of a thousand wolves. But wolves were new and easy to blame. Elk that had died of starvation and were curled up in the middle of the road were photographed by snowmobilers, and their deaths were blamed on wolves.

Hatred flared among hunters and livestock producers through the early 2000s while we were trying to get wolves delisted. Defenders of Wildlife, the group that Hank Fischer tried to bring to the middle with the ROOTS proposal for grizzlies, was adamant about keeping wolves on the endangered species list. They led the lawsuits against delisting. Suzanne Asha Stone, the new regional representative who replaced the more pragmatic Fischer when he retired, encouraged environmentalists and wolf supporters to express outrage whenever a wolf was killed or an attempt was made to delist.

Time and again, the USFWS efforts to delist were thwarted by Defenders' and several other environmental groups' lawsuits. All the while, hatred for a wolf population that was ten times higher than required for delisting burdened agencies, not only with the blame but also with constant management actions. Hunters, livestock producers, and politicians demanded action. Any public trust that might have existed in the federal government to delist any animal and do what they had promised waned.

It was apparent to those of us working in the middle of the wolf management and delisting debacle that environmental groups, in particular Defenders of Wildlife, were using wolves to raise money and membership—even though they knew full well that delisting wolves was needed to fulfill promises that Defenders and the government had made just a few years prior. At one time Suzanne Stone said that she didn't know what kind of back-door agreements Hank Fischer had made but that she was not responsible for them.[1]

All the animosity toward wolves during this time proved to undermine any effort by the USFWS to recover grizzly bears in the Bitterroots and probably also any ESA effort moving forward. They shot us all in the foot, while taking money from misinformed and well-meaning contributors. In our minds, they poisoned the well for future ESA recovery efforts for grizzly bears or any species and undermined the public's faith in not only the USFWS but also any federal or state agency. And Idaho government lost faith in the USFWS as well.

This intense pressure on predators and the sideshow on wolves led me to believe we were not doing enough for natural recovery of grizzly bears. IDFG did everything we could to increase the take of black bears, including providing free bags of dog food to use as bait. All the time, I worried about grizzly bears.

Prior to 2007, our information and education efforts for the BE did not include actually acknowledging that grizzly bears might exist there. We implemented an online grizzly bear identification test for the Selkirks and the Yellowstone Ecosystem, but did not suggest hunters in the BE take it. I had created a brochure about hunting in grizzly bear country for north Idaho and the area near Yellowstone, but we did not include units within the BE as part of the map where grizzlies might be located.

Although I had supported the use of baits for black bear hunting, I became increasingly concerned about what baiting would do to grizzly bear recovery. Every time I discussed the options of telling the public there might be grizzly bears in the BE, I was told that we would do nothing to discourage the taking of black bears. We did not allow baiting in Big Game Unit 1, where grizzly bears roamed near the Canadian border, nor did we allow it adjacent to Yellowstone. However, the wildlife bureau, the director, and the commission were very reluctant to do anything that might reduce black bear take in the Bitterroots. When complaints were filed by the USFS and wilderness users against baiting bears in the Selway-Bitterroot Wilderness, because of the impacts of outfitters' horses on muddy trails and their trashy bait sites, the commission turned a blind eye. Their immediate concern was not grizzly bears; it was predation on the once-prized Lolo and Selway-Bitterroot populations of elk. They had already dealt with Bitterroot grizzlies and set them aside.

I was feeling like a hypocrite at the BESC meetings, having to state where we stood on these issues. I was not getting any traction to make changes to protect grizzlies. Despite bears surrounding the BE, whenever I mentioned to IDFG leadership that there were potential Section 7 conflicts with natural recovery, my concerns were overridden as being in conflict with stated big-game management goals. At one of our BESC meetings, I volunteered to discuss this with my colleagues at the Governor's Office of Species Conservation and new IDFG Director Groen. The draft minutes were mailed for review, and they stated mistakenly that, "Steve would talk to the governor about Bitterroot grizzlies." Cal Groen and the commission saw the draft minutes before I could correct them and exploded, thinking I planned to go over their heads and knock on the governor's door and have a chat.

I eventually stopped pushing and, rather than preemptively promote natural movement of bears into the BE, I opted to wait until one was documented there before I argued for enhanced recovery efforts. I think the USFWS, USFS, and the BESC felt similarly because they did not want to upset their partnerships with IDFG. What we had theorized would be the case once their status changed to "natural recovery" was now reality and had, in fact, become the "no bear" alternative.

Over the next few years grizzly bears continued to knock on the door of the BE in both Montana and Idaho. There was good news and sad news, but until 2007, the USFWS made no changes to the status quo.

During the first few days of September 2007, along with other agency and carnivore biologists, I participated in a carnivore corridor workshop held by the Wildlife Conservation Society in Idaho Falls, Idaho. In that workshop, we were tasked with identifying important locations for preserving habitat and corridors that carnivores would use to travel between ecosystems. I remember drawing a circle on their map around Cache Saddle and the upper Kelly Creek area. I told the other biologists that this would be the first place a grizzly bear would be confirmed in the BE and thus needed to be protected as a corridor from Montana into north Idaho. When I got back to the office on Friday September 7, I found out a grizzly bear had been killed in the upper Kelly Creek area, right where I had drawn a circle the previous day.

CHAPTER 21

THE HUNTER

It was well past sunset and the night was taking control. Shadows were now indistinguishable from life forms.

THE 74-YEAR-OLD TENNESSEE HUNTER was sitting on the hillside, watching the bait. This was his third day on watch, but the bears had been mostly nocturnal, stealing the bait each night. The day before, they had seen three bears in the distance, and he had gotten a shot off on one as it approached the bait. The guide said he had wounded it, but not mortally, because he tracked him for a while and the blood trail eventually stopped. The guide reassured him that eventually a bear would step out during daylight and present a good target.

The hunter had done his homework before booking his trip. He checked for areas that allowed baiting because he knew he could only hunt over the long weekend and, at his advanced age, couldn't hunt over hounds or spot and stalk. He could sit on a bait, kill a bear, and be back to watch football in a few days. He had talked to the Montana outfitters, but Montana didn't allow baits, and the whole grizzly bear presence in Montana unnerved him. He wasn't sure he could tell the difference, and he surely didn't want to kill a grizzly and get crosswise with the feds. When he called the Idaho outfitter, he was told that grizzly bears don't live in the Bitterroots. The feds and the state Fish and Game Department said so. That was enough for him, and he booked the trip.

That evening, as darkness approached, he was wondering if, in fact, he would ever get to kill a bear. He had spent a few thousand dollars on the hunt and was determined to get one. Earlier, they had seen one about 400 yards away from the bait, but it was moving in the brush and too far for the old man to shoot.

It was well past sunset and the night was taking control. Shadows were now indistinguishable from life forms. The guide finally said the time was up and they needed to get back to camp. He briefly walked away from the hunter to get his pack, turned, and saw the hunter getting into the shooting position. The guide couldn't see what he was aiming at, but the hunter had seen a large dark form moving out of the trees toward the bait. It was a bear and, by the looks of it, a big one. Blood rushed to his head, and adrenaline pumped in his body as he leveled the rifle over the rock and put the crosshairs on the bear. The light-enhancing scope allowed him to see better than the naked eye despite the darkness, but all he could see was the rear end of a big bear. The bear form was moving slowly uphill toward the bait when he squeezed the trigger and the rifle kicked.

He may have rushed the shot a little, but he thought it might be that bear they saw earlier that had moved closer. When he put the scope back down, the bear was gone, but he heard it roaring and thrashing around not far from the bait. He knew he had hit it, but he didn't know if it was a mortal shot. The guide was agitated and yelled, "What did you shoot?" "Shot a bear, and a big one too!" the hunter exclaimed, while visibly shaking from the event. "He's down there thrashing around!" The guide listened and waited as long as they could for the thrashing to stop.

Finally, the bear's death moan shattered the quiet and rolled across the Bitterroot mountains, echoing back again and again, until finally fading like a great ship's light slowly disappearing on the horizon; and it rattled them both to the bone.

The guide knew that the moan meant it was over, but he hadn't heard one like this before; he approached the bear slowly, with his headlamp pointing the way. They both held their handguns in the ready position in case the bear had not yet died. They found the big bear at the end of the blood trail. The old man posed for a few pictures, then the guide began the slow process of skinning and removing the hide and head to pack out. When the guide got to the bear's feet, he noticed the long claws and started to worry. This looked different than all the black bears he had processed; but he was sure there were no grizzlies in the Bitterroots, so he thought maybe it was just a strange big black bear. Soon another guide showed up to help process the bear. They put the bear meat, hide, and skull on a mule and headed back to camp in the dark. The horses found their way, but they didn't get back until after midnight.

When they arrived back at camp and unrolled the hide to salt, the second guide shook his head and whistled. What he saw shocked him; it was the hide of a grizzly bear! The hairs had silver tips, but more importantly, the claws were a good two inches long. The longest black bear claws they had ever seen were about an inch and a quarter long. The guide was "all tore up," and neither he nor the client slept much that night, knowing what they'd done.

Now the guide had to tell the outfitter, his boss—something they all dreaded. The guide rode to the trailhead and called his boss. They feared the legal mess of killing a threatened species, one listed under the Endangered Species Act. The guide feared his license was at stake, and the client feared for his livelihood. He asked the outfitter if they had to tell—if they could just bury the thing and nobody would be the wiser for it. The outfitter thought about it for a while, but he knew this was a big event, a grizzly bear in the Bitterroots, and that someone would eventually find out—the guide or client drinking and bragging with friends, or an ex-wife of a guide or client telling law enforcement in revenge.

Secrets of this nature are almost never kept. The cover-up is always worse than the crime, and if someone found out he hid the fact that he had killed a grizzly, he would surely lose his business and probably a whole lot more. He decided to come clean. He got on the phone and contacted Fish and Game. The officer told him to pack out the hide and skull and have the shooter and guide meet him at the Lolo Hot Springs. He would have the feds there to look at the hide. The guide responsible for the bear stayed in camp, and another guide and the hunter rode out to the trailhead and drove to Lolo Hot Springs on Friday, September 7, to meet with the outfitter and law enforcement.

There they told their story and showed the hide and skull to Dr. Chris Servheen, the grizzly recovery coordinator, and to the Idaho Conservation Officer, an MFWP game warden, and biologist Jamie Jonkel. It was verified to be a grizzly, seized, and brought down to the Lewiston headquarters. The bear was estimated to be about six years old at the time, but a tooth was sent to the lab for accurate aging and it was determined to be only four years old.

No charges were filed. The grizzly was killed without penalty as a mistaken identity. The bear's death was not worth a ticket, not a trial, not even a misdemeanor or infraction. The Idaho Fish and Game Department and U.S. Fish and Wildlife Service felt that the agencies were negligent by telling the public there were no grizzly bears in the Bitterroots, so how could they press charges? Because it was a federal crime, they spoke with the federal prosecutor and the decision was made not to file charges. No jury would convict under the circumstances, and officials were feeling somewhat guilty themselves.

Many members of the public were outraged that a bear was killed and no penalty was incurred. Dan Johnson, the former ROOTS representative and current Idaho legislator, was furious that a grizzly was killed with no resulting penalty and asked what kind of message that sent.[1] The hunter said he felt very sorry, and offered to pay for a taxidermist to tan and create a life-size mount of the grizzly bear. IDFG never saw any money from the Tennessee hunter but did, however, have the Bitterroot grizzly bear mounted as a life-size display that is currently in the foyer at the IDFG office in Lewiston.

There was nothing that could be done about the Bitterroot Bear's death, but there was plenty that could be done to try to prevent a similar death from ever happening again.

Life-size display: the Bitterroot grizzly bear. At the IDFG office in Lewiston, Idaho.

CHAPTER 22

MY FINAL DAYS

On Labor Day 2007, a hunter from Tennessee mistakenly killed a grizzly bear in the upper reaches of Kelly Creek on the Clearwater National Forest. They had just confirmed the first grizzly in the Bitterroot in over 60 years, and it was now dead.

THE KILLING OF THE BITTERROOT GRIZZLY BEAR was big news to us. I spoke with Chris Servheen and Director Groen and immediately started handling calls from the media and other agency personnel. The BESC set up an emergency meeting for the next Tuesday in Lewiston where the bear had been taken. At the meeting, we discussed what this meant for recovery and what our next steps were to be. We were very upset that the first grizzly bear to be confirmed was a dead one. We had not done enough to protect his life or that of others trying to get to the Bitterroots. It was devastating!

269

We solemnly looked over the young grizzly bear's remains and took photos of his hide and skull. We discussed where to go from there and decided that we needed to intensify efforts to find bears that may have moved in over the past few years.

Servheen funded a DNA hair-collection and remote-camera study the following summer, hoping to find additional grizzlies. I developed signage to place at each of the trailheads where bears might be identified in the Bitterroot Ecosystem (BE). We developed brochures identifying the BE as a possible location for grizzly bears and cautioning hunters to be sure of their targets. Dave Cadwallader, the Regional Supervisor in Lewiston, was the new chairman of the Bitterroot Ecosystem Subcommittee (BESC) and supported the increased effort in his region to get the word out. The department, however, still did not support decreasing bear baiting in the area. At least we made information and education progress for the BE.

Author with hide of the Bitterroot grizzly bear that was killed in September, 2007, and the Bitterroot grizzly's skull.

As a former regional supervisor in the Clearwater, Director Groen was well aware of the grizzly bear situation but did not wish to make any unnecessary moves. Cal was as political a director as any we had over the years and was working to gain the support of the new governor, Butch Otter, and legislators. Dirk Kempthorne, the previous governor and grizzly bear nemesis, had become the new Secretary of the Interior under George Bush, replacing Gale Norton. We could expect nothing positive regarding grizzly bears from him.

When Cal became director in 2007, I knew I would miss my close relationship with Steve Huffaker. Steve and I had been partners in wolf and grizzly recovery, and he had my back at every turn, no matter what the commission or legislature said. I always respected him for supporting me. I worked hard for IDFG, getting our wolf management program off the ground, and now we were approaching delisting of wolves once again. I had worked closely with Cal over the previous years and felt we had a good working relationship as well. We had fished and hunted together and had what I thought was a solid relationship, and I believed he supported me in my job.

However, the day he was hired and moved to Boise, he came into my office, closed the door, and asked me, "Why does the commission think you're a wolf lover?" I pondered that for a minute, and then replied, "It's because I don't hate them. To the commission, anyone who doesn't hate them must be a wolf lover." Cal told me I needed to make a change so the commission wouldn't think that.

This was a clear warning from the new director. I told Cal that I could not do my job as wolf coordinator or grizzly or large carnivore manager if I did not have his full support. No one could. I told him that if I didn't have his support, I would begin looking for a new job. He asked me what I wanted to do.

So, it was finally happening after seven years as point man for wolves in the state. I had spent too much time before the commission and confronted them too many times while attempting to mitigate their constant anti-wolf (and grizzly bear) perspectives. My goal was to ultimately delist wolves and grizzly bears while maintaining the trust of the public and USFWS. If the commission constantly created turmoil, the public would not trust us and would continue to litigate and worry about these issues. I had developed and overseen the wolf program as the state's first wolf manager, and I had grown very weary of the constant attacks and bickering. It seemed appropriate and timely to move on. I was tired. In fact, we were all very weary of the wolf issue and just wanted it to normalize. But there was still work to do.

In 2007, I was named as Employee of the Year for Management/Leadership Coordination, a coveted award that had always been given to employees of a much higher pay grade than mine. It was given to me for my work with wolf and grizzly bear recovery and for cougar and black bear management, leadership, and coordination. The award was signed by IDFG Director Cal Groen and IDFG Commission Chairman Cameron Wheeler.

I finalized the first state Wolf Management Plan in 2008, in a coordinated effort with the public, the Legislative Oversight Committee, the governor's office, Fish and Game director and staff, and of course, the commission. I wanted to finish that and move on to the next phase of my career. The Plan was considered a real accomplishment by all of us. In fact, Chairman Cameron Wheeler told me it was actually the highlight of his entire career.

We got wolves delisted in March 2008, and with encouragement from Cal, I voluntarily gave up oversight of the program shortly thereafter. Because of his prior experience with wolves, I recommended they hire Jon Rachael as my replacement as wolf manager.

I was still the grizzly, black bear, and cougar manager, but now because of my wolf background, I was asked to get the first wolf hunting season off the ground. Cal told me to help my replacement, Jon Rachael, be successful. So, even though I was no longer the wolf manager, I was still doing the wolf work and training my replacement. It was difficult not calling the shots anymore and not being the focus of all things wolf for the State of Idaho, yet still doing the behind-the-scenes work. I had, however, brought us to the point where we wanted to be, so I had completed all I had set out to do for wolves. And, frankly, I enjoyed not being constantly stressed out.

In fact, the Yellowstone grizzly bear population was also briefly delisted in 2007; and, even though I had very little to do with it (most of the work was done at the regional and director's level), it was an accomplishment for our grizzly bear recovery efforts. I was quite proud that I had helped usher in a couple of the major endangered species accomplishments of the past few decades. And, coincidentally, the Bitterroot grizzly was killed the same year we delisted Yellowstone.

In early 2008, Cal and Jim Unsworth, the deputy director, decided that Jim would now take over all grizzly bear interactions with the Interagency Grizzly Bear Committee (IGBC) and the commission. They also told me I would no longer be overseeing grizzly bears for the state. They felt they needed more control of all the controversial species at their level and took most of the interactions with the commission and the governor's office out of my hands and the hands of all the biological staff. Grizzly bears had been relisted in Yellowstone, and the Bitterroot was now in the default mode of natural recovery. There was little I could do anyway.

Authority over recovery efforts had now moved from the staff biologist level up to the director and deputy director level. Even though as a regional supervisor Cal had always supported decentralizing power from headquarters to the regions, when he became director, he quickly centralized all authority at his level. Good or bad, decisions that were previously made by biologists or at the regional level quickly moved into the political arena and biologists merely provided input when asked.

While I was still overseeing grizzly bears in early 2008, I got some personally gratifying news. I had been selected to receive a career achievement award for management, coordination, and leadership in grizzly bear management and would receive the award from the IGBC at their summer 2008 meeting in Montana. This was the IGBC's 25-year anniversary, and they decided to recognize everyone who had significantly helped grizzly bear recovery over that period. I was one of three recipients for Idaho Fish and Game, along with Wayne Wakkinen for his Selkirk work and Greg Losinski for his efforts for the Yellowstone Ecosystem.

It was a true honor being recognized by my coworkers, grizzly bear managers across the West, and the IGBC for my 20-year career working on the Bitterroot recovery effort. It was also a fitting end to my work with the department on grizzly bears. This acknowledgment went a long way to relieving some of the anguish I felt over no longer being able to work toward grizzly recovery.

I refocused well, however, and even though I was no longer officially part of the BESC, I still remained in contact with them. Over the remaining ten years of my career with Fish and Game I continued to manage wildlife. I ran a black bear study for several years as the wildlife manager in the Southwest Region, looking into high rates of mortality and visiting dens to look at cub production. When I returned to headquarters, I oversaw the statewide moose program and ran a four-year study to determine what was causing our moose population to decline.

I retired from IDFG in 2017 and had enjoyed all my time with the outfit. I hold my head high because I feel like I did what I could, made a significant contribution to wildlife and to the people of Idaho and the country, and had fun doing it. I know that I was a burr under the saddle of the commission at times, and perhaps the directors, my supervisors, and most certainly the legislature; but

I think of that as a badge of honor! I stood up for wildlife, especially the controversial species like grizzly bears and wolves that most everyone else in the outfit tried to avoid. Because I was regularly quoted in news articles about wolves and grizzly bears, Director Groen once told me that I had more name recognition with the legislature than he did. I always did what I felt was right and necessary for wildlife and our mission. Wolves and grizzly bears are still controversial, but we have many more grizzly bears in Idaho now than when they were listed in 1975; and we have an entire species—wolves—reintroduced and recovered as a result of our efforts.

Time, they say heals all, and writing this story has been cathartic for me. While writing this book, I was able to reevaluate my perspective of these efforts over the years but found it has not changed. I think the work that was done by so many good people should not go unnoticed or unappreciated, even though in the end our efforts failed to bring back grizzlies to the Bitterroot Mountains. I hope and pray that a new generation of biologists and managers can succeed where we failed.

I dream of a warm summer day in the near future, on a high mountain pass leading into the edge of the Bitterroots, when a young female grizzly bear takes another historic step, this time for good.
And I, for one, will welcome her home.

Author Steve Nadeau returned to Kelly Creek in September 2019 — twelve years to the day — after the Bitterroot bear was killed.

CHAPTER 23

*Fallen leaves — The trees are now repaying
the earth with interest what they
have taken from it.*

— *Henry David Thoreau*

I FINISHED WRITING THIS BOOK in the spring of 2019, but
I had not completed my Bitterroot journey. Ever since the Bitterroot
grizzly bear was killed in 2007, I had wanted to take my horses into
upper Kelly Creek to visit the kill site. I knew I had to do it before the
book was published to take photographs of the site and gain a better
understanding of what happened there, so I could write a more accurate
portrayal for the book. The officers who investigated the incident and
wrote the report never did travel to the site, and as far as I know, no
official from the USFWS or IDFG ever has.

Despite a thorough review and report, in my mind there
were questions that needed answers, especially once I started writing

the story of the incident. I tried multiple times to contact the outfitter who still was licensed for the area, but he never responded. I spoke with his wife, but the outfitter never returned my calls—perhaps to avoid any notoriety or association with the incident. As a result, I had to describe the incident based only on what the officer's report indicated, and I doubt that was the entire story.

I also made some assumptions about what the outfitter, hunter, and guide may have thought, which I could not confirm. Without an actual interview, that part of the story could not be totally factual. Therefore, I used my experience with hunters and outfitters to depict what may have gone through their minds at the time they discovered they had illegally and accidentally killed a grizzly.

So on September 3, 2019, twelve years to the day after the Bitterroot bear was killed, Dave Cadwallader, the former Clearwater Regional Supervisor and past chairman of the Bitterroot Ecosystem Subcommittee, and I rode our stock into upper Kelly Creek. We came in from the Montana side, a grueling three-hour drive from Powell, over Fish Creek road and up a rutted and rocky Schley Mountain road to Schley Saddle. We loaded our gear into manties and panniers, and once the loads were well balanced on the stock, we started out.

We rode past Kidd Lake and down Kidd Lake Creek to the Middle Fork of Kelly Creek and then to the North Fork of Kelly Creek, where we set up camp five hours later, just before dark. The next morning, we rode past the vacant outfitter camp on the South Fork, then up to Williams Creek, where we tied the horses.

The officer's report mentioned a large house-sized rock up from the mouth of Williams Creek, where the bait had been placed in 2007. We found the rock, scrambled up a leaning log that had its branches sawn off to create a crude ladder, and found an old IDFG bait tag issued in 2012. This was the bait site and rock identified in the report. After taking some photos, we walked around the area and found a pile of rocks placed over a mound of dirt. This could have been where the guide left the remains of the bitterroot bear, but we were unable to verify that.

Photos from author's 2019 return to Kelly Creek. (1) View of Upper Kelly Creek area where the Bitterroot grizzly bear was killed in 2007. (2) Nadeau on large "house-sized" rock near the mouth of Williams Creek where bait had been placed in 2007, as identified in report. (3) Rock pile and mound near bait site, possible location of where the Bitterroot bear was killed. (4) IDFG bait tag issued in 2012, found in 2019.

During the trip, we found huckleberries everywhere, but especially at the mid to higher elevations. The lower elevation huckleberries were already gone. I had wanted to see what attracted the grizzly to the site, and the hillsides were very prominently covered with berry bushes. The outfitter's horses had pretty well consumed most of the grass between the outfitter's camp and the old bait site a couple of miles beyond, but other bear foods were plentiful. We surmised that shrubs had grown enough in the area to reduce visibility and, consequently, its quality as a bait site. But we had successfully found and photographed the area where the Bitterroot bear had been killed 12 years prior. We spent a few hours at the site, absorbing the scenery and what happened there. Then we returned to camp for the night and packed out the next morning. I had finally visited the site where the bear had been killed, completing my journey and the story of BB, the Bitterroot bear.

It was cathartic for me to visit the site and improve my understanding of what happened there in 2007. But more importantly, exciting news had reached me around that same time.

Two live grizzly bears had been verified in the Bitterroot recovery area that summer! The first was a radio-collared male grizzly that Wayne Kasworm, the Cabinet-Yaak grizzly bear biologist, had

Huckleberries, often found in the fall in higher-elevation forest habitats, are an important food source for grizzly bears.

radioed as part of their continued augmentation efforts in the Cabinet-
Yaak. He was able to monitor the bear as he made his way south from
his transplant site in the Cabinet mountains in Montana, along the
Bitterroot crest into the Bitterroot Ecosystem and recovery area south
of I-90. The bear then proceeded to make his way past Kelly Creek into
the Lochsa River drainage, where he spent much of September feeding
in the huckleberry fields of Spruce Creek and upper Storm Creek in the
Selway-Bitterroot Wilderness.

Remarkably, this was the same location of the grizzly bear
reported by Bud Moore in his book, *The Lochsa Story: Land Ethics
in the Bitterroot Mountains.* In the book, Bud said he found a grizzly
bear track one memorable day in 1946 that had been hardened in the
mud, "as if the mountains were trying to preserve the passing of the last

*Grizzly bear 927 moved from the Cabinet-Yaak ecosystem in Northwest Montana
and through Kelly Creek in June 2019, and then continued to move south to the
Selway-Bitterroot Wilderness in September before returning to the Cabinet-Yaak
in the fall to den. Trail camera photo courtesy Garrett Welling.*

grizzly bear." When the Bitterroot Chapter and EIS were written, that observation was considered the last verified evidence of a grizzly in the Bitterroots. If Bud were still alive, he would be happy to know a grizzly was making new tracks in his old haunts, the first to do so in that area in 73 years. This young male bear slowly made his way north, back to the Cabinet-Yaak ecosystem in October, where he eventually denned.

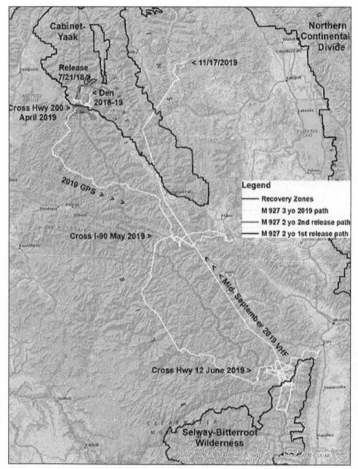

GPS satellite telemetry locations of grizzly bear 927 that moved from release site in the Cabinet-Yaak ecosystem in northwest Montana to the Selway Bitterroot Wilderness in 2019. Courtesy USFWS.

A second grizzly bear was identified in June 2019 by a black bear hunter who photographed it with a game camera at his bait site east of Grangeville and Whitebird. The hunter believed he had a grizzly coming to his site, so he set up the game cam and shared his photographs with an IDFG officer, who shared it with biologists. The bear was later verified by bear experts to be a grizzly. Where he came from and how long he had been there, no one knows. But considering the time of year the photograph was taken, it very easily could have been a bear that had spent the winter in the area. The snow in the high country would likely have prevented easy travel down from occupied grizzly bear habitat; therefore, the bear could potentially be a resident of the Bitterroot Ecosystem.

This is incredible and important news for recovery and very surprising if it is true. How did the bear get that far south and west? It was way outside of what was considered likely travel corridors and prime habitat for grizzly bears. We still have so much to learn about grizzlies, but it makes one wonder how many more that we don't know about may have found their way into the Bitterroot Ecosystem. They had been knocking on the door for some time.

In November 2019, I attended a Bitterroot Ecosystem Subcommittee meeting in Hamilton, Montana. I wanted to hear what, if anything, was being done to promote natural recovery in the ecosystem. Primarily, the subcommittee was in the information and education mode that they had been in for the past 12 years. Jamie Jonkel and Wayne Kasworm provided activity maps of several verified grizzly bears in and near the Bitterroots in Montana. James Teare, the Regional Supervisor for IDFG in Lewiston, spoke about several other recent probable and confirmed grizzly bear observations in the Clearwater that none of us in the meeting had previously heard about. And, incredibly, additional reports and photos are still being verified as of winter 2019-2020. It seems the dam has broken and the bears have decided that the Bitterroot ecosystem has suitable habitat after all. If you are a fan of grizzly bears, this is very exciting news!

So, things are happening in the Bitterroots, and agencies need to prepare. I hope they take the latest information and move with it. The Endangered Species Act (ESA) is clear in its requirements for a fully threatened species; and when the agencies pushed for natural recovery instead of reintroductions under Section 10(j) of the ESA, they were well aware of what that meant. They just didn't think it would happen.

Agencies cannot be caught unprepared again; it would be unconscionable. Section 7 consultation needs to be conducted. Road densities and linkage corridors need to be identified for grizzly bears. Bear baiting, food storage, and garbage management need to be addressed. Hunters, particularly bait hunters, must be informed of potential grizzly bear activity in the area; and they must be required to pass the online IDFG bear identification test and be given appropriate information. Perhaps baiting should be totally eliminated where grizzlies have most recently been verified, similar to game units near Yellowstone and in the Selkirk Mountains where grizzly bear populations exist. Signs, brochures, and other information efforts need to be implemented where appropriate. Perhaps wolf trapping, particularly snaring, should be eliminated there as well during bears' active seasons.

Or not....

Now we know that grizzly bears have secretly made it here through the Idaho and Montana gauntlet on their own, without our help. Maybe that is what they want most—just to be left alone. Even on our best days, we just can't seem to do that. At the very least, let us do our utmost to keep them alive now that they have, against all odds, made it back to the Bitterroots. They deserve that, at a minimum, and so do we.

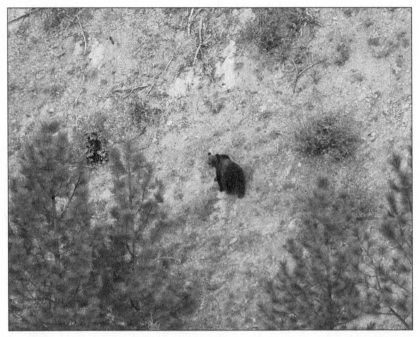

Bear 927 in Fish Creek, Montana, returning from the Bitterroots. Photo courtesy Liz Bradley, MFWP.

APPENDICES

APPENDIX A

INDEX OF NAMES USED IN THE NARRATIVE

APPENDIX A

France, Tom. Regional Director and Attorney for National Wildlife Federation, Missoula, MT. Pp. 123, 124, 128, 155, 169, 170, 213, 245, 319.

Gallagher, Dan. Associated Press (AP) Reporter. Pg. 174.

Gilbert, Barrie. Biologist, Researcher, Professor, Utah State University. Pp. 95, 96.

Gore, Jay. Biologist, USFWS, Boise, ID. Pp. 119, 150

Groen, Calvin. Director, IDFG. Pp. 216, 260, 269, 271, 272, 275.

Hamilton, Anthony. Biologist, Researcher, Alberta, Canada.

Hansen, Jerome. Biologist, IDFG. Pp. 51, 82.

Haroldson, Mark. Biologist, USGS. Yellowstone NP. Pg. 46.

Herrero, Stephen. Professor, University of Alberta, Calgary. Pp. 11, 48.

Hornocker, Maurice. Biologist, Researcher, University of Idaho. Pg. 100.

Huffaker, Steve. Director, IDFG. Pp. 254, 255, 256, 271.

Hugie, Roy. Biologist. Pp. 33, 39.

Hunt, Carrie. Biologist, Contractor. Pg. 46.

Johnson, Dan. Forester and Negotiator, ROOTS. Pp. 122, 127, 128, 267.

Jonkel, Chuck. Professor, University of Montana, Missoula, MT. Pp. 38, 46, 120, 154,167, 236, 318.

Jonkel, Jamie. Biologist, MFWP, Missoula, MT. Pp. 17, 38, 46, 167, 256, 266, 283, 314

Kaminski, Timm. Biologist, Contractor. Pp. 51, 82.

Kasworm, Wayne. Biologist, USFWS Grizzly Expert, Libby, MT. Pp. 118, 146, 147, 156, 157, 171.

Keane, Robert. Researcher, USFS Fire Lab, Missoula, MT. Pg. 232.

Kendall, Kate. Researcher, USGS. Glacier NP. Pg. 42.

Kempthorne, Dirk. Idaho U.S. Senator and Governor; Secretary of the Interior under President George W. Bush. Pp. 241, 242, 243, 244, 271.

Knick, Steve. Biologist, Researcher, USGS. Pg. 201.

Knight, Richard. Biologist, Researcher, Interagency Grizzly Bear Study Team.

Losinski, Greg. Information and Education Specialist, IDFG. Pg. 274.

Mace, Richard. Biologist, Researcher, MFWP, Kalispell, MT. Pp. 46, 156.

Mack, Curt. Biologist, Nez Perce Tribe. Pp. 146, 156.

Mallett, Jerry. Deputy Director, Acting Director, IDFG. Pp. 197, 198.

Manley, Tim. Biologist, MFWP, Kalispell, MT. Pg. 52.

Martinka, Cliff. Biologist, Glacier NP, MT. Pg. 47.

Mattson, David. Biologist, Researcher, University of Idaho. Pg. 201.

McLaughlin, Marguerite. Idaho State Legislator. Pg. 120.

McLellan, Bruce. Biologist, Researcher, BC Ministry of Environment. Pp. 49, 50, 118.

McLellan, Celine. Wife of Bruce McLellan. Pg. 50.

McPherson, Don. Retired IDFG Officer, President of Backcountry Horseman of Idaho. Pp. 151, 152.

Mealey, Stephen. Director, IDFG. Pp. 198, 199, 200, 201, 202, 203, 214, 215, 216, 230, 231.

Meiers, Richard. Commissioner, IDFG. Pg. 191.

Melquist, Wayne. Biologist, Nongame Manager, IDFG. Pp. 81, 119, 197, 201, 202, 235, 254.

APPENDIX A

Miller, Sterling. Biologist, Researcher, Alaska Dept. Fish and Game, Wildlife Federation, MT. Pp. 17, 154, 255.

Morgenweck, Ralph. USFWS, Regional Director, Region 6, Denver, CO. Pp. 144, 237, 238, 239.

Moore, Bud. USFS District Ranger, Powell, ID, Author. Pp. 80, 81, 281, 282.

Mulligan, Bill. Mill Owner, ROOTS, Lewiston, ID. Pp. 122, 169.

Munther, Sherri. Information Specialist, USFS, MT. Pg. 156.

Nadeau, Kara. Wife of Author Steve Nadeau. Pp. 17, 217, 220, 244, 245, 313.

Nez Perce Tribe.

Neher, Chris. Economist, University of Montana. Pg. 156.

Noh, Laird. Idaho State Legislator. Pp. 120, 174.

Norton, Gayle. Secretary of the Interior under President George W. Bush. Pp. 243, 244, 245, 253, 27.1

Nuss, Dale. NPS. District Ranger, Yellowstone NP. Pg. 38.

O'Gara, Bart. Professor, University of Montana, USFWS Cooperative Wildlife Research Unit. Pg. 47.

Peacock, Doug. Bear photographer and Author. Pp. 44, 45.

Peek, James. Biologist, Legislative Oversight Committee, Professor, University of Idaho. Pp. 120, 201.

Peterson, Joseph. Outfitter, Flying B, ID. Pg. 256.

Peyton, Bernie. Biologist. Unknown. Pg. 46.

Pinchot, Gifford. First USFS Chief under President Theodore Roosevelt.

Pollard, Herb. IDFG Regional Supervisor, Lewiston, ID.

Puchlerz, Tom. USFS Habitat Coordinator, Missoula, MT. Pg. 156.

Rachael, Jon. Biologist, Big game manager, IDFG, Boise, ID. Pg. 272.

Racicot, Marc. Governor of Montana. Pp. 127, 239, 242.

Roy, Johnna. Biologist, USFS, Writer/Editor of DEIS and FEIS for USFWS. Pp. 171, 176, 177, 214, 217, 218, 219, 220.

Ruesink, Bob. USFWS Idaho State Supervisor, Boise, ID. Pp. 216, 238.

Salwasser, Hal. USFS Regional Forester, Missoula, MT. Pg. 146.

Sando, Rod. Director, IDFG. Pp. 230, 238, 254.

Schlickensen, Roger. Defenders of Wildlife Director, Washington, D.C. Pg. 169.

Schwartzkopf, Norman. U.S. Army General, Retired, Bear Aware Campaign.

Serveen, Chris. Grizzly Bear Recovery Coordinator, USFWS, Missoula, MT. Pp. 46, 49, 53, 82, 118, 124, 130, 146, 147, 155, 156, 168, 170, 171, 176, 189, 238, 253, 266, 269, 270, 319.

Serveen, Gregg. Biologist, IDFG. Boise, ID. Pg. 235.

Siddoway, Cindy. Woolgrower. Legislative Oversight Committee. Idaho. Pg. 173.

Siddoway, Jeff. IDFG Commissioner, Idaho State Senator. Pp. 173, 174, 230.

Smith, Marty. Biologist. Pg. 46.

Stockton, Mike. Outfitter. Pg. 52.

Stone, Suzanne Asha. Wildlife Advocate. Defenders of Wildlife, Boise, ID. Pg. 258.

Teare, James. Regional Supervisor, IDFG. Pg. 283.

Thibodeau, Jeff. High school friend of Author Nadeau and travel buddy. Pg. 33.

APPENDIX A

Thier, Tim. Biologist, MFWP and USFWS. Pp. 46, 118.
Toweill, Dale. Biologist, IDFG, Boise, ID. Pg. 215.
Unsworth, James. IDFG Researcher, Big game manager, Wildlife Chief, Deputy Director. Pp. 254, 255, 273.
Vandehay, Ann. Biologist, USFWS. Pg. 118.
Waites, Lisette. University of Idaho Professor, DNA Expert. Pg. 236.
Waller, John. Biologist, GIS Specialist, University of Montana. Pp. 214, 215, 231, 243.
Wakkinen, Wayne. Biologist, Researcher, IDFG. Pp. 119, 150, 197, 274.
Weaver, John. Biologist, USFS Habitat Coordinator, DEIS team leader USFWS. Pp. 146, 156, 169, 170, 171, 200, 231.
Westfall, Roger. Senior Conservation Officer, IDFG. Pp. 217, 220.
Wheeler, Cameron. IDFG Commissioner, Idaho Legislator. Pg. 272.
Wozencraft, Chris. Professor, Lewis and Clark State College, Lewiston, ID. Pg 156.
Young, Don. Biologist. Alaska FG, USFWS. Pp. 46, 51, 82.

APPENDIX B

LIST OF BIOLOGICAL WORKING GROUP MEMBERS, BESC MEMBERS WHO WORKED ON CHAPTER AND EIS, AND CIG MEMBERS

Chapter, 1992-1993 — Biological Working Group
Allen, Harriet. Biologist, Washington Department of Wildlife.
Audet, Suzanne. Biologist, USFWS, Coeur d'Alene, ID.
Becker, Dale. Biologist, Salish-Kootenai Tribe, MT.
Blair, Steve. Forest Biologist, USFS, Nez Perce NF.
Claar, Jim. Habitat Coordinator, USFS, MT.
Davis, Dan. Forest Biologist, USFS, Clearwater NF.
Deibert, Jerry. Biologist, USFS Lolo N.F., Huson, MT.
Erickson, Glenn. Biologist, MFWP, Helena, MT.
Haas, Jeff. Biologist, USFWS, Olympia, WA.
Harms, Dale. Biologist, USFWS, Helena, MT.
Harrington, Paul. Biologist, USFS, Panhandle NF, Coeur d'Alene, ID.
Howard, Richard. Biologist, USFWS, Boise, ID.
Kasworm, Wayne. Biologist, USFWS Grizzly Bear Expert, Libby, MT.
Lawrence, Keith. Biologist, Nez Perce Tribe, Lapwai, ID.
McLaughlin, Marguerite. Idaho State Senator, Orofino, ID.
Melquist, Wayne. Biologist, IDFG Nongame program manager. Boise, ID.
Murphy, Maureen. Biologist, Colville Indian Tribe, WA.
Nadeau, Steve. Biologist, IDFG Lewiston, Boise, ID.
Nielsen, Lyn. Biologist, MFWP, Corvallis, MT.

APPENDIX B

Ormiston, John. Biologist, USFS, Bitterroot NF.
Servheen, Chris. Biologist, grizzly bear recovery coordinator, USFWS, Missoula, MT.
Servheen, Gregg. Biologist, IDFG, Lewiston, ID.
Thier, Tim. USFWS, Libby, MT.
Vandehey, Ann. Biologist, USFWS, Missoula, MT.
Wakkinen, Wayne. Biologist, researcher, chair, IDFG Bonners Ferry, ID.
Other Attendees:
Marty Almquist, Skip Kowalski, Art Callan, Margeret Gorski.

Bitterroot Ecosystem Subcommittee (Oversight Committee), *
Staff and Attendees, 1993-2000
Amos, Jeff. * USFS, Bitterroot NF, Hamilton, MT.
Becker, Dale. Kootenai-Salish Tribes, Pablo, MT.
Blair, Steve. USFS, Nez Perce, Grangeville, ID.
Caswell, Jim.* USFS, Clearwater NF, Orofino, ID.
Chatburn, John. Office of Governor, Boise, ID.
Claar, Jim. USFS, Region 1, Missoula, MT.
Clough, Rich.* MFWP, Missoula, MT.
Cottrell, Jane.
Cudmore, Pat. IDFG, Boise, ID.
Damon, Bill. USFS, Panhandle NF, Coeur d'Alene, ID.
Davis, Dan. USFS, Clearwater NF, Orofino, ID.
Daley, Diane. USFS/USFWS, Missoula, MT.
Deibert, Jerry. USFS, Lolo NF, Huson, MT.
Diamond, Seth. Intermountain Forest Industry Association, Missoula, MT.
Dude, Arnold. MFWP, Helena, MT.
Enneking, George. Idaho Co. Commission, Grangeville, ID.
Erickson, Glen. MFWP, Helena, MT.
Fischer, Hank. Defenders of Wildlife, Missoula, MT.
France, Tom. National Wildlife Federation, Missoula, MT.
Gore, Jay. USFWS, Boise, ID.
Gorski, Margaret. USFS, Clearwater NF, Powell, ID.
Green, Winn.* USFS, Clearwater NF, Orofino, ID.
Harm, Melinda. Idaho Conservation League, Moscow, ID.
Hetrick, Nicholas. USFS, Clearwater NF, Powell, ID.
Horn, Kirk*. USFS, Region. 1, Missoula, MT.
Hughes, Phil. IBEW Local #73, Lewiston, ID.
Johnson, Dan. ROOTS, Lewiston, ID.
Johnson, Minette. Defenders of Wildlife.
Jonkel, Jamie.* MFWP, Missoula, MT.
Kelly, Steve.* USFS, Bitterroot NF, Hamilton, MT.
King, Mike.* USFS, Nez Perce NF, Grangeville, ID.
Littlejohn, Bob. USFS Clearwater NF, Orofino, ID.
Lobdell, Chuck.* USFWS, Boise, ID.
Long, Mack.* MFWP, Missoula, MT.
Mack, Curt.* Nez Perce Tribe, Lapwai, ID.

Melquist, Wayne.* IDFG, Boise, ID.
McLam, Curt. Elk River, ID.
Miller, Damien. USFWS, Chubbuck, ID.
Nadeau, Steve.* IDFG, Lewiston, ID.
Ormiston, John.* USFS Bitterroot NF, Hamilton, MT.
Pollard, Herb.* IDFG, Lewiston, ID.
Prausa, Chuck.* USFS, Bitterroot NF, Hamilton, MT.
Puchlerz, Tom. USFS, Region 1, Missoula, MT.
Reilly, Tom.* USFS, Clearwater.
Robinson, Laird.* USFS, Region 1, Missoula, MT.
Roy, Mike. National Wildlife Federation, Missoula, MT.
Ruben, Adam. Wild Forever, Moscow, ID.
Ruesink, Robert.* USFWS, Boise, ID.
Servheen, Chris.* USFWS, Missoula, MT.
Solomon, Mark. Wild Forever, Moscow, ID.
Spoon, Chuck.* USFS, Lolo NF, Missoula, MT.
Their, Tim.* USFWS, Libby, MT.
Wakkinen, Wayne.* IDFG, Bonners Ferry, ID
Weaver, John.* USFWS, Missoula, MT.
Wilder, Chuck.* USFS, Salmon NF, Salmon, ID.
Wilson, Jim. Clearwater Co. Commissioner, Orofino, ID.

*BESC members, * Staff, and Attendees 2000-2007*
Amos, Jeff.*
Baker, Sundae. USFS, Region 1.
Bartlebaugh, Chuck. Center for Wildlife Information, Missoula, MT.
Beckes, Barb.
Bernhardt, Bruce.
Brewer, Elaine.
Brewer, Lorraine.
Bull, Dave. USFS.
Cadwallader, Dave.* IDFG, Lewiston, ID.
Carter, Marcie. Nez Perce Tribe, Lapwai, ID.
Claar, Jim. USFS, Region 1.
Crowser, Vivica.
Davis, Ellen. USFS, USFWS, IGBC.
Demick, Mike. IDFG, Lewiston, ID.
Foss, Jeff.* USFWS, Boise, ID.
Glacer, Minette. Defenders of Wildlife.
Groen, Cal.* IDFG, Lewiston, ID.
Gore, Jay.* USFWS, Boise, ID.
Hennessey, Carol. USFS, Orofino, ID.
High, Mary Ann. USFS. Nez Perce NF.
Jonkel, Jamie.* MFWP, Missoula, MT.
Johnson, Kimberly.
Hudson, Joe.

APPENDIX B

Keersemaker, John. USFS, Clearwater NF.
Long, Mack.* MFWP, Missoula, MT.
Miller, Damian.* USFWS, Chubbuck ID.
Miller, Sterling. National Wildlife Federation, Missoula, MT.
Nabozney, Sunni. USFS.
Nadeau, Steve.* IDFG, Lewiston, Boise, ID.
Peck, Brian.
Robinson, Laird.* USFS, Missoula, MT.
Servheen, Chris. USFWS, Missoula, MT.
Shoemaker, Rebecca. USFWS, Missoula, MT.
Schreck, Julie. USFWS, USFS.
Summerfield, Bob. USFS.

Citizens Involvement Group (CIG) 1992-1995
Almquist, Marty. Americans for Wilderness.
Ankney, Jeff. Culdesac, ID.
Bartlet, Paul. UPIU Local #712, Lewiston, ID.
Bieker, John. Idaho Trails Council, Moscow, ID.
Boehmier, Dick. Bitterroot Mission Group-Sierra Club, Missoula, MT.
Borowicz, James and Susan. Elk City, ID.
Brown, Ralph. Kooskia, ID.
Callan, Art. Ravalli County, Fish and Wildlife Association.
Callen, Ginger. Valley Cats Snowmobile Association, Kooskia, ID.
Callen, Jack. Blue Ribbon Coalition, Kooskia, ID.
Christopherson, Tim. Dabco Inc., Kamiah, ID.
Coffin, Angie. Alliance for the Wild Rockies.
Cole, Jack. Idaho State Snowmobile Association.
Fischer, Hank. Defenders of Wildlife, Missoula, MT.
France, Tom. National Wildlife Federation, Missoula, MT.
Galliard, Dave. Greater Yellowstone Coalition, Bozeman, MT.
Gunderson, Steve. Idaho State Trail Machine Association, Boise, ID.
Hanna, Mike. Empire Lumber, Kamiah, ID.
Harries, Dale. Great Burn Study Group, Missoula. MT.
Hartig, Ron. Road and Trail Committee, Pierce, ID.
Homsey, Alice. Kooskia, ID.
Hutchins, Elwin. Hutchins Lumber Inc., Weippe, ID.
Irby, Alex. Region 2 Wildlife Council, Orofino, ID.
Johnson, Dan. ROOTS.
Kidden, Jim. UPIU Local #712, Lewiston, ID.
Knight, Phillip. Predator Project, Bozeman, MT.
Krogh, Robert. Kooskia Inc., Grangeville, ID.
Latch, Al. Outfitter, Stites, ID.
Loftus, Bill. Lewiston Tribune Reporter, Lewiston, ID.
Lombardi, Lisa. Clearwater Forest Watch, Moscow, ID.

APPENDIX B

MacMenamin, Effie. Independent Miners Association, Grangeville, ID.
McDonald, Virginia. Boise, ID.
McPherson, Don. Backcountry Horsemen of Idaho.
Medberry, Mike. Idaho Conservation League, Ketchum, ID.
Milner, Doris. Montana Wilderness Association, Hamilton, MT.
Moore, Don and Jackie. Kooskia, ID.
Mulligan, Bill. Triple R Forest Products, ROOTS, Kamiah, ID.
Murphy, Stephanie. Idaho Conservation League, Ketchum, ID.
Nash, Herb. DAW Forest Company, Superior, MT.
O'Herren, Patrick. Missoula County Rural Planning Office, Missoula, MT.
Olsen, Marilyn. Wild Allan Mountain.
Quigley, Michael. Lewiston, ID.
Reed, Aaron. Clearwater Resource Coalition.
Reed, Cheryl. Clearwater Resource Coalition.
Renshaw, Linda. Outfitter, Kamiah, ID.
Riley, James. Intermountain Forest Industries Association, Coeur d'Alene, ID.
Shepherd, Jay. Orofino, ID.
Smith, Mike. Three Rivers Motel and Resort, Kooskia, ID.
Stamper, Dave. Ahsaka, ID.
Tennies, Helga. Kooskia, ID.
Wall, Bill. Potlatch Corporation, Lewiston, ID.
Watson, Greg. Plum Creek Forest Products, Missoula, ID.
Welling, Mike. Idaho Forest Industries, Coeur d'Alene, ID.
Wilhite, R.D. Shearer Lumber Products, Elk City, ID.
Wilson, V. James. Clearwater County Commissioner, Orofino, ID.
Wolke, Howard L. Wild Horizons Expeditions, Darby, MT.

Also on Mailing or Attendance List:
Alliance for the Wild Rockies, Missoula, MT.
Champion International Corporation, Missoula MT.
Empire Lumber Co., Kamiah, ID.
Friends of the Bitterroot, Hamilton, MT.
Hutchins Lumber, Inc., Weippe, ID.
Idaho Wildlife Federation, Lewiston, ID.
Mineral County Commissioners, Superior, MT.
Missoula County Commissioners, Missoula, MT.
Nez Perce Tribe, Lapwai, ID.

APPENDIX C

TIMELINE: GRIZZLY BEAR RECOVERY IN THE BITTERROOTS AND COINCIDENCES AND RELATIONSHIPS BETWEEN GRIZZLY RECOVERY AND MY LIFE EVENTS

1956   *Bud Moore credited with killing last grizzly bear in Bitterroots.* The year I was born. I spoke with Bud in 1994 and he clarified that he had, in fact, shot a large black bear in 1956. He was instead credited with last known sign of grizzly in 1946.

1975   *Grizzly bears were listed under the ESA as threatened. BE listed as a potential recovery area.* The year I graduated from high school. I receive my "totem" when a black bear stares me down in Maine.

1976   *USFWS implements first year of grizzly bear listing and plan development.* My first job out west in Yellowstone. Saw my first grizzly in Glacier NP.

1979   *Interagency Team identified to work on the Grizzly Bear Recovery Plan.* My second year in Yellowstone, relocating grizzly bears with Helitack team. Begin work on black bear study in Maine.

1980   *Interagency team begins Grizzly Bear Recovery Plan.* Graduated from University of Maine. I moved to Montana, worked in Glacier National Park studying mountain goats.

1981   *Worked on Admiralty Island, Alaska, worked among brown bears.* Got my first job on Glacier National Park bear team.

1982   *USFWS Grizzly bear plan finalized, identifies BE as potential recovery area needing more research.* As park bear management ranger, conducted my first study of bear movements near Granite Park Chalet.

1983   *U.S. Congress amends ESA to include Section 10, Experimental populations.* I led West Lakes bear team in Glacier National Park. Hired to spend winter 1983-84 in Selway-Bitterroot and Frank Church Wilderness areas to locate wolf sign.

1984   *Entered graduate school at University of Montana to study grizzly bears in Glacier.* Spent summer hiking Bitterroot Ecosystem looking for wolf sign.

1985   *Habitat studies began by Davis and Butterfield in Bitterroot Ecosystem.* Conducted my field studies in Glacier on habitat conditions leading to bear conflicts.

1986   *Worked for Bruce McLellan and Chris Servheen in North Fork Flathead River in British Columbia trapping grizzly bears.* On my 30th birthday, we captured three grizzly bears — one for each decade of my life.

APPENDIX C

1987   *Graduated with M.S. degree studying grizzly bears.*
Began career at IDFG.

1988-1989 *Moved to Powell, Idaho. My first patrol area as Conservation Officer
Became grizzly observation verifier for IDFG.* Patrolled Selway-Bitterroot
and throughout Bitterroot Ecosystem on foot, horse, pickup, fixed-wing,
and helicopter over next few years.

1990   *First remote sensor camera study in BE.* I assisted team.

1991   *IGBC declares BE a Recovery Area.* Additional camera study in BE.
Habitat studies completed and team of experts review and classify BE
suitable for recovery. Additional camera studies in BE. I leave enforcement and move to McCall as limited service biologist and explore
Frank Church Wilderness and southern end of BE.

1992   *USFWS begins recovery effort in BE.* Organize biological team and
Citizen's Involvement Group. Begin writing BE Chapter. I returned to BE
team as biologist in Lewiston.

1993   *We complete BE Chapter and submit to USFWS for signing.*
My limited service biologist position becomes permanent with IDFG.
I buy my first house.

1994   *IGBC votes to move forward with EIS for Bitterroot grizzly recovery at
summer meeting in Powell.* Powell was my old patrol area.

1995   *Interagency team works on EIS and citizens' involvement and education.*

1996   *Bitterroot Ecosystem Recovery Plan Chapter finalized and added as
Addendum to Recovery Plan in September.*

1997   *DEIS completed and submitted for public review.* Director Mealey removes
me from direct involvement as EIS team member, and attacks draft as
having "fatal flaws."

1998-1999 *FEIS finalized and released for internal and public comments with new
alternatives and added analyses.* I continue to work with team as advisor
and reviewer of documents but cannot speak with press.

2000   *EIS submitted to USFWS for final decision and implementation.*

2001   *USFWS changes decision from experimental non-essential population
reintroduction with CMC to Natural Recovery on June 22.* 98 percent
of comments oppose new decision for natural recovery. Secretary Norton
does not sign new ROD or fund old ROD. Natural recovery ensues, grizzly

bears approach BE in Montana. Change in listing status occurred one day before my wedding.

2002   *The Bitterroot Bear is conceived in the Selkirk Mountains.*
I move to Boise in April, for job as statewide large carnivore manager, oversaw grizzly bears, wolves, black bears and cougars for IDFG. Continued involvement with BESC, especially implementing bear-resistant sanitation, I&E.

2001–2006   *The Bitterroot Bear (BB) is born in 2003 and lives in the Selkirk Mountains, travels to the Bitterroots.* Several grizzly bears approach BE and are verified within a few miles of the BE borders. BESC continues to work on sanitation and information/education. I oversee grizzly recovery for state, help BESC maintain direction and conduct meetings.

2007   *Four-year-old grizzly bear killed in upper Kelly Creek on Clearwater National Forest within the BE.* First verified evidence of grizzly bear in 60 years. BESC team to implement many changes in signage, sanitation, brochures, education. Grizzly bears delisted in Yellowstone Ecosystem. This was my last year in charge of grizzly bears and working with the BESC. I received IDFG Employee of the Year award for management, leadership, and coordination for wolf, grizzly bear, black bear and cougar management efforts.

2008   *USFWS conducts camera and DNA study in BE, implements more standards in BE.* IGBC holds 25th Anniversary Meeting and awards individuals for major accomplishments in grizzly bear recovery. I receive IGBC lifetime award for grizzly bear management, leadership and coordination at IGBC 25-year anniversary meeting. Wolves are delisted and I change jobs. Am no longer in charge of wolves and grizzly bears for the state.

2009-2017   *Oversee implementing first wolf hunting season in Idaho, train new wolf manager.* Grizzly bear management and wolf management decisions now mostly all at director's office level and removed from staff. I take on new positions with IDFG and retire in 2017. No grizzly bear verified in BE between 2007 and 2018. But there was still hope…

2019   *I finished writing this book in the spring 2019.* Like always, as something ended in my story, something else happened with grizzly bears in the BE; three grizzly bears were separately verified in the Bitterroot Ecosystem throughout the summer of 2019. Grizzly bears are finding their way back, making central Idaho their home.

APPENDIX D

GLOSSARY OF TERMS

Adrenaline – A hormone secreted by the adrenal glands, especially in conditions of stress, increasing rates of blood circulation, breathing, and carbohydrate metabolism and preparing muscles for exertion.

Biomass – Total amount of organisms in an area. Ungulate biomass is the total amount of ungulate mass in an area.

Bitterroot Ecosystem – A grizzly bear ecosystem that is centered in the Selway-Bitterroot Wilderness Area.

Bitterroot Evaluation Area – A 5,500 square mile area within the BE that was delineated as a result of the Grizzly Bear Recovery Plan (1982) direction to evaluate and ascertain the suitability of the BE as a grizzly bear recovery area (*Figure 1*).

Blastocyst – Embryonic phase of a fertilized egg.

Citizens' Management Committee (CMC) – The proposed special rule for the preferred *Alternative 1* would authorize a 15-member panel to be appointed by the Secretary of Interior in consultation with governors of Idaho and Montana, and Nez Perce Tribe. They would be authorized to make management decisions leading to recovery.

Critical Habitat – As defined by the ESA: "the specific areas within or outside of geographical areas occupied by a species, at the time it is listed, on which are found the physical or biological features essential to conservation of the species..."

Delayed Implantation - Delayed implantation in bears describes a reproductive strategy where a fertilized egg (*blastocyst*) remains dormant and does not implant in the uterine wall, and subsequent pregnancy and development of the young are delayed until entering the den. This ensures the birth of young while the female is in the winter den and guarantees that the cubs will emerge from the den in the spring, when food is abundant. Implantation only occurs if the female is in good health.

Delist – To remove a species from ESA protections.

Ecosystem – An interacting set of organisms and their environment that persist, sustain life, and are bounded naturally for study or management purposes.

Environmental Impact Statement (EIS) — A document prepared by a federal agency proposing a major action, as mandated by the National Environmental Policy Act (NEPA), that describes environmental impacts of the action, alternative actions, the preferred alternative, a listing of public comments, and a Record of Decision.

Experimental Population – A 1982 amendment to the ESA established the Section 10j and defined experimental population as "...any population including any offspring

APPENDIX D

arising solely therefrom, authorized by the Secretary for release under paragraph (2), but only when the population is wholly separate geographically from nonexperimental populations of the same species."

Federal Lands - Areas under the administration of a federal agency such as the U.S. Forest Service, National Park Service, BLM, or USFWS.

Federal Register – A U.S. government publication where all major federal actions, rules, and regulations are announced.

Food-Conditioned (bear) – A bear that has learned to associate the presence of people and their activities or developments with food and may seek food from these areas.

Grizzly Bear Recovery Plan – A document prepared by a team of experts regarding biological and habitat requirements of grizzly bears, outlining tasks necessary to recover grizzly bears, initially completed in 1982, and revised in 1996 with the Bitterroot Chapter.

Habituated bear – A bear that has lost its fear of humans, their activities, or deveopments, and largely ignores people unless pressed.

Home range – An area where an animal spends about 90% or more of its time during a specific period, such as winter, summer, or year-round.

Hyperphagia – The period of extreme hunger and feeding when a bear can consume over 20,000 calories in a day and not feel full.

Induced Ovulation - Induced ovulation is the process whereby nervous stimuli from copulation pass to the brain, which, in turn, initiates events leading to the release of one or more *oo-cytes* (eggs) from the follicles allowing it to become fertilized.

Land-use Restrictions – Restrictions of human activities on public lands.

Linkage (habitat or ecosystem) – A land classification scheme in which large, core areas are connected to each other by areas with similar or slightly lower protection standards, with quality habitat and landscape features that allow for wildlife to travel through, or live within.

Listed Species – A species that has been classified as threatened or endangered by the USFWS under the ESA.

Livestock – Cattle, sheep, horses, and mules.

Lizard Brain - The most primitive part of the brain; the brain stem. Any part of a personality dominated by instinct or impulse rather than rational thought. The amygdala.

APPENDIX D

Metapopulation – As originally developed, a population composed of smaller distinct local populations that occasionally went extinct but were re-established by members dispersing from other local populations. Also, a set of spatially disjunct populations, among which there is some immigration.

Minimum Viable Population (MVP) – An MVP for any given species is the smallest isolated population having a given probability of survival for a given period of time despite the foreseeable effects of catastrophes.

National Environmental Policy Act (NEPA)- An Act passed by Congress in 1969 which is the basic national charter for protection of the environment. It requires consideration of environmental consequences for federal actions. It requires public involvement and detailed report summarizing these impacts (EIS is primary means of meeting NEPA).

New Westerners – As described in Michael Dax's *Grizzly West*, a philosophy that began establishing itself during the 1960s and 1970s when tourism boomed in the post-World War II era and environmentalism replaced utilitarian views of the land ethic. The New West population of immigrants wanted to protect the environments not only for the sake of harvesting its resources, but also because of the intangible, spiritual benefits it afforded in its natural state.

Non-Essential Experimental – Refers to an experimental population under Sec. 10j ESA, whose loss would not be likely to appreciably reduce the likelihood of the survival of the species in the wild.

Old Westerners – As described in Michael Dax's *Grizzly West* that refers to the culture and economy that took shape when white settlers moved into the region in the mid-to late nineteenth century. Most of these settlers were engaged in and reliant upon extractive industries.

Preferred Alternative – The alternative that the agency believes would fulfill statutory mission and responsibilities and meets purpose and need of NEPA document.

Prefrontal Cortex - Gray matter of the brain located in the anterior part of the frontal lobe that is highly developed in humans and plays a role in the regulation of complex cognitive, emotional, and behavioral functioning.

Public Land – Land under administration of federal agencies.

Recovery Goals – A specific set of targets identified in a recovery plan such that when a listed species reaches those targets, they will be considered recovered.

Recovery Plan – A document prepared by the USFWS for listed species, listing steps to be taken to recover the species.

APPENDIX D

Recovery Area – The Special Rule for reintroduction of an experimental population *(Alternative 1)* identifies the BE Recovery Area (instead of recovery zone) as the area recovery will be emphasized.

Recovery Zone – The area in which recovery parameters are monitored. Alternatives 2 and 4 have recovery zones identified. A recovery zone carries a list of restrictions affiliated with fully threatened status.

Reintroduction – The release of animals into an area that was part of their original geographic range, but from which they have declined or disappeared.

Roadless Areas – Areas of western national forests greater than 5,000 acres that do not contain any roads and have been inventoried by the USFS as to suitability and designated as Wilderness.

Rule ("Proposed," "Final") – Regulations developed by a federal agency that are published in the *Federal Register* either for public comment, or as adopted.

Special Rule – Developed for experimental populations by the USFWS and published in the *Federal Register* either for public comment, or as adopted.

Take – The ESA defines "take" as: to harass, harm, pursue, hunt, shoot, wound, kill, trap, capture, or collect, or attempt to engage in any such conduct.

Threatened Species – A threatened species is defined in the ESA as one that is likely to become endangered within the foreseeable future throughout all or a significant portion of its range.

Ungulate – A hoofed animal such as deer and elk.

Viable Population of Grizzly Bears – The number, distribution, and persistence of grizzly bears considered necessary for a grizzly bear population to have a reasonable likelihood of survival for the foreseeable future.

Wilderness Area – Area in the National Wilderness Preservation System that was established by the U.S. Congress and is managed under the provisions of the Wilderness Act.

APPENDIX E

LIST OF FIGURES

APPENDIX F

MAPS

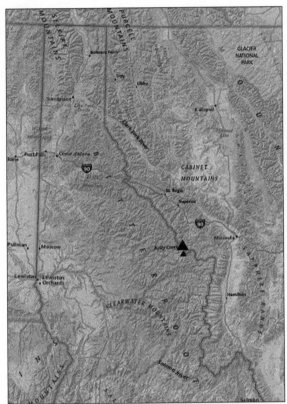

Map of northern Idaho. The Bitterroot bear was born in the Selkirk Mountains near Canada in January 2003 and journeyed to upper Kelly Creek, on the Clearwater National Forest, Idaho. The triangle marks where he was discovered. Courtesy Sonya Knetter.

Google Earth image of where the Bitterroot bear was killed in 2007, in the upper reaches of the South Fork of Kelly Creek, Clearwater National Forest, Idaho.

NOTES

Chapter 4: History of Grizzly Bears in the Bitterroots

1.Thwaites, G. R., L. L. D. 1959. Original journals of the Lewis and Clark Expedition 1804-1806. Antiquarian Press Ltd., NY.

2. Wright, W. H. 1909. *The Grizzly Bear.* Charles Scribner's & Sons, N.Y. 274 pp.

3. Moore, W. R. 1996. *The Lochsa Story: Land Ethics in the Bitterroot Mountains.* Mountain Publishing Co., Missoula, MT. 461pp.

4. Melquist, W. 1985. A preliminary survey to determine the status of grizzly bears (*Ursus arctos horribilis*) in the Clearwater National Forest of Idaho. Idaho Cooperative Fish and Wildlife Research Unit, University of Idaho, Moscow, ID. 54pp.

Chapter 6: The Recovery Effort Gets Underway in the Bitterroots

1. Scaggs, G. B. 1979. Vegetation description of potential grizzly bear habitat in the Selway-Bitterroot Wilderness Area, Montana and Idaho. M.S. Thesis. University of Montana, Missoula, MT. 148pp.

2. Butterrfield, B. R. and J. Almack. 1985. Evaluation of grizzly bear habitat in the Selway-Bitterroot Wilderness Area. Idaho Department of Fish and Game Project No. 04-78-719. Idaho Cooperative Fish and Wildlife Research Unit, University of Idaho, Moscow, ID. 66pp.

3. Davis, D. and B. Butterfield. 1991. The Bitterroot grizzly bear evaluation area: a report to the Bitterroot Technical Review Team. Interagency Grizzly Bear Committee, Denver, CO. 56pp.

4. Servheen, C., A. Hamilton, R. Knight, B. McLellan. 1991. Report of the technical review team: Evaluation of the Bitterroot and North Cascades to sustain viable grizzly bear populations. Report to the Interagency Grizzly Bear Committee. U. S Fish and Wildlife Service, Boise, ID. 9pp.

5. USFWS. 2000. Appendix 6, pg. 121, in: Final Environmental Impact Statement. Grizzly Bear Recovery in the Bitterroot Ecosystem.

6. IDFG. 2019. Idaho Department of Fish and Game Website: History.

NOTES

7. Gratson, M. W. and P. Zager. 2000. Elk ecology. Idaho Department of Fish and Game, Job Progress Report. Project W-160-R-27. Subproject 31. Study IV, Job 2. Boise, ID. 53pp.

8. USDA. 1999. BHROWS Assessment: North Fork Big Game Habitat Restoration on a Watershed Scale. Watersheds within the North Fork Clearwater River Basin. North Fork Ranger District, Clearwater National Forest, USDA. 129+ Appendices.

9. Culver, Lawrence. 2003. *Imagining the Big Open: Nature, Identity, and Play in the West,* edited by Liza Nicholas, Elaine M. Bapis, and Thomas J. Harvey. 161-180. Salt Lake City: University of Utah Press, UT. 2003.

10. Dax, Michael J. 2015. *Grizzly West: A Failed Attempt to Reintroduce Grizzly Bears in the Mountain West.* University of Nebraska Press. Lincoln, NE. 289pp.

Chapter 8: Creating the Bitterroot Chapter of the Grizzly Bear Recovery Plan
1. Letter to USFWS from John Burns, Salmon National Forest Supervisor, June 11, 1993.

Chapter 10: The Next Step: The Draft Environmental Impact Statement
1. Comments were accepted over a formal scoping for issues and alternatives that began with a notice in the *Federal Register,* opening a 75-day comment period. Only 80 comments were received.

2. Scoping sessions were held in Grangeville, Orofino, and Boise, Idaho; Hamilton, Missoula, and Helena, Montana; and Salt Lake City, Utah.

3. Duda, M. D. and K. C. Young. 1995. The public and grizzly bear reintroduction in the Bitterroot Mountains of Central Idaho. Responsive Management, Harrisonburg, Virginia. 141pp.

4. Local areas in Montana included Missoula, Mineral, and Ravalli counties; and in Idaho, Clearwater, Lewis, Nez Perce, and Shoshone counties were included. The regional area sample included the states of Idaho, Montana, Wyoming, Washington, Oregon, Utah, and Nevada. The national sample included the entire continental United States.

5. Backcountry Horsemen of Idaho letter signed by Steve Didier, Chairman. April 17, 1993.

6. Personal conversations with Don McPherson.

NOTES

Chapter 12: Competing Proposals – Learning Politics the Hard Way

1. Dax, M. J. 2015. *Grizzly West: A Failed Attempt to Reintroduce Grizzly Bears in the Mountain West.* University of Nebraska Press, Lincoln, NE. 289pp. Page 161.

2. Ibid. Pg 133.

Chapter 14: Idaho Department of Fish and Game, Politics, and the Draft EIS

1. Email from Wayne Melquist to Steve Nadeau, September 26, 1996.

2. Email from Steve Nadeau to Pat Cudmore, December 18, 1996.

3. Email from Steve Nadeau to Wayne Melquist, May 12, 1997, and personal notes.

4. Email from Wayne Melquist to Steve Nadeau, May 12, 1997.

5. Email from Wayne Melquist to Steve Nadeau, May 12, 1997.

6. Email from Wayne Melquist to Steve Nadeau. May 12, 1997.

7. Dax, M. J. 2015. *Grizzly West: A Failed Attempt to Reintroduce Grizzly Bears in the Mountain West.* University of Nebraska Press, Lincoln, NE. 289pp. Page 154.

Chapter 15: BB Enters the Bitterroot Recovery Area

1. Gratson, M. W. and P Zager. 2000. Elk ecology. Idaho Department of Fish and Game, Job Progress Report. Project W-160-R-27. Subproject 31. Study IV, Job 2. Boise, ID. 53pp.

2. Meintz, D. R. 2019. Elk. Statewide Report. Idaho Department of Fish and Game, Boise, ID 83707. 185pp.

Chapter 16: The Final EIS Conundrum

1. USDA. 1999. BHROWS Assessment: North Fork Big Game Habitat Restoration on a Watershed Scale. Watersheds within the North Fork Clearwater River Basin. North Fork Ranger District, Clearwater National Forest, USDA. 129 pp + Appendices.

Chapter 18: Fine-Tuning the Final EIS

1. Keane, R. E. and S. F. Arno. 2000. Whitebark Pine (*Pinus albicaulis*) in the Selway-Bitterroot Wilderness Complex: Ecology, Distribution and Health. Ch. 6, Appendix 3b, Final EIS on the Grizzly Bear Recovery in the Bitterroot Ecosystem. Pp 6-46.

NOTES

2. Melquist, W. 1985. A preliminary survey to determine the status of grizzly bears (*Ursus arctos horribilis*) in the Clearwater National Forest of Idaho. Idaho Cooperative Fish and Wildlife Research Unit. University of Idaho, Moscow, ID. 54pp.

3. Email to Steve Nadeau from Steve Huffaker, Wildlife Bureau Chief, IDFG, May 17, 1999.

Chapter 20: The Death of Recovery and the Bitterroot Bear
1. Personal communication with Rocky Barker, retired *Idaho Statesman* reporter, who reported on this event for the *Idaho Statesman*, Boise, ID.

Chapter 21: The Hunter
1. Personal communication with Idaho State Senator Dan Johnson, 2019.

PHOTO GALLERY

Author's early days packing and working in potential grizzly bear country: Frank Church and Gospel Hump, Idaho.

Steve Nadeau and wife Kara handling a Selkirk grizzly bear female in 2004.

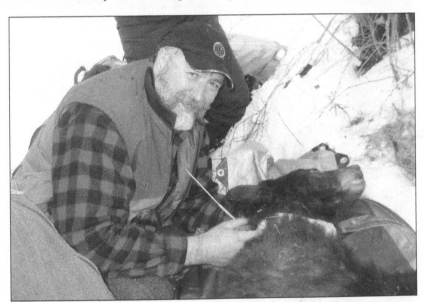

Nadeau replacing a radio collar on a black bear female at a den site in southwest Idaho, 2012. Study was to determine reproductive rates, health, and harvest rates in relation to productivity, and to test efficacy of remote cameras to determine population densities.

Grizzly bears often use scent posts for marking and scratching. Photo courtesy Jamie Jonkel, MFWP. 07.27.2014.

Three grizzly bears investigate a foot snare trap placed by USFWS researchers in the Cabinet-Yaak ecosystem. Researchers attempt to capture unmarked bears in order to place radio transmitters and identifying markers, check their health, and collect DNA samples and other biological data. Photo courtesy Justin Teisberg, USFWS. 09.19.2014.

Female grizzly bear with cub investigating a research hair collection site in Grass Creek, Selkirk Mountains, Idaho Panhandle National Forest, Idaho. A barbed wire corral surrounding a scent station is set up to capture hair in order to collect DNA. The cub finds the scent particularly appealing as the wary female looks on. Photo courtesy Jennifer Durbin, USFS, Panhandle NF. 06.15.2016.

Grizzly bear female with three cubs photographed at a USFWS research hair collection site in the Cabinet-Yaak ecosystem. Barbed wire corrals are placed around a scent that is attractive to bears but does not provide a food reward. When a bear crawls under the barbed wire, hair is collected on the barbs and photos are taken by the trail camera. DNA from the hair sample is then analyzed to compile information about individual bears as well as the population. Photo courtesy USFWS. 08.16.2017.

Grizzly bear female and young approaching scent station "hair grabber" in the Cabinet-Yaak Ecosystem near Keno Creek. Hair is collected from these barbed wire corrals for DNA analysis. Hair can be used to determine individuals and their ancestry. Photograph courtesy Wayne Kasworm, USFWS, set by Dustin Marsh. 08.19.2014.

Photo taken at Selkirk hair collection site near Boundary Creek, operated by IDFG volunteer Dave Gatchell as part of USFWS research in 2019. 08.21.2019.

Selkirk grizzly bear captured in Cow Creek, Idaho, June 2019. Tyler Vent preparing to radio collar bear No. 2003. Photo courtesy Alex Welander, USFWS.

Author Steve Nadeau on large rock near the mouth of Williams Creek bait site, possible location of where the Bitterroot bear was killed. Photo September, 2019.

Dr. Chuck Jonkel and son Jamie, with a friend. IGBC 2008.

L to R: Sterling Miller, (obstructed unknown), Tom France, Hank Fischer, and Chuck Bartlebaugh all receiving awards for work on grizzly bear recovery efforts. IGBC 2008.

Dr. Chris Servheen receiving award at IGBC 2008.

Author Steve Nadeau with black bear cub from IDFG study conducted in southwest Idaho, January 2011.

ABOUT THE AUTHOR

BIOLOGIST AND AUTHOR STEVE NADEAU was born in central Maine and grew up in Northern Maine on the Canadian border exploring the North Maine woods. He graduated from High School in 1975, the same year grizzly bears were listed under the Endangered Species Act. Bears became his totem following an encounter that set the direction of his career. He worked on the Maine bear project and moved west to work with and study grizzly bears in Yellowstone and Glacier National Parks, British Columbia and Alaska. He earned a B.S. from University of Maine in 1980 in Wildlife Management, an M.S. from University of Montana in 1987 studying grizzly bears in Glacier, followed by many various wildlife positions in his early career. Nadeau worked for the Idaho Department of Fish and Game for 30 years, enforcing laws, managing and researching wildlife, and focusing on large carnivores. He spent twenty of those years working on grizzly bear recovery in the Bitterroot Mountains of Central Idaho. He also was the State of Idaho's first wolf manager. Steve Nadeau lives with his wife, Kara, horses, and several pets in Boise, Idaho.

Steve Nadeau with his two favorite mountain horses, Tracker and Buddy, in 2016. He got Buddy in 1988 during his first year as a game warden. Buddy died at age 32, shortly after this photo was taken, which was Buddy's last trip. Tracker died one year later. Nadeau said, "Tracker was the smartest horse I ever knew." Photo taken in the Bitterroots at Elk Meadows, near the Montana border area where the "last" grizzly was verified in 1946, and where grizzly 927 was located in in 2019.

CPSIA information can be obtained
at www.ICGtesting.com
Printed in the USA
LVHW020731220620
658650LV00003B/150